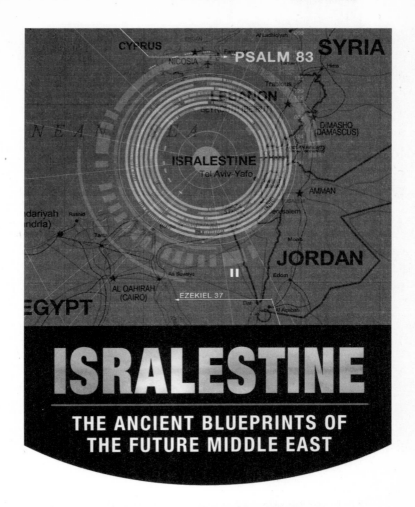

ISRALESTINE

THE ANCIENT BLUEPRINTS OF
THE FUTURE MIDDLE EAST

BILL SALUS

HighWay
A Division of Anomalos Publishing House
Crane

HighWay
A division of Anomalos Publishing House, Crane 65633
© 2008 by Bill Salus
All rights reserved. Published 2008
Printed in the United States of America
10 4
ISBN-10: 098149577X (paper)
EAN-13: 9780981495774 (paper)

Cover illustration and design by Steve Warner
Maps by Lani Harmony
Palestinian Refugee photos reproduced by permission from UNRWA

A CIP catalog record for this book is available from the Library of
Congress.

This book is dedicated to my wife, the love of my life, and best friend Toni. Thank you for leading me to Jesus and standing by my side for the past thirty-six years.

A further debt of gratitude is extended to my children, grandchildren, family, and friends who encouraged me to write Isralestine: the Koskys, Wheelers, Loyds, Fulmers, Oberneders, Campbells, Hodges, Lamberts, Hamons, Korbuts, Carrolls, Bartons, Hoergers, Goodrums, Marshs, Pettyjohns, and many others. All of your collective input has contributed to the inspiration of *These Ancient Blueprints of the Future Middle East.*

For nation will rise against nation,
and kingdom against kingdom.
And there will be famines, pestilences,
and Earthquakes in various places.
All these are the beginning of sorrows.
—JESUS CHRIST, MATT. 24:7–8

The Arab Kingdom will rise against the Jewish Kingdom.
—BILL SALUS, AUTHOR

CONTENTS

PREFACE

The book you hold in your hand contains highly sensitive subject matter. It began as a daily series of serious Bible studies after the terrorist events in New York on September 11, 2001. Those studies explored numerous Old Testament prophecies, which for centuries had bellowed out from the halls of obscurity, begging for their timely discernment. For the most part, expositors had either written off these prophecies as having been historically fulfilled, or haphazardly swept into the catchall closet of the "Tribulation Period," i.e., the end of the end-times.

During their formative periods, the author frequently shared these studies with professors, pastors, scholars, and the like, in an attempt to obtain consensus as to the accuracy of this author's interpretation. In fact, the material discovered, when viewed in its most literal interpretation, was found to be undeniably pertinent to the days in which we live. The information being deciphered was so astoundingly time sensitive that the author felt compelled to obtain these periodic professional confirmations.

It turns out that the Bible presents humanity with volumes of information intended to equip those who would but turn its pages with invaluable instructions on preparing for the dangerous period just around the corner. By the time the reader has traversed the pages of these studies, now fully grown into chapters, they should better understand how the Arab-Israeli Conflict, has created the world's new-found foe of terrorism and, as such, why the common man has a hard time smuggling a tube of toothpaste past security checkpoints at most international airports.

What an amazing analogy: the decaying Middle East is like one man's mouth full of rotting teeth. The entirety of humanity has now been affected one way or another by Middle East mayhem. Is there an end in sight or a way of escape from the evil escapades of world terror? Inside the pages of this book are some of the answers to what must certainly be the post-September 11 questions on your hearts and minds.

As stated earlier, due to the sensitive nature of this information, some readers may find some of the content of this book offensive. Please know it is not the author's intent to disturb, but rather to discern and disseminate. Scholars and nonprofessionals alike, from Christian, Jewish, Islamic, and even secular communities are invited to engage themselves in this book and find out for themselves what the God of the universe is preparing for the not-so-distant future.

Best Reading Regards,

Bill Salus

Author

ISRALESTINE

I t was 2:00 a.m. and there was no conjuring up the admission price for a good night's sleep. Editing deadlines had long since passed, and the full-court press was on for a specific, one-word title with an abbreviated subtitle for the book the future would not forget. It was now or never; this pitch-black morning required nothing less than heavenly manna to fall into the author's lap.

Five years had elapsed since the first prophetic words of his book had been penned, and again he found himself praying for a miracle. Let the Red Sea part, turn the water to wine, and help this foolish man to know: what was the title of his book going to be? Grasping for his last gasp of sanity, he cried out: "Please God, three-hundred plus pages later, I'm finally at a loss for words."

Suddenly, peace graced his soul as the Holy Spirit whispered into his heart, *Isralestine*. Finally, the gentle dove had landed upon his shoulder. It was time to write his first and final chapter, finish the editing, and inform the publisher it was time to design the book cover.

"Isral-a-what?" the publisher asked. "That's clever and catchy. I think I like it! Now what exactly does it mean?"

If you haven't guessed by now, the author and publisher are not fictional characters. What you are about to read is the true story of a former agnostic who late in life fell in love with Jesus Christ, and in the ensuing process may have stumbled upon a significant missing piece of today's Middle East puzzle.

Although I can expound for hours about the prophetic content of this manuscript, perhaps the definition of this curious word *Isralestine*, is best left for the imagination of the reader. *Isralestine* may be too big a word to be boxed in by one man's understanding. At first glance, it becomes apparent that *Isralestine* merges Israel into Palestine. It has the appearance of a perfect fit. It has the audacity to present itself as the simple solution to the world's most complicated problem. If only it could be so easy! The definition of *Isralestine* starts here and expands further throughout this book. It represents the author's interpretation and is not intended to circumvent the reader's imagination.

Isralestine: The Ancient Blueprints of the Future Middle East regards itself with Bible prophecy. It invites the reader to take an adventure with the author through time—past, present, and future. The first destination is the Old Testament, where the ancient Hebrew prophets inscribed invaluable insights intended to be unveiled and understood in these present times.

The clock then advances centuries forward to display the hours and minutes leading up to May 14, 1948, when most of the international community invited the Jewish people to set out their welcome mats and hang their shingles in a place called Palestine. The turmoil that erupted made humanity pause to wonder if the hourglass had made its final turn that day. Now, with wristwatches held close, mankind listens intently for the ticking of the second hand and wonders if the sands of time are nearing their end in the Middle East.

What, where, when, how, who, why? The fountain of questions never ceases to flow from the world's most problematic region. A long time ago, people referred to the land in question as Canaan. It later became Israel and eventually was renamed *Palestine* by the Romans around AD 135. Miraculously, the world has dug into the archives, dusted off the shelves, and put the ancient name of Israel back on the map.

As far as history and prophecy are concerned, it is a done deal; the United Nations legislated Israel to become not *a*, but *the* Jewish State.[1] The declaration became effective on May 14, 1948, and it affected the land of Palestine. The surrounding Arab nations have lodged their vehement protest and the land with the longest standing history has become the most disputed real estate in the world today.

Isralestine sets before the investigative eyes of the world the ancient blueprints drafted for these specific times and begs humanity to dust for the divine fingerprints. The rest of this chapter has been intentionally omitted, offering the reader an opportunity to decide upon the broader reaching definitions of *Isralestine*. Upon reading the entire book, I invite you to make your way back to this first chapter and draft its final page. Please submit your ideas to www.isralestine. net for thoughtful consideration and universal communication on the World Wide Web.

Isralestine is: _____

_____

_____

THE MISSING PUZZLE PEACE

There is an abundance of prophetic content about the "end-times" contained within the scriptures. Information that not only authenticates the sovereignty of God, the only true Author of prophecy, but is furthermore intended to prepare humanity for the times in which they live. The intent of this book is to explore Bible prophecies that receive little regard, which are extremely relevant today.

It is not difficult to find prophetic Christian commentaries written about the Rapture of the Church, whereby Jesus Christ returns "in the twinkling of an eye" to miraculously remove from the Earth millions, perhaps billions, of His true believers.[2] Nor are writings scarcely scattered upon the shelves of bookstores regarding the coming Russian-Iranian led confederate invasion of Israel, commonly referred to as the Magog Alliance.[3]

It is also easy to find exposition explaining the epic events of the Tribulation Period and the one-thousand-year Messianic Kingdom period to follow.[4] But is a chapter missing—a concealed matter in desperate need of being searched out? Is it a chapter unfolding before our eyes, yet remaining virtually unnoticed? In light of the events developing on the world scene these days, prophetic scriptures exist that command equal attention!

Indeed, this missing chapter is the critical component that completes the final piece of the prophetic puzzle. Until we understand it, the events listed above find themselves out of chronological sorts. Far too often, we sweep misunderstood prophecy into the final seven-year Tribulation Period. Though many significant events will manifest during that period, expositors would do well not to make that window of time the catchall closet for misunderstood prophecy.

The Bible tells of a time in the world's future when Israel amasses an "exceedingly great army." This army develops out of the need for national defense to protect against the continued advance of Arab aggression. At some point, this finely tuned military instrument unleashes deadly force against its aggressors to achieve a decisive victory. Because of this Israeli conquest over the inner circle of the core surrounding Arab populations of Palestinians, Syrians, Saudi Arabians, Egyptians, Lebanese, and Jordanians, Israel's borders are enlarged, prosperity increases, and national stature is enhanced.[5]

Israel as a nation experiences a condition of regional superiority, which enables it to dwell securely in an otherwise insecure neighborhood. The Jews still dispersed throughout the world at that time will flow back into their safe haven of Israel. With this influx of Jewish population, the Jews will exploit the resources of the conquered Arab territories and the people will be set to experience the "restoration of their fortunes."[6] At that time Israel will become one of the wealthiest nations in the world, perhaps the wealthiest of them all.

When Israel finds itself in this prosperous condition, the aforementioned prophetic events are set forth for their final fulfillment. This book explores the lines connecting the end-times in order to locate the missing puzzle peace of Bible prophecy.[7] The appropriate time placement of this information enables Christians to intelligently answer the questions being asked of them in these days, and in so doing bring glory to the sovereignty of God and the authority of His word.

The terrorist events that occurred in New York on September 11,

2001, whereby the world witnessed the collapse of the Twin Towers, not only took America and the secular world by surprise, but it also caught the Church of Christ off guard. Catholics, Protestants, and the like were found wanting, wondering if these attacks and terrorism in general had biblical significance.

In essence, the puzzled world population imposed upon the Church the need to do its job and seriously search the scriptures for the appropriate answers. This book is a start in that direction. Passages populating these pages clearly evidence that the LORD did not forget to foretell the perils of our time.

The twentieth century Church should have predicted Jews would experience the horrifically grave circumstances of the Holocaust, and that from those dry bones conditions the Jewish people would be restored into the Holy Land of Israel.[8] Furthermore, the Church should have known from scripture that part and parcel with the rebirth of the nation of Israel would come the protests of neighboring Arab nations. Modern history clearly evidences the occurrence of these events.

The Middle East mayhem that scripture clearly predicted is the present thorn in the world's side. Terrorism has become the by-product of this conflict, and has extended its ugly embrace deep into the international community. What the world fails to recognize is that divine foreign policy, established ages ago, still exists, fully capable of resolving this most unfortunate form of misbehavior.

Now is the time for the Church to seize the opportunity and answer the questions on the hearts and minds of the masses. As of this book's writing, the world wages war against terror and wonders of its outcome. The reader will find God has not left the results of this episode in human history to random chance; rather, an end is in sight. As you explore the following pages you will come to understand the origin and the intent of terrorism, but, more importantly, you will find comfort in the knowledge of its outcome.

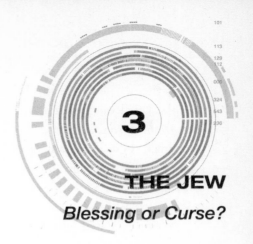

3

THE JEW
Blessing or Curse?

Newsworthy Middle Eastern events relentlessly stream from our television sets, computers, and newspapers, causing humanity to consider the Arab-Israeli crisis and its imposing effects on daily life. From its inception in 1948, the re-established State of Israel has presented the world with an inescapable question: Are the Jewish people and their re-established State of Israel a blessing or curse? Let us not forget that hundreds of prophecies exist within the Bible pertaining to the descendants of Abraham, Isaac, Jacob, and his twelve sons. Many of these prophecies concerning the Jewish people remain unfulfilled. We find one such prophecy in the book of Ezekiel.

Also He [God] said to me [Ezekiel], "Prophesy to the breath, prophesy, son of man, and say to the breath, 'Thus says the LORD GOD: "Come from the four winds, O breath, and breathe on these slain, that they may live."'" So I prophesied as He commanded me, and breath came into them, and they lived, and stood upon their feet, an *exceedingly great army.* Then He said to me, "Son of man, these bones are *the whole house of Israel.* They indeed say, 'Our bones are dry, our hope is lost, and we ourselves are cut off!' Therefore prophesy and say to them, 'Thus says the LORD GOD: "Behold, O My people, I will open your graves and cause you to come up from your graves, and bring you into the land of Israel. Then you shall know that I am the LORD, when I have opened your graves, O My people, and brought you up from your graves."'" (Ezek. 37:9–13, NKJV; emphasis added)

As previously stated, one only need turn on a television or read the newspaper to recognize the Jewish people have been brought back into the land of Israel and, furthermore, that they have formed a formidable army. It has been about 1800 years since the Holy Land saw such a sight, a Jewish army functioning in the land of Israel. In AD 70, the Romans destroyed Jerusalem and the second Jewish temple. Subsequently, in AD 135, they defeated the Bar Kokhba revolt, and in so doing eliminated the final Jewish military presence of any significance in Israel. At that point in history, the land of Israel was renamed Palaestina and the Jewish people were essentially evicted from the Holy Land.

Since the secular world at large was not aware of Bible prophecy at the time, the international mindset assumed the God of the Jews was a weak god. A god by definition was supposed to possess supernatural strength, which would protect and preserve a people in their homeland. But it appeared as though the Roman Empire was more powerful than the Jehovah of the Jews. What the world failed to recognize was that the Romans did not eradicate the Jewish requirement contained within Bible prophecy; they merely served as an instrument of prescribed prophecy.[9]

Henceforth fulfilled was the foretold worldwide scattering of the Jewish people. They became refugees, fleeing from their ancient homeland, grasping for ethnic survival. The Bible spoke of a time when the Jewish people would encounter this fate. In accordance with the Mosaic Law as specified in Leviticus 26:30–33, a desolation of and dispersion from the land was required whenever the nation strayed into an irreversible condition of apostasy. This national condition occurred and prompted the Leviticus clause into action.

For centuries, the Jews unsuccessfully attempted to amalgamate with the Gentle nations of the world. Finally, on May 14, 1948, with the general consent of the international community, they began to return to the ancient land of Israel. Upon their return, a most hostile welcoming committee promptly greeted them: the armies of the surrounding Arab nations. Miraculously, the Jewish people assembled a rag-tag army and successfully defeated their Arab aggressors.

"Miraculously" may appear too powerful a word for this event, but history reminds us that more conventional Arab assaults against the reborn Jewish nation met with similar results in 1956, 1967, and 1973. When the Jewish people were destined to descend from the Holy Land, no military effort could delay the inevitable. Similarly, now that the Jews are set to ascend back into the land of Israel, no military effort can prevent it. With abundant authority, Bible prophecy spoke of both episodes: the disciplinary descent of the Jew out of the land of Israel, and their subsequent ascribed ascent back into the Holy Land.

Few would question the need for an Israeli army today. If not for these forces, Israel would, as many of their Arab neighbors wish, be deleted from the landscape of the Middle East. However, you know at least one Jewish prophet foretold the emergence of this army centuries ago. As you read on, you will see that Ezekiel was not the only Jewish prophet made aware of the arrival of this Israeli "exceedingly great army."

From the time God made a covenant with Abraham up to the era in which we now live, the prophetic program for Abraham and his descendants has continued to play out as prescribed. The forthcoming fulfillment of prophecies regarding the Jewish people should be understood with finality. This is it—there is no turning back the tides of the prophesied times in which we live.

God is not done with the Jew. Consider the grave refugee conditions of their reentry into their ancient homeland of Israel. Ponder the pounding they withstood from their ancient Arab enemies upon their return. Then appreciate the fact that, in order to survive, they have had to emerge as an "exceedingly great army" foretold by the prophet Ezekiel.

> So I prophesied as He commanded me, and breath came into them, and they [the Jewish people] lived, and stood upon their feet, an *exceedingly great army.* (Ezek. 37:10, NKJV; emphasis added)

This Israeli army has become a finely tuned military instrument, emerging for the primary purpose of preserving the nation of Israel as a Jewish state. The army will accomplish four additional feats. First, the facilitation of the safe passage of world Jewry back into the land of Israel. Second, the protection from and the ultimate conquest over Israel's hostile Arab neighbors. Next, the ushering in of the conclusion of the "perpetual enmity" harbored by Israel's ancient enemies.[10] And finally, the restoration of Jewish fortunes.[11]

Only once prior in history has a band of refugees who existed outside of their homeland for four hundred years or longer ever transformed as promptly into an effective war machine—it was the selfsame nation, Israel. During the Hebrew exodus out of Egypt, Moses (later succeeded by Joshua) "miraculously" conquered the enemies who attempted to stand in the way of their return to the Holy Land.

The Red Sea parted and the walls of Jericho tumbled down as the ancient Hebrews made their ascent back into the Promised Land. Similarly, modern history saw the defeat of the German army, the disbanding of the Soviet Union, the fall of the Iron Curtain, and the collapse of the Berlin wall. Each of these episodes inspired the return of the Jews back into the land of Israel.

Some may wonder why anyone would want to return to a land plagued by conflict and hostility. It is generally unsafe to visit any public place in Israel, for at any time one could lose his or her life to a suicidal Islamic militant with a bomb. Yet terror does not dissuade Israelis entirely; it is set in their hearts and minds that they will return to the Holy Land of their ancient patriarchs, Abraham, Isaac, and Jacob. Against all odds, they return to Israel suggesting that their God still has plans for their future.

> "So I will make *My holy name* known in the midst of *My people Israel*, and I will not let them profane *My holy name* anymore. Then *the nations shall know that I am the LORD*, the Holy One in Israel. Surely it is coming, and it shall be done," says the LORD GOD. (Ezek. 39:7–8, NKJV; emphasis added)

> Thus says the LORD, "Who gives the sun for a light by day, The ordinances of the moon and the stars for a light by night, Who disturbs the sea, And its waves roar" (The LORD of hosts is His name): "If those ordinances depart From before Me," says the LORD, "Then the seed of Israel shall also cease From being a nation before Me forever." (Jer. 31:35–36, NKJV)

Scripture suggests it is virtually impossible for God to eliminate the Jew from His prophetic program. Certainly, the Palestinians will not be able to strip the "ordinances" referenced above from the hands of God. Perhaps they believe their god Allah is able to do so, but in Isaiah we find,

> I *am* the LORD, and there is no other; There is *no God besides Me*. I will gird you, though you have not known Me, That they may know from the rising of the sun to its setting That there is none besides Me. I am the LORD, and there is no other. (Isaiah 45:5–6, NKJV; emphasis added)

The million-dollar question all the world's inhabitants must answer is: Does God's Genesis 12:3 declaration still hold true almost four-thousand years later? The following passage is what God instructed Abraham would become His divine foreign policy throughout time, for the entirety of humanity.

I will bless those who bless you, And I will curse him who curses you; And in you all the families of the Earth shall be blessed. (Gen. 12:3, NKJV)

We understand the "you" of this important passage to be not only Abraham, but all of his descendants that would follow through the lineages of his son Isaac and grandson Jacob. This makes the Jewish people of today the recipients "you" of this ancient decree.

Therefore, if this divine foreign policy is still operable, one must intelligently determine if the Jew is a blessing or a curse. The answer is, in both instances, yes. The Jew is a blessing to those who bless him or her, and a curse to those who behave to the contrary.

Therefore, with this precept in place, we understand that the Arabs assault the Jews at great risk to themselves and induce upon themselves enormous potential for peril. In so doing, they subject themselves to the divine foreign policy established centuries ago through the Abrahamic covenant.

YISRAEL YASHAB BETACH
Israel Dwelling Securely

Recently there has been much talk centered on the future timing of the Russian-and Iranian-led invasion of Israel foretold in the Bible episode of Ezekiel 38 and 39. Due to the newsworthy events presently occurring, whereby Russian and Iranian relationships are ever strengthening, prophecy buffs are appropriately attempting with god-speed to connect the prophetic dots. As such, we must carefully consider the four prerequisite conditions by which the world must characterize the nation of Israel before any such invasion will occur.

1. A nation re-established as a sovereign Jewish state.
2. A nation militarily secure
3. A nation at peace in the Middle East
4. A nation of restored fortune

After many days you will be visited. In the latter years you [Russian-Iranian led coalition] will come into the land of those brought back from the sword and gathered from many people on the mountains of Israel, which had long been desolate; they were brought out of the nations, and now all of them dwell safely. (Ezek. 38:8, NKJV)

This passage informs us God will gather Jewish people from the nations of the world and bring them back to the "mountains of Israel." This does not imply that all Jews will migrate into the mountainous areas of Israel; rather, it alludes to the Jewish people forming a sovereign state. Although the Bible often refers to mountains in a literal, geographical sense, it may also allude to the leadership or government of a nation in the typological sense. In this instance, the inference is an independent Jewish entity over which a sovereign government presides.[12] Since this government is associated with "the mountains of Israel," we can safely surmise that the location of this restored sovereign Jewish Sate is Israel.

Furthermore, the Bible depicts the Jewish people as dwelling in a condition of security. Ezekiel declares that as a nation they "all" "dwell safely." He uses the Hebrew words *Yashab Betach* to highlight this point.[13] The Bible uses these Hebrew words in tandem elsewhere in the Old Testament, to identify the sovereign State of Israel dwelling in a condition of military security.[14]

> Thus says the LORD GOD: "On that day it shall come to pass that thoughts will arise in your mind, and you will make an evil plan: You will say, 'I will go up against a land of unwalled villages; I will go to a peaceful people, who dwell safely, all of them dwelling without walls, and having neither bars nor gates to take plunder and to take booty, to stretch out your hand against the waste places that are again inhabited, and against a people gathered from the nations, who have acquired livestock and goods, who dwell in the midst of the land.'" (Ezek. 38:10–12, NKJV)

Ezekiel expounds further upon the conditions of Israel at the time of the advance of the Russian-Iranian led coalition. They will, he says, be "a peaceful people, who dwell safely (*yashab betach*), all of them dwelling without walls." Israel will be a nation at peace in the Middle

East. Ezekiel's description of a nation dwelling without walls emphasizes a condition of national security.

Throughout time, humans constructed fortified walls to prevent enemy intrusions and enforce separation between two diverse population groups. The Chinese built the Great Wall around 200 BC to protect China's northern borders from intruders. The Germans erected the Berlin wall in 1961 in order to separate the Communistic political system of the East from the capitalism spreading in the West. Likewise, Israel has today constructed its own fortified wall intended to prevent the terrorist element of the Palestinian population from intruding into Israel proper. This wall reaches up to twenty-five feet and is projected to span at least 403 miles upon completion. As such, Israel today is not a nation dwelling without walls as described in Ezekiel 38:11.

Note that the previous passage references "a people gathered from the nations, who have acquired livestock and goods." Israel acquires livestock, representing agricultural wealth, and goods, representing commercial wealth. This condition of restored fortune will resemble the period of Israel's history around 1000 BC, when King Solomon reigned over the nation.[15] As was the case then, Israel will become one of the wealthiest—if not *the* wealthiest—of the world's nations.

In his next verse, Ezekiel informs us that Israel's restored fortune is what the Russian-Iranian-led coalition aspires to attain. Sheba and Dedan, which likely represent the modern nations of Yemen and Saudi Arabia, along with other merchant and military populations, question the coalitions motivation and in so doing enlighten us as to its true intention.

Sheba, Dedan, the merchants of Tarshish, and all their young lions will say to you, "Have you come to take plunder? Have you gathered your army to take booty, to carry away silver and gold, to take away livestock and goods, to take great plunder?" (Ezek. 38:13, NKJV)

The Russian-Iranian coalition targets the livestock, goods, and other "great plunder" acquired by Israel. That Israel possesses great plunder further emphasizes the idea of a wealthy nation.

The present international prescription for Israel to accomplish the four characteristics listed above and become "a peaceful people, who dwell safely, all of them dwelling without walls" is to make sweeping political and real estate concessions with the Palestinians and their Arab cohorts. In return, Israel expects international security assistance and acceptance by more members of the Arab League for the right to exist as a sovereign Jewish State. However, this international solution is not biblically endorsed.

The Bible states that the nation of Israel accomplishes its four prerequisite conditions via a military solution. The Israeli Defense Force will become engaged in a serious regional conflict. In victory, they will become primed for the future events of the Russian-Iranian coalition destined to form against them.

Turning back a few pages from the Ezekiel passages quoted above to Ezekiel Chapter 28, we discover that God will come to the defense of Israel.

And there shall no longer be a pricking brier or a painful thorn for the house of Israel from *among all who are around them, who despise them.* Then they shall know that I *am* the LORD GOD. Thus says the LORD GOD: "When I have gathered the house of Israel from the peoples among whom they are scattered, and am hallowed in them in the sight of the Gentiles, then they will dwell in their own land which I gave to My servant Jacob. And they will dwell safely there, build houses, and plant vineyards; yes, they will dwell securely, when I execute judgments on all those around them who despise them. Then they shall know that I *am* the LORD their God." (Ezek. 28:24–26, NKJV; emphasis added)

Simply paraphrased: "Yes, they will dwell securely (*yashab betach*), when I (God) execute judgments on all those (Arab nations) around them who despise them." Ezekiel reminds us that the national security Israel so desperately seeks today occurs via the judgments executed "on all those around them who despise them."

Surprisingly, "all those (Arab nations) around them who despise" the emerging Jewish State of Israel, are conspicuously absent from the Russian-Iranian-led coalition which includes Ethiopia, Libya, and Turkey along with several modern nations.[16] Prophecy buffs have wondered why this would be the case, since presently "all those (Arab nations) around them who despise" the emerging Jewish State are Israel's most observable opponents.

Coincidentally, the Arab nations in question are enlisted members of the distinctly separate and yet-to-be-fulfilled prophecy described in Psalm 83:

> Do not keep silent, O God! Do not hold Your peace, And do not be still, O God! For behold, Your enemies make a tumult; And those who hate You have lifted up their head. They have taken crafty counsel against Your people, And consulted together against Your sheltered ones. They have said, "*Come, and let us cut them off from being a nation, That the name of Israel may be remembered no more.*" For they have consulted together with one consent; They form a confederacy against You: The tents of Edom and the Ishmaelites; Moab and the Hagrites; Gebal, Ammon, and Amalek; Philistia with the inhabitants of Tyre; Assyria also has joined with them; They have helped the children of Lot. *Selah.* (Psa. 83:1–8, NKJV; emphasis added)

The adversaries of Israel who seek to cut the Jews off from being a nation will form their own coalition. Unfortunately for them, they are described in Ezekiel 28:24–26 as "all those around them who despise them." They are those upon whom God will execute devastating judgments prior to the formation of the Russian-Iranian coalition.

We can safely presume the execution of the judgments upon the surrounding Psalm 83 nations will occur before the coalition in question forms. We deduce this by recollecting that the Russian-Iranian-led coalition will attempt to invade a militarily secure Israel. This condition of security becomes a reality only subsequent to the judgments executed upon the surrounding Psalm 83 nations.

The modern equivalents of the Psalm 83 confederates are: tents of Edom (Palestinian Refugees and Southern Jordanians), Ishmaelites (Saudi Arabians), Moab (Palestinian Refugees and Central Jordanians), Hagrites (Egyptians), Gebal (Northern Lebanese), Ammon (Palestinian Refugees and Northern Jordanians), Amalek (Arabs South of Israel), Philistia (Palestinian Refugees and Hamas of the Gaza Strip), inhabitants of Tyre (Hezbollah and Southern Lebanese), Assyria (Syrians and perhaps Northern Iraqi's), and the children of Lot (Moab and Ammon above).[17]

Because of the judgments made upon the Arabs who despise them, Israel will attain the autonomy required to set the stage for the Russian-Iranian-led attack. The world will internationally esteem Israel as the sovereign Jewish State, and the Arab-Israeli conflict we witness today will be finally resolved. As such, Israel will be a nation of peace achieved via their military might. It is the "exceedingly great army" of Israel foretold in Ezekiel 37:10 that is the instrumental tool utilized in the execution of the judgments against the surrounding Arab nations.[18] The Jewish State will seize and exploit much of the conquered Arab territory, and as such, their fortunes will be greatly restored.

Before we develop further the theme of the Israeli conquest "on those around them who despise them," let us first come to appreciate the reason for the Restoration of the Nation Israel as the Jewish State, which occurred May 14, 1948, and the rationale behind the pending

Russian-Iranian invasion of the Jewish State of Israel. Largely, God intends both of these monumental events to serve the same divine purpose, which is:

> "So I [God] will make *My holy name* known in the midst of My people Israel, and I will not *let them* profane My holy name anymore. Then the nations shall know that I am the LORD, the Holy One in Israel. Surely it is coming, and it shall be done," says the LORD GOD. "This *is* the day of which I have spoken." (Ezek. 39:7–8, NKJV; emphasis added)

With the help of their God, the Jews defeat the Russian-Iranian coalition during the events described in Ezekiel 39:3–6, and in 39:7 we see that through these events God makes His "holy name" known throughout the nations of the world. Similarly, in Ezekiel 36:22–24 we learn that the Restoration of the Nation Israel as the Jewish State serves the same purpose.

> Therefore say to the house of Israel, "Thus says the LORD GOD: 'I do not do *this* for your sake, O house of Israel, but for *My holy name's* sake, which you have profaned among the nations wherever you went. And I will sanctify *My great name*, which has been profaned among the nations, which you have profaned in their midst; and *the nations shall know* that *I am the LORD*,' says the LORD GOD, '*when I am hallowed in you* before their eyes. For I will take you from among the nations, gather you out of all countries, and bring you into your own land.'" (Ezek. 36:22–24, NKJV; emphasis added)

Furthermore, it is noteworthy that God intends to be "hallowed" by the Jewish people in the sight of the international community. The Hebrew word for "hallowed" is *qadash*, and it is the same word utilized in Ezekiel 36:23 and Ezekiel 28:25. In both instances, it emphatically highlights the Restoration of the Sovereign Jewish State of Israel as an epic and holy event.

Miraculously, in modern history the call of Zionism has tugged adamantly upon the hearts of the Jewish people, who for centuries lived dispersed throughout the nations of the world. Israel became a nation in 1948, and the Jewish people have responded to the Zionistic inclination implanted within them individually and corporately. Many of them have answered the sacred call, and have migrated back into the land that 1,878 years prior had bid them a hostile farewell.

Yes, the Jews have returned and "all those (predominately Arabs) around them who despise them" have attempted to prevent the prescribed process. Therefore, as we reread Ezekiel 28:24–26 with this hallowed understanding, we can conclude that the judgments destined for the surrounding Arab nations are justified.

> "And there shall no longer be a pricking brier or a painful thorn for the house of Israel from among all *who are* around them, who despise them. Then they shall know that I *am* the LORD GOD." Thus says the LORD GOD: "When I have gathered the house of Israel from the peoples among whom they are scattered, and am hallowed in them in the sight of the Gentiles, then they will dwell in their own land which I gave to My servant Jacob. And they will dwell safely there, build houses, and plant vineyards; yes, they will dwell securely [*yashab betach*], when I execute judgments on all those around them who despise them. Then they shall know that I *am* the LORD their God." (Ezek. 28:24–26, NKJV; emphasis added)

What we can glean from all of this is that God is presently preparing to make His Holy Name known throughout the nations of the world. He is gathering the Jewish people and forming them into an exceedingly great army. The execution of judgments on many Arabs will be a humbling and hallowing event in the world's future history. Gentiles will consider the Jews, the Jewish sovereign state, and most importantly, the holy name of their God Jehovah.

What the world now witnesses in the theater of the Middle East is the stage setting for the marquee event, whereby the holy name of God features prominently before the international audience. The Arab-Israeli conflict, the Iranian nuclear concerns, the oil recently found in the Caspian Sea between the borders of Russia and Iran, and many other events are but opening acts in God's grand show.

Due to the strengthening relationship between Russia and Iran, prophetic scholars are rightfully discerning the world's nearness to the fulfillment of the events described in Ezekiel 38 and 39. They will indeed occur soon, however, not necessarily next. Prior to this, the nation of Israel must display sovereignty, peace, security, and fortune. "All those around them who despise them" presently oppose these four conditions.

The LORD will soon execute judgments upon these enemies! These judgments will be fashioned in the manner prescribed by God, who is presently poised to sanctify His Holy Name. Approximately four-thousand years ago, God spelled out His international foreign policy through Abraham, as contained in Genesis 12:3.[19] He promises blessings to those who bless the Jewish descendants of Abraham, and curses those who curse them.

The same recipe for Jewish disaster the surrounding Arab nations concoct will be redirected against them in like fashion. This punishment will highlight the curse-for-curse in kind component of the Abrahamic Covenant.[20] The Arab Kingdom will come against the Jewish Kingdom in fulfillment of the prophecy of Jesus Christ.

> For nation will rise against nation, and [Arab] *kingdom against* [Jewish] *kingdom.* And there will be famines, pestilences, and Earthquakes in various places. All these *are* the beginning of sorrows. (Matthew 24:7–8, NKJV; emphasis added)

In World War I and World War II, nation rose against nation. This set the stage for the restoration of the nation Israel and the re-establishment of the Jewish Kingdom. The Arab nations bordering Israel have proven their dissatisfaction with the re-emergence of the Jewish Kingdom in their area of the world. They will ultimately confederate in the fulfillment of Psalm 83, and, in that unified condition will represent the sentiment of the broader Arab Kingdom.

> They [the Arab Kingdom] have said, "Come, and let us cut them off from being a nation, That the name of Israel [the Jewish Kingdom] may be remembered no more." (Psa. 83:4, NKJV)

When the Jewish Kingdom prevails militarily over the Arab Kingdom, the fulfillment of Ezekiel 28:24–26 will occur, as God executes the "judgments on all those around them who despise them." The deliverance of these devastating judgments via the mighty means of the Jewish Kingdom will display that the divine foreign policy contained in the ancient decree of the Abrahamic Covenant is still effectually in tact. The Abrahamic Covenant, will at that time, nullify all incompatible international foreign policy relating to the Arab-Israeli conflict.

After digesting this information, the reader might consider that there is indeed a God, and that His name is holy. Enormous events on a David-and-Goliath scale continue to unfold in the Middle East and directly affect our daily lives. Terrorism, primarily born from Middle East mayhem, has extended its ugly embrace around our lives. Try carrying a tube of toothpaste onto an airplane. It has become a major ordeal as tight airport security has become unavoidable. Who among us would have foreseen that a basic element of personal hygiene would become an advanced tactical weapon in the arsenal of terrorism?

Now is the perfect time to consider the significance of the re-establishment of Israel, Jesus Christ (the Jew who claimed to be the

Messiah and the Son of God), and the holy name of God, our Heavenly Father. Let us continue to delve into the Bible to discover more about the days in which we live. Let us be active participants in keeping His book in its rightful position at the top of the best-seller list.

THE FOUR-TOLD QUESTIONS

In this chapter, we will answer four of the most logical questions regarding today's return of the Jewish people into the land of Israel. We find these answers in the Old Testament book of Ezekiel. The prophet Ezekiel formatted his prophetic book in such a way as to stimulate the curiosity of his readers to the point that they feel compelled to ask themselves four basic questions.

After one reads Ezekiel Chapters 1–34, he or she becomes aware that the Jewish people were to undergo dispersion out of their homeland into the nations of the world. Chapter 34 declares that the Jewish people would then be re-gathered out of the nations of the world and brought back into their homeland, and, furthermore, that they would ultimately be ushered into the Messianic Kingdom. The Messianic Kingdom is the high point of Old Testament Jewish prophecy. In short, there would be dispersion, gathering and an ushering into the Messianic Kingdom.

Ezekiel assured us that the return of the Jews back into the land of Israel would not occur randomly. Rather, it would be an enormous undertaking orchestrated by God. With the magnitude of this event at the forefront of his reader's mind, he foresaw that the four following questions would arise. The thought process should go something like this:

Wait a minute. Before I read Ezekiel Chapters 35–39, let me ask a few questions!

1. How will Israel's historical enemies respond to their return?
2. What will be the condition of the Holy Land upon their return?
3. When will this gathering take place?
4. Why will this gathering take place?

We know today that the worldwide dispersion occurred between the years of AD 70 and 1948. We also realize the return of the Jews to the land of Israel officially commenced on May 14, 1948, the date the United Nations formally recognized Israel as the Jewish state. According to Ezekiel, this return will ultimately produce a faithful final remnant of Jews.

This remnant represents an ethnic contingency of Jews who survive the disasters associated with the Tribulation Period, realize Jesus Christ is the Messiah, and accept him as their personal Savior. Many Christian scholars refer to the Tribulation Period as the final seven years of the earth's timeline. They also suggest Christ returns to the Earth at the end of the Tribulation, defeats the Antichrist and his armies, and subsequently establishes a Messianic Kingdom for one-thousand years.[21]

1. HOW WILL THE HISTORICAL ENEMIES OF ISRAEL RESPOND TO THEIR RETURN?

Before Ezekiel 35–39 unfolds, the first legitimate question for the reader to ask regards how would their Arab neighbors, who throughout history harbored hatred towards the Jewish people, greet them upon their collective return back home into the Middle East. Would this ancient hatred expire due to sympathy for the Jewish people's dispersion plight? Perhaps a harsher reality would await them upon their return.

The answer is contained in Ezekiel 35:1–36:15. Upon their return, Ezekiel said, the latter would be the case. The surrounding Arab nations would protest the national return of the Jew into the region. Israel's enemies would revive the ancient hatred and oppose severely the Jewish people.

Ezekiel used clear terms in describing the hostility the Jewish people would face upon their return. Their enemies would hate them and shed their blood, according to Ezekiel 35:5. They would contest the Jews' right of return into, and their sovereignty over, the land of Israel, says Ezekiel 35:10. The entire process would be plagued by blasphemous propaganda (Ezek. 35:12). The Arabs would proudly boast "Aha" in a public proclamation as Israel's enemies (Ezek. 36:2).

Ezekiel foretold the events surrounding the Jews' return to the land of Israel in 1948, and what remains today. The historical enemies of Israel never abandoned their ancient hatred, even though 1,878 years had elapsed since the Jews left their homeland.

Unsuccessful conventional wars in 1948, 1956, 1967, and 1973 gave rise to the unconventional method of warfare we call terrorism. In conjunction, propaganda arose contesting the claims of the Jewish people's right to return to their ancient homeland. Both are products of the surrounding Arab nations, all of whom were historical enemies of Israel. Ezekiel got it right on the first question. Let's see how he fares on the next three.

2. WHAT WILL BE THE CONDITION OF THE HOLY LAND UPON THE JEWS' RETURN?

What would become of "the mountains, the hills, the rivers, the valleys, the desolate wastes, and the cities that have been forsaken, which became plunder and mockery to the rest of the nations all around?"[22]

Would the LORD restore the land to a condition capable of facilitating the massive influx of returning Jews?

We find the answer in Ezekiel 36:1–12. The land would be tilled and sown facilitating an abundance of agriculture as per Ezekiel 36:9. Men would be able to multiply, they would inhabit the cities, and they would rebuild the ruins (Ezek. 36:10). Human and animal life would thrive, and the general living conditions would be better there than before (Ezek. 36:11). Regarding the land, Ezekiel 36:12 tells us: "Yes, I will cause men to walk on you, *My people Israel*; they shall take possession of you, and you shall be their inheritance; no more shall you bereave them *of children.*"[23]

Indeed, Ezekiel predicted the land would be capable of supporting the return of millions of Jewish migrants. In fulfillment of numerous prophecies, the Jews are returning to the land promised to their patriarchs, Abraham, Isaac, and Jacob. I believe the parting of the Red Sea at the time of the Exodus of the Jews from Egypt pales in comparison to the miraculous navigation of millions of Jews back to Israel. Out of persecution and poverty into riches, Israel's doors have parted wide to bid them welcome. Though they met with Arab resistance, this should not overshadow the spectacle of their return.

So, Ezekiel is two-for-four. Israel now sustains Jewish life and endures Arab assault, and nations throughout the world recognize it as a productive nation. Let's see what Ezekiel says about the time of the gathering, which began in 1948.

3. WHEN WILL THE GATHERING TAKE PLACE?

Ezekiel does not answer this question in terms of time, but rather in terms of condition. He suggests that the Jewish people would find themselves in a horrifically grave condition, and that this would be their restoration point. The Jews would experience this fate while they, as a people, resided outside the land of Israel, scattered among the nations of the world.

Then He said to me, "Son of man, these bones are the whole house of Israel. They indeed say, '*Our bones are dry, our hope is lost, and we ourselves are cut off.*' Therefore prophesy and say to them, 'Thus says the LORD GOD: "*Behold, O My people, I will open your graves and cause you to come up from your graves, and bring you into the land of Israel.* Then you shall know that I *am* the LORD, when I have opened your graves, O My people, and brought you up from your graves. I will put My Spirit in you, and you shall live, and I will place you in your own land."'" (Ezek. 37:11–14, NKJV; emphasis added)

Ezekiel told us the LORD would bring the Jews into the land of Israel, meaning that they as a people would still be residing outside the land at the time. His usage of such descriptive terms as "dry bones," "lost hope," "cut off," and "grave," portrays the national condition of the Jewish people at the end of their dispersion. They would fall victim to a helpless and hopeless Holocaust condition whereby if God did not intervene they would be exterminated ("cut off"). Thus, their helpless condition entirely defined the metric of time.[24]

We now know from history that the Holocaust fulfilled Ezekiel's "dry bones" prophetic vision (Ezek. 37:1–14), and the answer to the question, "when will the re-gathering take place?" The hope of the Jewish people was lost as the events of World War II abruptly postponed their Zionist movement and their focus shifted from the homeland, naturally, to the Holocaust. The re-gathering took place immediately after the horrific conditions Ezekiel foretold.

Thus, Jewish people found themselves in such a grave situation that if their God did not intervene and return them to their homeland, their enemies would have completely exterminated them. Their God had long before promised their patriarchs Abraham, Isaac, and Jacob that the Jewish people would never be extinguished, but would be as the "stars of the heaven and as the sand which is on the seashore."[25]

God utilized the Allied forces of World War II to preserve the Jewish race.

Just as Ezekiel predicted, "a horrifically grave situation" victimized the Jewish people. It was evident that God needed to intervene for the sake of His Holy Name, or the world would face the possibility that every last Jew would be "cut off," at which point the great God Jehovah could be made a liar. Ezekiel accurately predicted it would come to that fatal point whereby God would have to move to protect the descendants of Abraham, Isaac, and Jacob.

> Therefore say to the house of Israel, "Thus says the LORD GOD: 'I do not do this [protect and restore] for your sake, O house of Israel, but for My holy name's sake, which you [Jews] have profaned among the nations wherever you went.'" (Ezek. 36:22, NKJV)

World War II concluded and the Jewish exterminators, the Nazis, met with defeat. Thus, the attempted genocide of the Jewish people also ended. General international sympathy for the oppression of the Jews by the Nazis led the United Nations to legislate the reestablishment of the nation of Israel.

As we see, Ezekiel accurately accessed the situation for us about 2,500 years before it occurred. As stated earlier, he declared in Ezekiel 37:12: "I will open your graves and cause you to come up from your graves, and bring you into the land of Israel." This prophecy did not regard itself with resurrection, but rather restoration. It predicted divine intervention for the ultimate prevention of Jewish genocide, coupled with the facilitation of Jewish return to the land of Israel.

Furthermore, Ezekiel stated: "I do not do this for your sake, O house of Israel," indicating that in the years leading up to the Holocaust, the Jews would do nothing notable on the world scene to cause other nations to esteem them as the client nation "My people Israel." In essence, their behavior would convey a national lack of belief in God.

From the Chosen People, disbelief would serve to defame the holy name of God. In this condition, the Jewish people would give the nations of the world no reason to respect their God, and would subject them to terrible treatment like that which they ultimately received during the Holocaust. This would be an intolerable situation for God, considering He had always advised that He was the only God. How could any god call himself God if his own people were without homeland, faith, righteous behavior, and divine protection?

> "When they [the Jews] came to the nations, wherever they went, they profaned My holy name—when they said of them, 'These *are* the people of the LORD [My people Israel], *and* yet they have gone out of His land.' But I had concern for My holy name, which the house of Israel had profaned among the nations wherever they went. Therefore say to the house of Israel, 'Thus says the LORD GOD: "I do not do this for your [unbelieving] sake, O house of Israel, but for My holy name's sake, which you have profaned among the nations wherever you went. And I will sanctify My great name, which has been profaned among the nations, which you have profaned in their midst; and the nations shall know that I *am* the LORD," says the LORD GOD, "when I am hallowed in you before their eyes. For I will take you from among the nations, gather you out of all countries, and bring you into your own land." (Ezek. 36:20–24, NKJV; emphasis added)

God's point here is that the Jews would return from the nations of the world in essentially the same spiritual condition as when they left. Nearly two-thousand years would come and go without an effectual religious change in the national condition of the Jewish people. They would regroup in a condition of unbelief, emphasizing that their God Jehovah would take responsibility for their return. God would need to restore His Holy Name after the centuries of damage done to it during the Jewish dispersion.

4. WHY WILL THE GATHERING TAKE PLACE?

This question leads Ezekiel to prophesy the momentous event that would have to occur to restore the holy name of God.

> "And I will sanctify My great name, which has been profaned among the nations, which you have profaned in their midst; and the nations shall know that I *am* the LORD," says the LORD GOD, "when I am hallowed in you [Jews] before their [Gentile nations] eyes." (Ezek. 36:23, NKJV; emphasis added)

It would only be fitting that along with the restoration of the Jewish people would come the restoration of the holy name of their God Jehovah. But how would God perform such a miracle? One would think that the mere rescue of the Jews from the genocide of the Holocaust, or perhaps the miraculous restoration process currently in place, would have been sufficient. However, as we look around, we see that the nations of the world are not cognizant of the conspicuous fingerprints of God all over the restoration process.

Therefore, Ezekiel describes something even greater—an event to come that is so spectacular the Gentile nations will take notice of the Jewish people and the holy name of their God.

> "So I will make My holy name known in the midst of My people Israel, and I will not *let them* profane My holy name anymore. Then the nations shall know that *I am* the LORD, the Holy One in Israel. Surely it is coming, and it shall be done," says the LORD GOD. "This *is* the day of which I have spoken." (Ezek. 39:7–8, NKJV; emphasis added)

God intended to make His Holy Name known in the midst of his people, Israel. Before reading the description of this event, let the reader recognize that at this point the Jewish people are classified as "My people Israel!"[26] This means God again recognizes the Jewish people as the Client Nation, the Chosen People of God. It also suggests that at this time, when God sanctifies His great name in the midst of "My people Israel," the Church is absent. Presently, the Church is esteemed as the people of God.

So where is the Church when God's people, Israel, once again take the front-and-center position in the divine plan of God? One possible answer is that the Rapture of the Church precedes the spectacular event whereby God upholds His Holy Name.

Ezekiel describes the main event by which God upholds His Holy Name in Chapters 38 and 39, a section commonly referred to as the Magog Invasion. While it is not the intent of this book to describe in detail this spectacular event, good commentary describing the event can be accessed through Dr. Arnold Fruchtenbaum's Ariel Ministries, as well as Chuck Missler's Koinonea House Ministry.[27]

The Magog Invasion occurs after the Holocaust, at some point during the period of the gathering of Jewish people into Israel. Ezekiel 38:8 describes the Jews as a people recovered from war, dwelling securely in the latter days in the mountains of Israel. The Jews dwell securely in villages without walls, gates, bars (Ezek. 38:11). They possess great spoils because of the success of their exceedingly great army over the Palestinians, and the surrounding Arab nations of Egypt, Saudi Arabia, Gaza, Jordan, Syria, and Lebanon.[28]

The Magog Invasion will team Russia, Iran, and several other modern-day, predominately Islamic, nations, but is devoid of the surrounding Arab nations of Egypt, Saudi Arabia, Gaza, Jordan, Syria, and Lebanon, in a confederated attempt to rise against the Jewish people. The Jewish people will find themselves residing in conditions we've already covered. Israel will bask in the glory of its military might and regional superiority when this formidable and unimaginable confederacy comes against them. The expanding nation of Israel will be no match for this offensive.

The chapter entitled *The Future Maps of Isralestine* contains projected maps depicting the Middle East geography as it should exist at the time of the Magog Invasion.[29] Refer to those maps now for a better understanding of the enormity of the event through which God will uphold His Holy Name.

Ezekiel 38:4 tells us that God stages this massive invasion: "I will turn you [invaders] around, put hooks into your jaws, and lead you out." It is an event specifically designed to be significant enough in scope to accomplish the divine protection of God, over His "Client Nation," i.e. "My people Israel."

To the spectator it would appear as though the whole ordeal is entirely disproportionate: the big Russia and Friends rising against tiny Israel, who is on its own. However, we are not to forget that the establishment of the means justifies God's desired end. In order for God to uphold His Holy Name after thousands of years of defamation, He obviously feels compelled to create an even greater storyline than David meets Goliath.

"And you, son of man, prophesy against Gog, and say, 'Thus says the LORD GOD: "Behold, I *am* against you, O Gog, the prince of Rosh, Meshech, and Tubal; and I will turn you around and lead you on, bringing you up from the far north, and bring you against the mountains of Israel. Then I will *knock the bow out* of your left hand, *and cause the arrows to fall* out of your right hand. *You shall fall upon the mountains* of Israel, you and all your troops and the peoples who are with you; *I will give you to birds of prey* of every sort and to the beasts of the field to be devoured. *You shall fall on the open field;* for I have spoken,"'" says the LORD GOD. "*And I will send fire on Magog* [Russia] and on those who live in security in the coastlands. Then they shall know that I *am* the LORD. So I will make My holy name known in the midst of My people Israel, and I will not *let them* profane My holy name anymore. Then the nations shall know that *I am* the LORD, the Holy One in Israel. (Ezek. 39:1–7, NKJV; emphasis added)

As Ezekiel states, God will uphold His Holy Name by conquering this momentous event. God intends to let the nations of the world know that Israel is indeed the client nation, "My people Israel," and that the holy name of God is alive and well after experiencing centuries of dismissal throughout the dispersion of the Jewish people.

God's followers did not entirely dismiss His name during this time. He did have adequate representation of His Holy Name in the Church during the long years of Jewish dispersion. However, the Church in general regressed throughout its existence in its understanding of the Jew's role in God's prophetic plan. In so doing, it de-emphasized the relationship between God and the Jewish people. This is problematic, because it minimizes the importance of the Jewish element within the Abrahamic Covenant. This unconditional covenant that God made with Abraham outlines divine policy regarding human existence.[30]

The nations of the world were left free to establish their own forms of international behavior, without regard for the Abrahamic Covenant. This created a most unfortunate situation, because, in essence, it has allowed the international community to function independently of divine rule. This would be acceptable only if divine rule did not exist; however, it does, and it cannot be ignored indefinitely. Thus, we understand the importance of God reestablishing the nation Israel as the Client Nation, and, in so doing, putting the world once again on notice that the God of the Jews is the only God, and that His name is holy.

In summary, we see that Ezekiel foretold the answers to the four questions surrounding the return of the Jew into the land of Israel: they would meet with resistance by the surrounding Arab nations; the land would be fitted to facilitate the massive migration of Jewish people destined to return to the Promised Land; the Jews would emerge from a horrific Holocaust, which would evidence the conclusion of their dispersion sequence; and, lastly, they would re-establish themselves as the Client Nation "My people Israel" and through them their God would again uphold His Holy Name.

ISRAEL'S EXCEEDINGLY GREAT ARMY

So I prophesied as He commanded me,
and breath came into them, and they lived,
and stood upon their feet, an exceedingly great army.

—EZEK. 37:10, NKJV

E zekiel 37:10 informs us that Israel, rising from a seemingly helpless fate, will establish for itself an "exceedingly great army." The Jews will change from victims to victors, from destroyed to destroyers, and from hunted to hunters. Today we witness the doors to the Holy Land, which approximately 2000 years ago bid them a hostile farewell, re-opening. One by one, they come home to Israel. With the Holocaust behind them and their ancient enemies before them, they arrive with one eye on the farm and the other on the fight.

The Jewish army rises to power to fulfill a specific purpose found within the prophetic plan of God. The outline below chronicles the events scheduled to occur as foretold by the prophets:

1. God gathers the Jews into the land of Israel from the four corners of the Earth.
2. Jews rebuild ruins and inhabit formerly abandoned cities.
3. They meet with Arab resistance.
4. Israel establishes an army in self-defense.
5. Surrounding Arab nations form a confederacy.
6. The confederacy plots to destroy Israel.
7. War starts between the confederacy and Israel.
8. Israel regains the title "My people Israel."
9. Israel decisively defeats the confederacy.
10. Israel takes prisoners of war.
11. The region is reshaped.
12. Israel expands its borders.
13. Israel dwells securely in the land.
14. Israel has become an "exceedingly great army."
15. This segment of the plan of God is fulfilled!

A primary purpose of this prophetic period is casting judgment upon the animosity established in ancient times toward the promises God made to Abraham. Long ago, Hagar, Ishmael, Esau, Moab, and Ammon formed adversarial attitudes toward God and His covenantal promises.[31] Throughout the years that followed, their descendants perpetuated this hatred and propelled this disposition across the region. Other historical enemies of Israel found it favorable to embrace this attitude. In time, this "ancient hatred" became cleverly enveloped into a religion, known as Islam.

1. GOD GATHERS THE JEWS INTO THE LAND OF ISRAEL

This gathering is foretold in numerous scriptures, just a few of which I will list. This present *Aliyah* process, whereby the world is witnessing the immigration of world Jewry back into the land of Israel, is the fulfillment of this gathering.[32]

For I will take you from among the nations, gather you out of all countries, and bring you into your own land. (Ezek. 36:24, NKJV)

Therefore prophesy and say to them, "Thus says the LORD GOD: 'Behold, O My people, I will open your graves and cause you to come up from your graves, and bring you into the land of Israel.'" (Ezek. 37:12, NKJV)

These passages from the prophet Ezekiel describe in detail the return of the Jews to the Holy Land. He declares that the Jewish people will come out from "among the nations," alluding to the fact that the Jewish people were dispersed worldwide. Secondly, God is rescuing these returning Jews from a horrifically grave Holocaust-type condition.

It shall come to pass in that day *That* the LORD shall set His hand again *the second time* To recover the remnant of His people who are left, From Assyria and Egypt, From Pathros and Cush, From Elam and Shinar, From Hamath and the islands of the sea. He will set up a banner for the nations, And will assemble the outcasts of Israel, And gather together the dispersed of Judah *From the four corners of the Earth.* (Isa. 11:11–12, NKJV; emphasis added)

Isaiah informs us the LORD will set His hand a second time to recover the remnant of His people from "the four corners of the Earth." To set "His hand" refers to an event that occurs because of divine orchestration. In this instance, God takes the responsibility to ensure the survival and return of a remnant of Jewish people. Isaiah declares that it is "a second time;" there is no third, fourth, or fifth occurrence referenced in scripture, making the second time both significant and final. There are theories as to what constitutes the first and the second times, and they are further discussed in the chapter *The Second Time: A Jewish Sequel.* Isaiah's use of the four corners idea signifies that the extent of the gathering is worldwide.

> That the LORD your God will bring you back from captivity, and have compassion on you, and gather you again [a second final time] from all the nations where the LORD your God has scattered you. If *any* of you are driven out to the farthest *parts* under heaven, from there the LORD your God will gather you, and from there He will bring you. Then the LORD your God will bring you to the land which your fathers possessed, and you shall possess it. *He will prosper you* [Jews] and multiply you more than your fathers. (Deut. 30:3–5, NKJV; emphasis added)

This Deuteronomy passage prescribes not only the worldwide gathering, but also the restoration of Jewish fortunes. This is another purpose for the rise of the exceedingly great army. This army will be instrumental in the recapture of the real estate of the Promised Land, and as such, the inherit resources and wealth therein.

2. THEY REBUILD RUINS AND INHABIT FORMERLY ABANDONED CITIES

During the dispersion period, the cities of Israel were forsaken and reduced to ruins. Cultural landmarks were laid to waste. Surrounding nations swallowed the country from every side, and in so doing gave themselves the land promised to Abraham and his descendants, the Jewish people. The prophet Ezekiel presaged this scenario over 2,500 years ago.

> And you, son of man, prophesy to the mountains of Israel, and say, "O mountains of Israel, hear the word of the LORD!

Thus says the LORD GOD: 'Because the enemy has said
of you, "Aha! The ancient heights have become our possession,"'" therefore prophesy, and say, "Thus says the LORD
GOD: 'Because *they made you desolate and swallowed you up
on every side*, so that you became the possession of the rest of
the nations, and you are taken up by the lips of talkers and
slandered by the people therefore, O mountains of Israel, hear
the word of the LORD GOD!'" Thus says the LORD GOD
to the mountains, the hills, the rivers, the valleys, the desolate
wastes, and the cities that have been forsaken, which became
plunder and mockery to the rest of the nations all around
therefore thus says the LORD GOD: "Surely I have spoken in
My burning jealousy against *the rest of the nations and against
all Edom*, who gave *My land* to themselves as a possession,
with wholehearted joy and spiteful minds, in order to plunder
its open country." (Ezek. 36:1–5, NKJV; emphasis added)

The key phrases in these scriptures are the "rest of the nations
all around," "all Edom," "My land," and "they made you desolate
and swallowed you up on every side." The surrounding Arab nations,
including Edom, took full advantage of the land of Israel while the
Jewish people were reduced to absentee owners during their centuries of worldwide dispersion.[33] In essence, they homesteaded the Holy
Land.

At the heart of the conflict in the Middle East today is this Holy
Land. The return of the Jew has meant the eviction of Arab trespassers.
Many have become homeless refugees, and the surrounding nations
from which their ancestors came have not facilitated their return. Israel
seeks acceptance among these nations for the mere right to exist as a
nation. In order for these nations to concede this right, they must forfeit much of what they consider their real estate holdings in the Holy
Land of Israel. "They have not conceded," nor will they, according to
the prophecy of Psalm 83, apart from the Israeli conquest over them.

The Arab trespassers expect to extract a heavy price for this real estate, and until they receive this ransom, they systematically terrorize the Holy Land. Ultimately, scripture suggests that whether or not the price is honored, Jews will remain the victims of the ancient hatred infecting the region[34]. Regardless of the formidable opposition awaiting the Jewish people upon their return to the land of Israel, from their trespassing Arab neighbors Ezekiel further prophesies that the cities shall be reclaimed and the ruins rebuilt.

> But you, O mountains of Israel, you shall shoot forth your branches and yield your fruit to *My people Israel, for they are about to come.* For indeed I am for you, and I will turn to you, and you shall be tilled and sown. I will multiply men upon you, all the house of Israel, all of it; and *the cities shall be inhabited and the ruins rebuilt.* (Ezek. 36:8–10; NKJV, emphasis added)

3. THEY MEET WITH RESISTANCE IN THE REGION

Enemies unsuccessfully advanced at least three primary assaults against Israel in 1948, 1967, and 1973. Islamic nations have embraced the unconventional method of terror as an alternative to failed conventional warfare. Scripture suggested this would be the case.

> *The terror you* [Edom–Palestinian Refugees] *inspire* and the pride of your heart have deceived you, you who live in the clefts of the rock, who hold the height of the hill.[35] Although you make your nest as high as the eagle's, from there I will bring you down, says the LORD. (Jer. 49:16, NRSV; emphasis added)

> I have heard the reproach of Moab [Central Jordan], And the insults of the people of Ammon [Northern Jordan], With

which *they have reproached My people* [Israel], *And made arrogant threats against their borders.* (Zeph. 2:8, NKJV; emphasis added)

Thus says the LORD GOD: "Because the enemy has said of you [Israel], 'Aha! The ancient heights have become our possession,'" (Ezek. 36:2, NKJV)

Thus says the Lord GOD: "Because of what Edom [Southern Jordan] did against the house of Judah, by taking vengeance, and has greatly offended by avenging itself on them." (Ezek. 25:12, NKJV)

For violence against your [Esau] brother Jacob [Israel], Shame shall cover you, And you shall be cut off forever. (Obad. 1:10, NKJV; emphasis added)

Because you have had an ancient hatred, and have shed the blood of the children of Israel by the power of the sword at the time of their calamity, when *their iniquity came to an end.* (Ezek. 35:5, NKJV; emphasis added)

As a people, the Jews had been led apostate by their leaders leading up to and during the first advent of Christ. This resulted in the national rejection of Christ as their Messiah. This national and unpardonable sin detailed in Matthew 12:24–31 was the iniquity referenced by Ezekiel, an iniquity that ended with the Holocaust. This event was the climactic, catastrophic event that concluded the discipline of the Jewish people. From the point of Israel's national rejection of Christ forward, in fulfillment of Hosea 1:9–10, the title "My people Israel" began to slip away from the Jews, as Christ turned His future efforts toward both Jew and Gentile. He began speaking in Parables in Matthew 13, evidencing His ministerial turnabout.

The Hebrew word for iniquity is *avon*, and is first used in Genesis 4:13 with regard to the punishment of Cain for the shedding of his brother Abel's blood. Hebrews 12:24 declares that a better blood than Abel's was shed upon the cross.

> To Jesus the Mediator of the new covenant, and to the blood of sprinkling that speaks better things than *that of* Abel. (Heb. 12:24, NKJV)

All the guilt for the righteous bloodshed, even Abel's, was to be measured against the Jewish generation present at the time of the first coming of Christ. The client nation the world knew for the longest time as "My people Israel" had become a brood of vipers. The Jewish leadership were likened to serpents who would ultimately shed the blood of Christ like their fathers before them shed the blood of the prophets who foretold of Christ.

> Therefore you are witnesses against yourselves that you are sons of those who murdered the prophets. *Fill up, then, the measure of your fathers' guilt.* Serpents, brood of vipers! How can you escape the condemnation of hell? Therefore, indeed, I send you prophets, wise men, and scribes: *some* of them you will kill and crucify, and *some* of them you will scourge in your synagogues and persecute from city to city, *that on you may come all the righteous blood shed on the Earth, from the blood of righteous Abel to the blood of Zechariah*, son of Berechiah, whom you murdered between the temple and the altar. Assuredly, *I say to you, all these things will come upon this generation.* (Matt. 23:31–36, NKJV; emphasis added)

The connection of brother spilling brother's blood and receiving *avon*, or punishment, for it is as follows: Cain was Abel's older brother. Cain was jealous of Abel's fellowship with God, because his works were evil and Abel's works were righteous. As such, Cain spilled the blood of his brother.[36] For this Cain received avon:

> And Cain said to the LORD, "My punishment *is* greater than I can bear! Surely You have driven me out this day from the face of the ground; I shall be hidden from Your face; I shall be a fugitive and a vagabond on the Earth, and it will happen *that* anyone who finds me will kill me." (Gen. 4:13–14, NKJV)

Likewise, His Jewish brethren—playing the role of jealous older brother—spilled the blood of Christ. Their ways and deeds were evil like Cain's, and the works of Christ were righteous like Abel. Their sacrificial offerings, much like those of Cain, fell short of God's acceptance in that they lacked true repentance. Their Mosaic law, which they had reduced to a condition of hypocrisy, eventually passed away and was replaced by the better "New Covenant."[37] Christ was, and still remains, a Jew. He therefore justifiably considers the Jewish people His brethren.[38]

> So I scattered them [The Jews] among the nations, and they were dispersed throughout the countries; *I judged them* according to their *ways* and their *deeds*. (Ezek. 36:19, NKJV; emphasis added)

As punishment, the LORD drove Cain out from the face of the ground. Similarly, the avon of the Jewish people were driven from the face of the land of Israel. Cain became a fugitive and a vagabond on the Earth, always under threat of persecution. "I shall be a fugitive and a vagabond on the Earth, and it will happen that anyone who finds me will kill me."[39] We can make a comparison to the Jewish people during their centuries of worldwide dispersion. Some glaring examples of Jewish persecution during the dispersion period were the Spanish expulsion of 1492 and the Holocaust, concluding in 1944.

Lastly, Cain complained, "I shall be hidden from Your face." This was the like predicament of the Jewish people; they became "not my people," seemingly hidden from the face of God.[40] Ezekiel 36:19 informs us that the Jewish people have been judged. They have been judged severely for "their (avon) iniquity," and though they remain in the national condition of unbelief in the Messiah, God is moving forward with His prophetic program.

4. ISRAEL ESTABLISHES AN ARMY IN SELF-DEFENSE

Israel has become a sharpened military instrument as a result of the Arab assaults against them. Its army has arisen, unbeknownst to the masses, in preparation for the fulfillment of the sworn oath of God foretold by Ezekiel.

> Therefore thus says the LORD GOD: "I have raised My hand in *an oath* that surely the nations that are around you [Israel] shall bear their own shame." (Ezek. 36:7, NKJV; emphasis added)

By way of review, God had Ezekiel prophesy that the Jews would find themselves in a grave-like condition; this was fulfilled 24 centuries later at the time of the Holocaust. Prior to Ezekiel, Isaiah had informed them that they would be restored as a people and brought back into the land of Israel a second time, of which the first phase is ongoing today.

God also had Ezekiel declare that the land upon which the Jews were to return was swallowed up and homesteaded by the surrounding Arab nations "all around." As a result, the land of Israel bore the shame of those neighboring Arab nations:

> Therefore prophesy concerning the land of Israel, and say to the mountains, the hills, the rivers, and the valleys, "Thus

says the LORD GOD: 'Behold, I have spoken in My jealousy and My fury, because you have *borne the shame of the nations.*'" (Ezek. 36:6, NKJV; emphasis added)

God raises His hand in an oath to reverse the direction of shame placed upon Israel. He declares through Ezekiel: "Surely the nations that are around you shall bear their own shame." God will execute the shame of those hostile Arab nations that "are around" Israel in compliance with the curse-for-curse-in-kind clause inscribed in Genesis 12:3. This clause is the historically proven foreign policy procedure of God toward the Gentile nations. The reversal of shame will involve the shedding of Arab blood, as they are guilty of shedding Jewish blood. It will involve placing portions of Arab lands under Jewish sovereignty, as they had done to the land of Israel, and it will involve the taking of the spoils of war. The condition the Jewish people find themselves enjoying subsequent to these things above is what the Magog alliance appears to be after.

After many days you will be visited. In the latter years you will come into the land of those brought back from the sword *and* gathered from many people on the mountains of Israel, which had long been desolate; they were brought out of the nations, and now all of them dwell safely. (Ezek. 38:8, NKJV)

Thus says the LORD GOD: "On that day it shall come to pass *that* thoughts will arise in your mind, and you will make an evil plan: You will say, 'I will go up against a land of unwalled villages; I will go to *a peaceful people, who dwell safely,* all of them dwelling without walls, and having neither bars nor gates—to take plunder and to take booty, to stretch out your hand against *the waste places that are again inhabited,* and against *a people* gathered from the nations, *who have acquired* livestock and goods, who dwell in the midst of the land.'

Sheba, Dedan the merchants of Tarshish, and all their young lions will say to you, 'Have you come to take plunder? Have you gathered your army to take booty, to carry away silver and gold, to take away livestock and goods, to take *great plunder*?'" (Ezek. 38:10–13 NKJV; emphasis added)

These excerpts summarize well the point of Israel's condition prior to this Russian-Iranian Magog advance.[41] "In the latter years those brought out of the nations, a peaceful people, who dwell safely, the waste places that are again inhabited, a people who have acquired great plunder."

This condition is for the most part the result of the Israeli Conquest over the Psalm 83 confederacy, of the surrounding Arab nations. Sheba and Dedan, which are ancient cities most likely representing the countries of Yemen and Saudi Arabia, acknowledge the great plunder Israel has acquired through the defeat of these Arab nations. They, along with the young merchants of Tarshish, appear to abstain from enjoining themselves with the Russian-Iranian Magog alliance.

As pointed out in a previous chapter, the Psalm 83 confederate Arab nations are absent from the Russian-Iranian alliance.[42] Some commentators have found it interesting that Palestinians, Lebanese, Syrians, Jordanians, Saudi's, and Egyptians, who are presently the most observable opponents of the Jewish state, appear to opt out of this advance. The logical explanation for their transparency would be their prior defeat at the hands of Israel's exceedingly great army.

Further on in this book we find passages that appear to depict these Arab peoples displaced from their homelands. Many of their citizens are killed, displaced, or captured and placed in internment camps. The exceedingly great army of Israel seizes their land, livestock, and wealth. Israel, no longer living under Arab threat, becomes a peaceful state dwelling in unwalled villages in the latter years.

Presently there is little doubt among any nation in the region or the world as to which Middle Eastern nation is most militarily dominant. It is Israel, who has risen to this position of prowess in less than sixty years. They have had to—their survival as a nation depended upon their ability to fight off numerous Arab assaults. It is becoming increasingly clear that Israel has rapidly been fashioned into the military instrument prophesied about in Ezekiel 37:10. All that stands between them and the title an "exceedingly great army" is the Israeli Conquest over the Psalm 83:6–8 Arab confederacy.

5. THE SURROUNDING ARAB NATIONS FORM INTO A CONFEDERACY

Lebanon to the north, Syria to the northeast, Jordan to the east, Saudi Arabia to the southeast, Gaza to the west, and the Sinai Peninsula and Egypt to the south all number themselves among the confederacy. [43] Hints of this confederacy surfaced during the Arab advances against Israel in 1948, 1956, 1967, and 1973. However, none of these fits the description of the final fulfillment of the Psalm 83:1–8 prophecy.

6. THE CONFEDERACY MUTUALLY CONSENTS TO DESTROY THE NATION ISRAEL

To date, the consensus among these nations is to reject Israel's right to exist. There is mounting international pressure upon these Arab nations to change this attitude and to accept Israel's nationhood. Perhaps the international community will succeed in forcing these nations to accept Israel's right to exist, though at some point in the not-so-distant future these nations will assemble into a confederacy whose mandate is nothing less than the extermination of the Jewish people and the recapture of the Holy Land of Israel.

> Do not keep silent, O God! Do not hold Your peace, And do not be still, O God! For behold, Your enemies make a tumult; And those who hate You have lifted up their head. They have

taken crafty counsel against Your people, And consulted together against Your sheltered ones. They have said, "Come,
and let us cut them off from *being* a nation, That the name of
Israel may be remembered no more." For they have consulted
together with one consent; They form a confederacy against
You...(Psa. 83:1–5, NKJV; emphasis added) Who said, "Let
us take for ourselves the pastures of God for a possession."
(Psa.83:12, NKJV)

These nations will confederate in an attempt to promote the
spread and dominance of Islam, the destruction of the Jewish people
and their religion, and of course the possession of the property of Israel with all of its recently rebuilt ruins and revitalized interests.

7. WAR BREAKS OUT IN THE MIDDLE EAST BETWEEN THE CONFEDERACY AND ISRAEL

Soon to come is a major and devastating war in the Middle East between the confederacy of Psalm 83:5–8 and the exceedingly great
army of Israel. The previous Arab advances against Israel will be child's
play compared to this final confederate attempt.

"Therefore behold, the days are coming," says the LORD,
"That I will cause to be heard *an alarm of war* In Rabbah
[Amman, Jordan] of the Ammonites; It shall be a desolate
mound, And her villages shall be burned with fire. *Then Israel
shall take possession* of his inheritance," says the LORD. (Jer.
49:2, NKJV; emphasis added)

Behold, he [the confederacy of Esau] shall come up like a lion
from the floodplain of the Jordan Against the dwelling place
of the strong [the army of Israel]; But I will suddenly make

him [Esau] run away from her [Israel]. (Jer. 49:19, NKJV, abbreviated)

Flee, turn back, dwell in the depths, O inhabitants of Dedan [Saudi Arabia]! For I will bring the calamity of Esau [Southern Jordan] upon him [Esau's descendants], The time that I will punish him. (Jer. 49:8, NKJV)

These three scriptures, along with many more scattered throughout this book, point to a Middle-Eastern war that many Bible scholars do not appear to recognize is coming. Among those who do, many place its occurrence in the final seven-year tribulation period—I respectfully disagree. This event will occur soon, well in Advance of both the Russian-Iranian Magog invasion and the seventieth week of Daniel (i.e., the Tribulation). During the Tribulation Period, this army, having previously won the acclaimed title of being exceedingly great, will be sidelined for the first three-and-one-half years while a false and temporary peace accord is confirmed.[44] Then, in the second three-and-one-half years, this army is defeated, and the Jews flee Israel for safety elsewhere, as the Antichrist advances in an attempt to destroy them.[45]

8. ISRAEL REGAINS THE TITLE "MY PEOPLE ISRAEL"

Somewhere, in the midst of events listed in this chapter, the Jewish State of Israel rises to its former status as the "Client Nation," chosen of God. When this occurs, the nation will again be identified as "My people Israel". The next chapter is dedicated to describe the significance of this national name-changing event. The compilation of scriptures contained in the following chapter encourages the placement of this episode here chronologically. I reference it now to introduce the topic, but defer to the forthcoming *My People Israel* chapter for further details.

9. ISRAEL DECISIVELY DEFEATS THE CONFEDERACY

The army of Israel will defeat the Psalm 83 confederacy, and as a result God will fulfill the oath He made in Ezekiel 36:7. The confederacy of Arab nations will be humiliated for their attempt to expire the Jewish race. Historians will record their failed attempts alongside those of Hitler at the time of the Holocaust, and Pharaoh at the time of the Hebrew Exodus out of Egypt. Additionally the divine foreign policy contained in the Genesis 12:3 clause of the Abrahamic covenant, will be demonstrated again to the watchful eyes of humanity.

The passages below pertain to the Israeli conquest over their ancient enemies.

> The house of Jacob shall be a fire, And the house of Joseph a flame; But the house of Esau shall be stubble; They shall kindle them and devour them, And no survivor shall remain of the house of Esau, For the LORD has spoken. (Obad. 1:18, NKJV)

Israel, represented by the house of Jacob and Joseph reduces Southern Jordan, which is represented by Esau, to rubble. This defeat is thorough leaving no survivor.

> Then your mighty men, O Teman, shall be dismayed, To the end that everyone from the mountains of Esau May be cut off by slaughter. (Obad. 1:9, NKJV)

Obadiah 1:9 describes the soldiers of Teman, which was an important city in Edom, as having been slaughtered.[46] This emphasizes the severity of Israel's defeat over the Palestinian descendants of Edom. Teman's modern equivalent may be Taiwan, about 3 miles (5 km) east of Petra. However, Teman and the mountains of Esau appear to be representative of the entire region of Edom in this passage.[47]

Therefore thus says the LORD GOD: "I will also stretch out My hand against Edom, cut off man and beast from it, and make it desolate from Teman; Dedan [Saudi Arabia] shall fall by the sword. I will lay My vengeance on Edom by the hand of My people Israel [Israeli Defense Force I.D.F.], that they may do in Edom according to My anger and according to My fury; and they shall know My vengeance," says the LORD GOD. (Ezek. 2513–14, NKJV)

The same hand that God lifted up in a sworn oath he will stretch out in order to lift up the great army of Israel. This army will execute God's revenge against the Arabs who attack the Jews and, in so doing, assault the Abrahamic covenant. This war extends into Saudi Arabia, as the army of Israel advances beyond the Southern border of Jordan into northwest Saudi Arabia, represented by Dedan.

Therefore hear the counsel of the LORD that He has taken against Edom, And His purposes that He has proposed against the inhabitants of Teman: Surely the least of the flock shall draw them out; Surely He shall make their dwelling places desolate with them. The Earth shakes at the noise of their fall; At the cry its noise is heard at the Red Sea. (Jer. 49:20–21 NKJV)

The results are devastating for the descendants of Esau; even the least of the Jews possesses dominance over them, or draws them out. This is a possible reference to the capture process resulting from the military defeat. Israel will take prisoners of war. The noise refers to this war and all of its thundering sounds. This war does not limit its battleground to southern Jordan, but extends as far south as the Red Sea. This places the confederate members of Saudi Arabia, Southern Jordan, and Egypt within its scope. Jeremiah says the Earth shakes at the sound of their fall. This shows the magnitude of the affect that the

Israeli Conquest over the Arab nations will have upon the international community. The Hebrew word used is "raash," which reflects the trembling experienced during a devastating earthquake and its aftershocks.

> But I have made Esau bare; I have uncovered his secret places, And he shall not be able to hide himself. *His descendants are plundered,* His brethren *and his neighbors,* And he is no more. (Jer. 49:10, NKJV; emphasis added)

Israel makes barren the territory of southern Jordan because of this war. The Israelis plunder the descendants of Esau and his genealogy appears to end. The Jews also plunder the neighboring confederate nations involved in the conflict.

> He will set up a banner for the nations, And will assemble the outcasts of Israel, And gather together the dispersed of Judah From the four corners of the Earth. Also the envy of Ephraim shall depart, And *the adversaries of Judah shall be cut off;* Ephraim shall not envy Judah, And Judah shall not harass Ephraim. But *they shall fly down upon* the shoulder of the Philistines toward the west; Together they shall *plunder* the *people of the East;* They shall lay their hand on Edom and Moab; And the people of Ammon shall obey them. (Isa. 11:12–14, NKJV; emphasis added)

The army of Israel will cut off its confederate adversaries, and then come down upon the Gaza territory. In continuing their conquest, they plunder the people of the East, which, according to its first scriptural usage in Genesis 29:1, would be Syria. They then lay their hands on all of Jordan, causing its capitol to fall under Jewish sovereignty. Ammon represents northern Jordan, the location of the capital city of Amman. Isaiah says the people of Ammon shall obey them, depicting the surrender of Jordanian sovereignty.

The burden against Damascus. Behold, Damascus will cease from *being* a city, And it will be a ruinous heap. (Isa. 17:1, NKJV)

The city with the longest standing history of civilian habitation will be extinguished. It, like much of Jordan, will be reduced to rubble.[48] Presently, almost every known Middle Eastern terrorist organization has representation in Damascus. Soon, they will have none. How fitting that the city most adversarial to the nation of Israel will cease to exist.

Against Damascus. "Hamath and Arpad are shamed, For they have heard bad news. They are fainthearted; There is trouble on the sea; It cannot be quiet. Damascus has grown feeble; She turns to flee, And fear has seized her. Anguish and sorrows have taken her like a woman in labor. Why is the city of praise [Jerusalem] not deserted, the city of My joy? Therefore her young men shall fall in her [Damascus] streets, And all the *men of war* shall be cut off in that day," says the LORD of hosts. (Jer. 49:23–26 NKJV; emphasis added)

In that day, Egypt will be like women, and will be afraid and fear because of the waving of the hand of the LORD of hosts, which He waves over it. And the land of *Judah will be a terror to Egypt*; everyone who makes mention of it will be afraid in himself, because of the counsel of the LORD of hosts which He has determined against it. (Isa. 19:16–17, NKJV; emphasis added)

Even Egypt will be in the sights of the exceedingly great army of Israel. The picture Isaiah aptly portrays is that of a fragile, unarmed female fighting a skilled male warrior wielding a mighty sword. The woman is frightened as the warrior waves his sword in the air.

10. ISRAEL TAKES PRISONERS OF WAR

"Wail, O Heshbon, for Ai is plundered! Cry, you daughters of Rabbah, Gird yourselves with sackcloth! Lament and run to and fro by the walls; For Milcom shall go into captivity With his priests and his princes together...But afterward I will bring back The captives of the people of Ammon," says the LORD. (Jer. 49:3,6, NKJV)

"Woe to you, O Moab! The people of Chemosh perish; For your sons have been taken captive, And your daughters captive. Yet I will bring back the captives of Moab In the latter days," says the LORD. Thus far is the judgment of Moab. (Jer. 48:46–47, NKJV)

Leave your fatherless children [descendants of Esau], I will preserve them alive; And let your widows trust in Me. (Jer. 49:11, NKJV)

Israel will establish future detention camps in the regions of Southern Lebanon and the Negev. Israel is accustomed to imprisoning known Palestinian terrorists. This process will greatly intensify as Israel captures prisoners of war from the various Psalm 83 confederate nations.[49]

The captivity of Milcom, the Ammonite god, and Chemosh, the Moabite god, may have interesting ramifications. Presently, the god served by most Jordanians is Allah. The Islamic faith emerged subsequent to the writings of these prophecies. Islam put under a monotheistic umbrella the polytheistic practices of the Arabs in the region. Estimates that as many as 360 various gods celebrated by the Arabs in the Middle East were packaged into one god named Allah. Prophetic phrases like Milcom shall go into captivity, and Chemosh perish, may imply the diminished scale of Islam, at least in the Middle East.

This they shall have for their pride, Because they have reproached and made arrogant threats Against the people of the
LORD of hosts. The LORD *will be* awesome to them, For
He will reduce to nothing all the gods of the Earth; People shall
worship Him, Each one from his place, Indeed all the shores
of the nations. (Zeph. 2:10–11, NKJV; emphasis added)

11. THE REGION IS RESHAPED

Due to the magnified scope of Israel's military campaign, the region
will experience severe damage. Israel will levy a series of decisive
blows, and gain sovereignty over much of the Middle East. In the
passages below, Syria, Jordan, and the Gaza Strip come under serious
attack, and what were once thriving cities or territories become desolate wastelands.

The burden against Damascus. "Behold, Damascus [Syria]
will cease from being a city, And it will be *a ruinous heap.*"
(Isa. 17:1, NKJV; emphasis added)

"Therefore behold, the days are coming," says the LORD,
"That I will cause to be heard an alarm of war In Rabbah
[Northern Jordan] of the Ammonites; It shall be *a desolate
mound,* And her villages shall be burned with fire. Then Israel
shall take possession of his inheritance," says the LORD. (Jer.
49:2, NKJV; emphasis added)

But I have made *Esau bare;* [Southern Jordan] I have uncovered his secret places, And he shall not be able to hide himself.[50] His descendants are plundered, His brethren and his
neighbors, And he is no more. (Jer. 49:10, NKJV; emphasis
added)

For *Gaza* shall be *forsaken,* And *Ashkelon desolate*; They [Israeli Defense Force] shall *drive out Ashdod* at noonday, And *Ekron shall be uprooted.* (Zeph. 2:4, NKJV; emphasis added)

12. ISRAEL EXPANDS ITS BORDERS

The result of a military conquest is sovereignty over the affected territories. This rule of thumb appears to apply in this case. Israel will begin to resemble the tribal territories of old.[51]

The South shall possess the mountains of Esau (southern Jordan), and the Lowland shall possess Philistia (Gaza Strip). They shall possess the fields of Ephraim and the fields of Samaria (West Bank). Benjamin shall possess Gilead (West Bank & Golan Heights). (Obad. 1:19, NKJV)

The Negev will possess Southern Jordan, and the lowland of Judah will possess the Gaza Strip and the southern parts of the West Bank. Northern Israel will possess the northern part of the West Bank, the Golan Heights, much of northern Jordan, and southern Syria.

"Therefore behold, the days are coming," says the LORD, "That I will cause to be heard an alarm of war In Rabbah [Northern Jordan] of the Ammonites; It shall be a desolate mound, And her villages shall be burned with fire. Then *Israel shall take possession of his inheritance*," says the LORD. (Jer. 49:2, NKJV; emphasis added)

Much of modern-day Jordan was once part of the inheritance of Israel. The tribes of East Manasseh, Gad, Benjamin, and Reuben, once possessed land that is presently under Jordanian Sovereignty.

In that day five cities in the land of Egypt will speak the language of Canaan [Hebrew] and swear by the LORD of hosts;
one will be called the City of Destruction. In that day there
will be an altar to the LORD in the midst of the land of
Egypt, and a pillar to the LORD at its border. (Isa. 19:18–19,
NKJV)

Isaiah appears to suggest that the Expansion of Israeli sovereignty
in the region will burden even Egypt to some degree. Five Hebrew-
speaking cities will develop in the land of Egypt. In the center of the
country, an altar will be erected to Jehovah, and at the border, a pillar
will be erected to the God of the Jews. The altar may be built to offer
sacrifices to Jehovah, which was often the scene in the days of old
when Mosaic Law was operative.

13. ISRAEL DWELLS SECURELY IN THE LAND

Israel is elevated to a condition of regional superiority due to their
decisive victory over the confederacy of the surrounding Arab nations.
As such, they dwell securely in the Middle East for a time, a point
already detailed in the chapter entitled *Yisrael Yashab Betach: Israel
Dwelling Securely.*[52]

14. ISRAEL BECOMES AN EXCEEDINGLY GREAT ARMY

So I prophesied as He commanded me, and breath came into
them, and they lived, and stood upon their feet, an exceedingly great army. (Ezek. 37:10, NKJV)

Undeniably, the result of all the events outlined in this chapter
earns Israel the right to classify its defense force (IDF), as an "exceedingly great army." To genuinely achieve such a title, it is required that

the army delivers a decisive victory in a full-scale war. The Psalm 83 confederate advance against tiny Israel will be considered by the international community a full-scale war. Repeating Jeremiah 49:21: The Earth shakes at the noise of their fall; At the cry its noise is heard at the Red Sea.

15. GOD FULFILLS THIS SEGMENT OF HIS PLAN

Again, the purpose of this segment was to judge the animosity established in ancient times and perpetuated through the ages to the covenantal promises God gave to Abraham. The Psalm 83 confederate advance is a direct assault against the Abrahamic covenant. It is an attempt to kill the Jewish people and confiscate the land of Israel. The preservation of both are critical elements contained within the covenant.

Furthermore, if the enemies of the Jews succeeded in exterminating them, there would be no remnant left to fulfill the mandate of the second coming of Christ, which is the Jewish remnant to repent and beckon His return.[53] Likewise, the return of the Messiah fulfills the Davidic aspects of the covenant and the New Covenant, which is an amplification of the entire Abrahamic covenant. God promised Abraham a people, a place, and an eternal throne; unfortunately for the Arab confederacy, the survival of this covenant is non-negotiable.

MY PEOPLE ISRAEL

God formally recognized the descendants of Abraham, Isaac, and Jacob in scripture as His people in Exodus 3:7. God declared: "I have surely seen the oppression of my people who are in Egypt."[54] More than three-hundred years had passed after the death of Jacob, and God, in remembrance of His covenant with Abraham, put the world on notice that these people were "My people."

Not long before, Pharaoh of Egypt had attempted to weaken God's people with his campaign to kill their newborn male children.[55] This act, along with his stepped-up enslavement of the Jews, provoked the contents of the Abrahamic Covenant into enactment.[56] The historical events that followed evidenced the supremacy of God and His faithfulness to His covenant with Abraham. Everything subsequently fashioned by Pharaoh to harm God's people boomeranged back to harm Pharaoh and his people in a like manner.

The world saw that these, the descendants of Abraham, Isaac, and Jacob, were the people of God. Nothing could suppress their supreme God from fulfilling His unconditional covenant custom made for Abraham and his descendants, the Jews.

> For you *are* a holy people to the LORD your God; the LORD your God has chosen you to be a people for Himself, a special

treasure above all the peoples on the face of the Earth. The LORD did not set His love on you nor choose you because you were more in number than any other people, for you were the least of all peoples; but because the LORD loves you, and *because He would keep the oath which He swore to your fathers,* the LORD has brought you out with a mighty hand, and redeemed you from the house of bondage, from the hand of Pharaoh king of Egypt. (Deut. 7:6–8, NKJV; emphasis added)

These passages from Deuteronomy adequately describe the preferred client-nation status once bestowed upon Israel. They were the least of all peoples, but because God loved them and swore an oath to their patriarchal fathers Abraham, Isaac, and Jacob, they would one day become a holy people. They would be the chosen people of God, treasured above all the peoples on Earth. People throughout the world would come to know them as "My people Israel."

As we study the history of the Jewish people, we see a continual love-hate relationship with God developed amongst their culture throughout time. When they were in love with God they were obedient to His callings and were blessed accordingly. They were mighty and prosperous, and the land of Israel produced bountifully. However, when they were indifferent toward God and had digressed into idolatrous practices, God severely disciplined them. Jewish leadership misdirected the nation, the military experienced defeat, rain did not fall in due season, and the land failed to produce.

Several Old Testament passages remind us that their dominant tendency was to be fickle, rather than faithful to their calling as the client nation.[57] As such, God gave official notice through Hosea the prophet that a time would arrive whereby the client nation Israel would become "not my people," and would be stripped of their coveted "My people Israel" title.[58] The ramifications of the fulfillment of this prophecy were staggering! Humans could question the very character of God's covenant-making capabilities if indeed God disinherited the true descendants of Abraham, Isaac, and Jacob.

> Then the Angel of the LORD called to Abraham a second time out of heaven, and said: "*By Myself I have sworn*, says the LORD, because you have done this thing, and have not withheld your son [Isaac], your only *son* [not Ishmael]—blessing I will bless you, and multiplying *I will multiply your descendants as the stars* of the heaven *and as the sand* which *is* on the seashore; and your descendants shall possess the gate of their enemies. In *your seed* all the nations of the Earth shall be blessed, *because you have obeyed My voice.*" (Gen. 22:15–18, NKJV; emphasis added)

The Angel of the LORD, which scholars commonly teach to be an Old Testament reference to the pre-incarnate Jesus Christ, tells Abraham that God has sworn by nothing less than His own righteous character that because Abraham obeyed God, Abraham's descendants would multiply without end. In those days, the numerical equivalent to infinity was the innumerable number of the stars of heaven or the grains of sand on the seashore.

This scripture offers no opt-out clause. God based this sworn oath to multiply the descendants of Abraham upon an obedient act of Abraham "because you have done this thing, and have not withheld your son, your only son," and no matter how many the disobedient acts of his descendants that followed may have been, this promise was understood to be irreversible.

The question then arises: Could it be that the multiplication of Abraham's descendants will never cease, but unlike their father Abraham, they as a people might reach a point of hardening or callousness toward God? Those who recognized the contents of the Abrahamic covenant could not conclude this definitively, because through one of his descendants, his "seed," all the nations of the Earth were to be blessed.

To the spectator, it would appear as though God had indeed painted Himself into a corner by Hosea's prophecy. Hosea declares that the God of Abraham will at some point cease to be the God of Abraham's descendants, the Jewish people.

> Now when she had weaned Lo-Ruhamah, she conceived and bore a son. Then *God* said: "Call his name Lo-Ammi, For you *are not My people*, And I will not be your *God.*" (Hosea 1:8–9, NKJV; emphasis added)

Then, almost in the next breath, Hosea quotes the multiplication of Abraham's descendants clause:

> Yet the number of the children of *Israel Shall be as the sand of the sea*, Which cannot be measured or numbered. And it shall come to pass In the place where it was said to them, "You *are* not My people," *There* it shall be said to them, "*You are* sons of the living God." (Hosea 1:10, NKJV; emphasis added)

There appeared to be an identity crisis in the making: on the one hand, Jews were the blessed "My people Israel," because God swore an oath to Abraham. On the other, because as a people they generally disobeyed God, He would disqualify them at some point from that coveted title. They would be known as "not My people," though they would never face ultimate extermination as they were still promised to multiply without end. Lastly, as a nation the LORD would classify them as "sons of the living God."

What was happening here? It was as if the Jewish people were playing Russian Roulette with their heritage. How was this turn of events prophetically scheduled to occur? To understand this better, it is important to go back historically to the point whereby "My people Israel" became "not My people."

Though Hosea 1:9–10 speaks of a time when Israel would be

reclassified as "not My people," this declassification did not find final fulfillment during Hosea's time, whose ministry spanned from 750 to 725 BC. Rather, is was a prophecy of events to come. The title "My people Israel" continued to apply even during the time of the prophet Jeremiah, whose ministry began in the thirteenth year of Josiah (628 BC). They continued to hold the title even during the Babylonian captivity, evidenced by the fact that Daniel was still prophesying from within Babylon during that period.

It is not plausible to think that the Jewish people lost this coveted title during the post-exilic period after the Babylonian captivity, which ended in 536 BC, as they were instructed in the Old Testament book of Nehemiah to return to their homeland Israel and rebuild their temple in Jerusalem. During that time, God was still communicating with His people of Israel through the post-exilic prophets Haggai, Zechariah, and Malachi. Even up to the time of the first advent of Christ, they were still operating in the official capacity of "My people Israel," as evidenced by the fact that John the Baptist, also a Jewish prophet, continued to disseminate prophecy.

For over seven-hundred years, the inference inherent in this prophecy haunted the Jews. Then came "the seed," Christ. Until that point, the Jews continually wondered when they would become "not My people." What generation would be stripped from the responsibilities of the adoption, the glory, the covenants, the giving of the law, the service of God, and the promises given by God to Abraham, Isaac, and Jacob?[59] All these were appointed to the people of God, "My people Israel."

Could it be that Gentiles would someday replace the Jews in God's eyes? As preposterous as the thought appeared, Old Testament prophecies familiar to the Jews spoke of the Messiah being a light to the Gentiles.[60]

This is an important area of study, because the assumption within the preponderance of the Church today is that this was exactly what happened. Many believe that God is done with the Jew, and that the

Jewish people are no longer "My people Israel." They believe that the Jew has no further place within the overall prophetic plan of God. They surmise that the Church has replaced them as the people of God. Estimates tell us this dangerous misconception, known as Replacement Theology, is held by as much as 85 percent of the visible Church.

We must now look at when the nation of Israel lost its coveted title. God finally fulfilled his prophecy in the generation that rejected Christ (Matt. 12:24). This was when the nation Israel committed the unpardonable sin—the denial of Christ as Messiah based on demon possession. From that time forward the title began to wane, and beginning in AD 70 and continuing into the centuries of worldwide dispersion that followed, the Jews assumed the title "not My people."

The fulfillment of Hosea's prophecy had finally come, and the Abrahamic covenant hung in the balance . Would God abandon the covenant He made with Abraham and, in so doing, disinherit Abraham's children, the Jewish people? Perhaps He would replace the true descendants of Abraham with Gentiles. It would be highly unlikely He would choose the former, because to abandon an unconditional covenant would be to defame His own character as the true God over all creation. One can bet that Satan and his fallen angels packed the theater at that time to see God work His way out of this quandary.

The answer everyone awaited finally came in one of the eight mysteries of the New Testament (a mystery is the revealing of information in the New Testament that hadn't been disclosed in the Old Testament). Years later, Paul resolved the dilemma by introducing the mystery.

So that you may not claim to be wiser than you are, brothers and sisters, I want you to understand this mystery: *a hardening has come upon part of Israel,* until the full number of the Gentiles has come in. (Rom. 11:25, NRSV; emphasis added)

It was no mystery that Israel would become hardened. After all, they would eventually become so calloused that they would become "not My people." Neither was it a mystery that God would call a full number of Gentiles to be saved.[61] However, it was indeed a mystery that "not all Jews" would be classified as "not My people."

God's surprise was keeping the Abrahamic covenant in tact by holding onto a believing faction of the Jews as the true descendants of Abraham. These believing Jews never assumed the title "not My people." They were simply reclassified from "My people Israel," to "My people the Church." Hence, we must now touch upon a second of the New Testament's mysteries, the fellowship mystery.

> By which, when you read, you may understand my knowledge in the mystery of Christ, which in other ages was not made known to the sons of men, as it has now been revealed by the Spirit to His holy apostles and prophets: *that the Gentiles should be fellow heirs, of the same body,* and partakers [with the believing Jews] of His promise in Christ [the seed of Abraham] through the gospel. (Eph. 3:4–6, NKJV; emphasis added)

We therefore understand that "God is not done with the Jew" as the apostle Paul so aptly asserted in Romans Chapters 9–11. Paul specifically reminds us in Romans 9:25–26 of what Hosea 1:9–10 disclosed.

> As He says also in Hosea: "I will [yet again] call them My people [Israel], who were not my people, And her beloved, who was not beloved. And it shall come to pass in the place where it was said to them, 'You are not My people,' There they shall be called sons of the living God." (Rom. 9:25–26 NKJV)

We see that, as He promised their father Abraham, God will never be done with the Jews.[62] Though the greater part of the client nation, the hardened part, was temporarily stripped of the coveted title "My people Israel," until the full number of Gentiles has come in, the Jews were never erased entirely from God's last will and testament. In addition to being heirs of the unconditional Abrahamic covenant, they will be the recipients of numerous Old and New Testament end-time prophecies yet to occur.

The hardness or blindness of the nation of Israel will end after "the fullness of the Gentiles has come in" (Rom. 11:26). Furthermore, we know that ultimately "all Israel will be saved." The national salvation of Israel occurs with the second coming of Christ, and from that point forward, all of Israel remains saved throughout the Messianic Kingdom. It is at that point that the world comes to know them as "sons of the living God." Yet several scriptures inform us that before this happens, the Jewish people will go from their present "not My people" status, to their former world-renowned title "My people Israel."

We need, then, to determine when the Jewish people, who are presently "not My people," become "My people Israel." Ezekiel wrote several prophecies clearly identifying the Jewish nation in advance of the second coming of Christ as "My people Israel."

But you, O mountains of Israel, you shall shoot forth your branches and yield your fruit to My people Israel, for they are about to come. For indeed I *am* for you, and I will turn to you, and you shall be tilled and sown. I will multiply men upon you, all the house of Israel, all of it; and the cities shall be inhabited and the ruins rebuilt. I will multiply upon you man and beast; and they shall increase and bear young; I will make you inhabited as in former times, and do better *for you* than at your beginnings. Then you shall know that I *am* the LORD. Yes, I will cause men to walk on you, My people Israel; they shall take possession of you, and you shall be

their inheritance; no more shall you bereave them *of children.*
(Ezek. 36:8–12, NKJV)

Ezekiel 36:8–12 re-introduces the Jewish people as "My people
Israel." Twice within these passages they are referred to this way. The
first usage suggests they have returned to God's favor even before their
return to the land of Israel in 1948. Ezekiel writes: "For they are about
to come." The second usage portrays the Jewish people as walking
upon the Holy Land of Israel, in full possession of it.

The Hebrew words translated as "about to come" are *qarab bo,* and
can also be translated as "draw near to attain." The first Ezekiel usage
may imply that the Jewish people, formerly recognized as "My people
Israel," but better known in their dispersion as "not My people," draw
near, to re-attain their client-nation status. The second usage, however, makes clear that when Israel takes possession of the land and the
land becomes their inheritance, their God once again recognizes them
as "My people Israel."

Describing the gathering, Ezekiel also uses the phrase "all the
house of Israel, all of it," alluding to two things: first, that the gathering would be worldwide and, secondly, that the Jewish people would
no longer be a divided kingdom as in the times between the Northern
Kingdom (Samaria) and the Southern Kingdom (Judah). This is a
point also prophesied in Isaiah 11:12–13 and Ezekiel 37:15–22.

To date, it is at least clear that the Jewish people have drawn near
to attain full autonomy over the Promised Land . We can also surmise
that they are a united people, no longer dividing allegiance to a northern or southern kingdom. The land is productive, the Jewish people
are reproductive, and the cities are inhabited as in former times. It is
debatable, however, as to whether or not they fully possess the land, a
critical condition that must be in place when the Jews once again are
seen as "My people Israel."

Another Ezekiel passage describes the Jewish people as an extension of God's hand in judgment against Arabs. This passage likewise

identifies the Jews as "My people Israel" in advance of the second coming of Christ.

> "I will lay My vengeance on Edom [Southern Jordan] by the hand of My people Israel, that they may do in Edom according to My anger and according to My fury; and they shall know My vengeance," says the LORD GOD. (Ezek. 25:14, NKJV)

In a major campaign to extinguish all the Jewish people, Edom forms a confederacy with the other Arab nations that presently border the land of Israel. The Bible describes this confederacy and their campaign in Psalm 83:1–8, 12. The judgment Ezekiel describes is, in part, God's response to this confederate effort. The Arabs come against the Jewish people at a time when they are gathering back into the land and have become, or will soon again become, known as "My people Israel."

Though there have been serious attempts in 1948, 1956, 1967, and 1973 by one or more of these Arab countries to destroy the restored nation of Israel, the attempts do not serve as the final fulfillment of this Psalm 83 confederate effort. When the Psalm 83 campaign finally arrives on the world scene, the Jewish people will rise up and rain God's vengeance upon Edom according to His anger and fury. After this Israeli Conquest, the Jewish people will walk in full possession of the land. At that point, if not before, they will undoubtedly be again classified as "My people Israel."

> "I have heard the reproach of Moab, And the insults of the people of Ammon, With which they have reproached My people, And made arrogant threats against their borders. Therefore, as I live," Says the LORD of hosts, the God of Israel, "Surely Moab shall be like Sodom, And the people of Ammon like Gomorrah— Overrun with weeds and saltpits,

And a perpetual desolation. The residue of My people shall plunder them, And the remnant of My people shall possess them." (Zeph. 2:8–9, NKJV)

The execution of vengeance extends beyond Edom into Ammon and Moab. Thus, all of modern-day Jordan will be vanquished by Israel. Ammon and Moab are enlisted members, along with Edom, in the Psalm 83 confederacy. As this book points out, this will be in addition to the confederate territories of Lebanon, Syria, Saudi Arabia, Egypt, West Bank, and the Gaza Strip, who will all come under some form of military domination from Israel's exceedingly great army.

The point here is that, as it was during the early campaigns of "My people the Hebrews," the exodus from Egypt, and the migration into the Promised Land, God will endow the present Jewish generation with the strong arm of His might. All present Arab attempts against the successful return of the Hebrews into the Holy Land of Isralestine, and the reclamation of their coveted title "My people Israel" are beyond futile; they will prove to be fatal. Present Arab aggressions provoke the providential protection with well-known historical Hebrew precedent. Soon the world will experience the Jews coming into possession of much of the Promised Land through the strength of the exceedingly great army prophesied in Ezekiel 37:10.

Subsequent to the fulfillment of Ezekiel 25:14, "The Israeli Conquest," the Russian-Iranian Magog alliance described in Ezekiel 38 and 39 will confront the Jewish people. The world will know the Jews by this time as "My people Israel."

Therefore, son of man, prophesy and say to Gog, "Thus says the LORD GOD: 'On that day when *My people Israel* dwell safely, will you not know *it?*" Then you will come from your place out of the far north, you and many peoples with you, all of them riding on horses, a great company and a mighty army. You will come up against *My people Israel* like a cloud, to cover the land. It will be in the latter days that I will bring you against My land, so that the nations may know Me, when I am hallowed in you, O Gog, before their eyes. (Ezek. 38:14–16, NKJV; emphasis added)

So I will make My holy name known in the midst of *My people Israel*, and I will not *let them* profane My holy name anymore. Then the nations shall know that *I am* the LORD, the Holy One in Israel. (Ezek. 39:7, NKJV; emphasis added)

Ezekiel 38:14, 16, and Ezekiel 39:7 also refer to the Jewish people as "My people Israel." God endows the Jewish people with this title at a time when He has re-gathered them from the nations back into the land of Israel in the latter years. They have come out of the Holocaust, and dwell securely in the land, due to the fact that by this point they have executed vengeance on the Psalm 83 confederacy and in so doing have established themselves as an exceedingly great army.

One might justifiably question the whereabouts of the church at this time. If Israel is at some point again called "My people Israel," then where on Earth are "My people the Church?" The church is thought to be the people of God in these days; could it be they will be raptured on or near the time of Israel regaining their client nation status? After all, the Church came into being around the same time Israel lost their favored-nation status.

One might find the answer to this question in the understanding of what Paul meant by the term "fullness of the Gentiles." Expositors like Adam Clarke, Warren Wiersbe, and many more believe Paul meant this to represent the Gentile believers during the Church age, i.e., the Bride of Christ.[63] They advocate that when the rapture occurs, the "fullness of the Gentiles" has come in. As such, the stage begins to set for the LORD to save all of Israel. However, we know that all of Israel will not be saved for at least seven years, a period which encompasses the "Seventieth Week of Daniel," i.e., the "Tribulation." It will actually be longer than seven years, because it is not the rapture that will set the seven-year clock ticking; rather, it is the signing of the false covenant by Israel, confirmed by the Antichrist.[64]

So we are left to wonder what occurs between the time of the rapture, if that is when the "fullness of the Gentiles has come in," and the end of the Tribulation Period whereby "all Israel shall be saved." Many things happen, but for the purposes of this study, we are concerned with the reclassification of the client nation status to "My people Israel."

During that window of time, Israel will be restored to its client nation status. They will be "My people Israel." There appears to be some time correlation between the calling out of the 144,000 Jewish witnesses of Revelation 7:1–8 and the reinstatement of the "My people Israel" title. These are clearly Jews called to the service of God. They come on the scene at a very interesting time and represent Israel again in a preferred national condition. They are clearly identified genealogically from their ancestral Jewish tribes, and the ordering of the usage of their tribal names, though puzzling, may have ministerial meaning.

The Bible calls these 144,000 Jews "the servants of our God" in Revelation 7:3. They receive their ministry after the Church is raptured. According to many, the simple interpretation of Revelation 2 and 3 represents the Church on Earth, and Revelation 4 and 5 represents the Church, raptured and residing in heaven. Revelation 7 starts with the Greek words "meta tauta," interpreted in English as "after these things." After the summation of events of the Church age on Earth and the rapture of the Church, the events of Revelation 7 occur. This adds credence to the fact that, if the "fullness of the Gentiles" is the Church, then the fullness of the Gentiles has been completed and it is time for "My people Israel" to again take front-and-center stage as God's people.

For the most part, all Jewish tribal genealogical records were destroyed in AD 70, yet a Revelation 7:5–8 prophetic event still to occur distinctly identifies the emergence of twelve thousand members from each of their twelve ancestral tribes. [65] This is not a random selection; rather, God orchestrated it and ordained it by the angel having the "seal of the living God." It is not accident there are not 11,999 from one tribe and 12,001 from another. There are exactly 12,000 from each tribe sealed for service. From these specifics, we can assume God is administering His Earthly program once again through the Jewish people. This safely suggests that these Jews are not "My people the Church," which by this time have likely been raptured. Rather, they represent a significant component within "My people Israel."

These 144,000 servants minister after the Church age and are familiar with the gospel and the mystery of fellowship quoted earlier from Ephesians 3:4–6. Thus, they know—and therefore teach—that salvation now comes through faith in Christ and not the Mosaic Law. They also teach that it is God's will that Gentiles should be partakers along with the Jews through the gospel. With this understanding, we can interpret the possible ministerial message within the ordering of the names of the twelve tribes in Revelation 7:5–8.

> of the tribe of *Judah* twelve thousand *were* sealed;
> of the tribe of *Reuben* twelve thousand *were* sealed;
> of the tribe of *Gad* twelve thousand *were* sealed;
> of the tribe of *Asher* twelve thousand *were* sealed;
> of the tribe of *Naphtali* twelve thousand *were* sealed;
> of the tribe of *Manasseh* twelve thousand *were* sealed;
> of the tribe of *Simeon* twelve thousand *were* sealed;
> of the tribe of *Levi* twelve thousand *were* sealed;
> of the tribe of *Issachar* twelve thousand *were* sealed;
> of the tribe of *Zebulun* twelve thousand *were* sealed;
> of the tribe of *Joseph* twelve thousand *were* sealed;
> of the tribe of *Benjamin* twelve thousand *were* sealed.
> (Rev. 7:5–8, NKJV; emphasis added)

The names of the twelve tribes are listed in this non-chronological order, perhaps to describe the ministerial purposes of the 144,000 Hebrew Christian witnesses of Revelation 7:5–8. Normally, the Bible lists descendants in the chronological order of their birth. However, the apostle John lists these tribes out of order, apparently giving us insight into the ministry of these witnesses.

The tribe of Judah is listed first in Revelation 7:5, however, in birth order, Judah was the fourth son. Similarly, the Bible lists the other tribes out of order in Revelation 7:5–8. An astute student of the Word watches for these abnormalities within the scriptures and, as such, is always encouraged to dig deeper in order to discover what the Holy Spirit intends for him or her to understand relative to the text.

THE MEANINGS OF THE NAMES:

Judah (Praise God), *Reuben* (behold a son), *Gad* (good fortune), *Asher* (happiness), *Naphtali* (my wrestling), *Manasseh* (God has caused me to forget), *Simeon* (hearing), *Levi* (joining or adhesion), *Issachar* (God hath given me my hire, or man for hire), *Zebulun* (elevated or elevated dwelling), *Joseph* (adding or increaser), *Benjamin* (son of the right hand).

THE MESSAGE OF THE NAMES:

Praise God! Behold! a son of good fortune and happiness. My wrestling God has caused me to forget. Hearing of our joining, God hath given me my hire and elevated dwelling increased by the son of the right hand.

What we might surmise from these names is their individual understanding of their subject ministries. Praise God for the gospel of Christ, a son of good fortune and happiness. My wrestling with sin and the Mosaic Law, God has caused me to forget. Hearing the mystery of our joining with the Gentiles God hath given me my hire.

He has elevated me, a Jew reinstated with "My people Israel" status, back into ministry and has increased the number of those being saved through Christ, the son of the right hand.

> These are the ones who were not defiled with women, for they are virgins. These are the ones who follow the Lamb wherever He goes. These were redeemed from *among* men, being firstfruits to God and to the Lamb. And in their mouth was found no deceit, for they are without fault before the throne of God. (Rev. 14:4–5, NKJV; emphasis added)

These 144,000 servants become "firstfruits to God and to the Lamb," suggesting that after the rapture the subsequent dispensation has the 144,000 as its firstfruits, and they are firstfruits to God and to the Lamb, (Jesus Christ).[66] This further suggests that at that time God will again administer His sovereign program through "My people Israel." These 144,000 servants likely represent the first crop of harvested souls subsequent to the Rapture of the Church. They are the first of many saved souls which were foretold to follow the sudden disappearance of the Christian Church.[67]

FIRSTFRUITS

The choice examples of a crop harvested first and dedicated to God. In accordance with Mosaic law, individual Israelites brought to the house of the LORD "the first (that is, 'the best') of the firstfruits of thy land." (Ex. 23:19; 34:26)[68]

ISRALESTINE

God's Roadmap Plan for Peace

sralestine is a new word construct used for the purposes of this book. Throughout the book, it is utilized in multiple ways to define present and future geopolitical concepts. Its usage in the chapter title is intended to illustrate the return of the Jewish people into the land of Palestine in fulfillment of biblical prophecy. The ancient name of the territory was Israel; Palestine became a superseding name imposed upon the land by the Romans in AD 135. Therefore, the Jewish State of Israel became re-established on land formerly recognized as Palestine. *Isralestine* merges the terms Israel and Palestine in an attempt to give the reader further insight into the subject matter of this chapter.

Presently the International Community has drafted a potential plan for peace in the Middle East. Their roadmap plan, presently on the negotiating block, attempts to resolve the ongoing conflict between the Jews and the Arabs.[69] This struggle preoccupies the world at large, which has precluded that in order to achieve peace in the Middle East, it must first settle the continuing saga between the Jews and the Palestinians.

We gain insight from Jeremiah that God already has His own roadmap plan in place. Over 2,500 years ago, God told Jeremiah that at the appointed time, the Jews would be re-established in the land of ancient Israel, regardless of how their Arab and Persian partners in the neighborhood feel about the matter.

> Thus says the LORD: "Against all *My evil neighbors* who touch the inheritance which I have caused My people Israel to inherit—behold, *I will pluck them* [the Arabs] *out* of their [the Jews] land [Israel] and pluck out the house of Judah from among them [the surrounding Arab nations]. Then it shall be, after I have plucked them out, that I will return and have compassion on them and bring them back, everyone to his heritage and everyone [Jew and Arab] to his [respective] land. And it shall be, if they [the resettled Arabs] will learn carefully the ways of My people, to swear by My name, 'As the LORD lives,' as they taught My people to swear by Baal, then they shall be established in the midst of My people.[70] But if they do not obey, I will utterly pluck up and destroy that nation," says the LORD. (Jer. 12:14–17, NKJV; emphasis added)

God proposes His own compassionate, peaceful political solution to the potential regional problem of the return of the Jew into the Holy Land. He would cause the corridors to be open for the Arabs to leave the land destined to become the Jewish state and return to the lands of their ancestry. In addition, He would resettle the Jews out of the surrounding Arab nations, and bring the Jews back into their homeland Israel. As each ethnic group migrated they would vacate homes and jobs enabling the returning peoples economic opportunities, and in some cases already existing communities to inhabit. It had the makings of a perfect Isralestine plan.

These passages represent ancient blueprints, divinely designed to insure the successful return of the Jewish people back to the land of their heritage. God's Roadmap Plan to Peace took into consideration that there would be "evil neighbors" homesteading the holy land. He foreknew they would have to be relocated to make way for the return of the Jewish people.

The Middle East conflict that confounds politicians today has not caught God off guard. Provisions were included in Jeremiah's prophecy for their future as well. They would be "plucked out" and escorted back to the lands of their ancestry. A fertile future awaited them, if they entreated their affections to Jehovah, the God of the Jews, and Architect of this Isralestine plan.

In apparent fulfillment of the Jeremiah 12:14–17 prophecy, there are millions of Arabs "plucked out" from the territory formerly recognized as Palestine. For approximately sixty years, these uprooted Arabs have been unable to relocate to an alternative homeland. They have been reduced to refugee status because their Arab relatives have shut their national doors to them. These refugees remain strategically deployed by their Arab partners close to the borders of Israel.

These Arab nations have cleverly managed to shift the burden of responsibility for the relocation of these refugees into the lap of the international community—the same community that legislated the re-establishment of the nation Israel as the Jewish State, implemented in 1948. UNRWA, the United Nations Relief and Works Agency, was established May 1, 1950, to find a solution to the refugee problem.[71]

By not taking responsibility for absorbing Palestinian refugees into their societies, these Arab nations are in severe breach of God's Roadmap Plan to Peace. They have decided against worshipping Jeremiah's God, and implementing the ancient blueprints, specifically designed for the political architects of our time. This is a terrible mistake, which we will discuss at the conclusion of this chapter.

DIVINE INTERNATIONAL INTERVENTION?

As we review the events leading to the restoration of the nation Israel, we see God perhaps causing international efforts to facilitate this divine program. Shortly after the conclusion of World War I, the Middle

East changed. In succession Egypt, Saudi Arabia, Iraq, Lebanon, and Syria, all received their independence after four hundred years of Turkish domination.[72] This began to pave the way for the return of Arab peoples back to their ancestral homelands.

Additionally, the League of Nations drafted the Balfour document in 1917. This document in its original draft referenced Palestine as the intended location for the re-establishment of the Jewish State.[73] It conceded land east and west of the Jordan River for this specific purpose. This land mass represented all of modern-day Israel, and Jordan. This document would enable the Jewish people to come out of the neighboring nations and resettle into their own state. It appeared as though the world was unknowingly reorganizing the Middle East in fulfillment of Jeremiah's prophecy.

However, certain influential Arabs, due to their relationship with Britain, were able to convince the British to act unilaterally to separate the land east of the Jordan River out of the Jewish state and to place it into Arab sovereignty. In 1922, the land east of the Jordan River came to be called Transjordan, and fell under Arab rule. Britain relinquished its control over Transjordan on March 22, 1946. Today, we call Transjordan the Arab nation of Jordan.

Palestine, which in 1917 was to include approximately 46,000 square miles extending from the Mediterranean Sea on the West, Eastward to Iraq, and was intended to be the entire Jewish state as per the Balfour Document, fell to less than 9,000 square miles. It included only the land west of the Jordan River.

Then in 1947, United Nations General Assembly approved Resolution 181, which called for the establishment of a Jewish State. This "Partition Plan," was intended to establish the small notch of unclaimed land west of the Jordan River, into two co-existing states. They drafted it as a Two-State Solution intended to allow the Arabs and Jews to co-exist peacefully in their ancestral lands.

Unfortunately, the Jewish people, who were still recovering from the attempted genocide of the Holocaust, had two more huge obstacles to overcome. First, the Partition Plan left them with only a "small notch" of land, in which to establish their Jewish State, and secondly the Arab Kingdom promptly rejected the Partition Plan. As such when the Jewish people attempted to claim their land west of the Jordan River in May of 1948, they had to fight the previously established Arab nations of Lebanon, Syria, Iraq, Jordan, and Egypt for it.

As a result of the Partition Plan, the Arabs were appropriated even more land, approximately 2,409 square miles, which is the general land mass associated with the Gaza Strip (146 sq. miles) and the West Bank (2263 sq miles). In fact, within the twenty-seven years that followed the collapse of the Turkish Ottoman Empire, the Arabs and their Islamic Persian cohorts became sovereign over approximately 2,309,000 square miles.[74]

This enormous amount of land was generally delivered to these predominately-Islamic populations via the means of the international community. This same international community attempted to present in the same spirit, a small sliver of territory, which had 1,878 years prior been occupied by their Jewish ancestors, to a group of Jewish Holocaust refugees. Today the Jews inhabit this "small notch" of land, approximately the size of the state of New Jersey, if you include the Palestinian territories of the Gaza Strip and the West Bank, under general Arab protest.

It is indeed a sad story that the Arab Kingdom will not withdraw its protest regarding Israel's right to exist. However, God's Roadmap Plan considered this. Someday the Arab Kingdom will concede, as pointed out further on in this chapter.

By May 14, 1948, when the Jewish state officially arrived, what was left of the 46,000 square miles designed for them as per the international community back in 1917, was a meager 5,591 square miles, excluding the Gaza and West Bank territories, and even then this real estate had to be fought for. Immediately in 1948, the nations of Egypt, Jordan, Syria, Lebanon, and Iraq attacked the tiny Jewish state.

As such, they evidenced their true title given in the Jeremiah 12:14 prophecy "My evil neighbors."

The Arab disposition caused a suspension in the divine compassionate peaceful political approach, and forced God's military plan into effect. Still, the prophetic plan moved forward as the attackers instructed those Arabs residing within the tiny Jewish state to vacate temporarily, while their militaries could destroy the newly forming nation.

At the same time, the Jews in Arab lands were forced out of their jobs, homes and communities, leaving them no choice but to resettle in their ancient homeland Israel. Hence, the "pluck-out" process began, as the evil neighbors were routed out of Israel and the Jews were uprooted from their century-old communities established in the neighboring Arab lands.

As we know, the Jewish state was not destroyed and, therefore, it became the burden of those neighboring Arab nations to assimilate these refugees into their lands. Henceforth, and continuing today, is the Palestinian refugee problem. Unlike the unsettled Arab crisis, which has burdened the United Nations for over fifty years, the Jewish refugees have been welcomed and absorbed into Israeli society.

Even still God stated through Jeremiah that if these Arabs would "swear by My name," that they would "be established in the midst of My people." However, on the flip side, "if they do not obey," God "will utterly pluck up and destroy that nation." In other words, a peaceful co-existence could still occur in the region if these Arab nations would comply with God's holy program. But if they persist as "evil neighbors," they will provoke upon themselves their own destruction.

The use by Jeremiah of the words "pluck out," and "evil neighbors" gave prior indication that the resettling process would not be a cooperative effort. The Hebrew word for "pluck out" is *nathash* and its primary scriptural usages point to an involuntary uprooting of a people out of a land.

Thus, we see that a two state solution, more commonly referred to these days, as the Roadmap is not a new concept. However, as time elapses and the ruins of Israel are rebuilt, the cities are inhabited, and the desolate wastes become prosperous places, these Arabs covet the land their ancestors homesteaded all the more.

That tiny, less than 13 percent of what remained of Palestine, now called Israel, is under constant threat of evil neighbors. The Arabs have been conducting their own plucking process. They are attempting to pluck out the client nation Israel, the apple of Gods eye.[75] In so doing, they seal their own fate: God "will utterly pluck up and destroy that nation!"

WHO-DOMITES?

Who Are the Edomites Today?

The present conflict in the Middle East between the Israelis and Palestinians is proof positive that we are nearing the end of times. The Bible foretold the face off between these two ethnic groups to occur in the last days! Scripture informs us that it will be resolved through a sizeable regional war in the Middle East, whereby Israel forms their exceedingly great army.[76] They then execute the vengeance of their God on the Palestinians and their coalition of Arab allies.[77] The historical equivalents to the Palestinians, at least in part, are the ancient Edomites.

Regarding the Edomites, there are numerous scriptures in the Bible written by various prophets that predict their present participation in the Middle East crisis. These prophecies, when appropriately discerned, present us with invaluable insights into the cause, details, duration, and resolve of the conflict at hand. As such, this prophetic information has direct and specific application to this present generation.

This chapter is committed to the study of the Edomites and boldly attempts to connect part of their genealogy to the modern-day ethnic group commonly referred to as the Palestinians. Unless you are a Middle East historian or an avid student of the Bible, you likely run the risk of not knowing whom the Edomites were and, therefore, what some of the Palestinian ancestry was. The Edomites have for the most part long been forgotten. However, they and their former homeland of Edom, which is modern-day Southern Jordan, fill many pages of end-times Bible prophecy.

WHO-DOMITES?

- Did you know that in the last days scheduled for the Earth we presently occupy, the land of modern-day Southern Jordan, the ancient homeland of the Edomites, is the predetermined stage for the return of Jesus Christ and His face-off with the Antichrist and the armies participating in the campaign of Armageddon?[78]
- Did you know that before the Armageddon campaign, the Palestinians will enjoin the nations of Egypt, Saudi Arabia, Jordan, Syria, and Lebanon in a confederate attempt to extinguish the Jewish people, hoping to cause the name "Israel" to be "remembered no more?"[79]
- Did you know that at least some of the Palestinian suicide bombers blowing themselves up in the Middle East today are likely of Edomite descent? That's right. Contained within the Palestinian population of today resides a remnant of people who are of Edomite descent.

WHO ARE THE EDOMITES?

Simply put, they are the descendants of Esau, the twin brother of the infamous Jacob of the Old Testament.[80] Jacob was later known as Israel, and from his twelve sons came the formation of the nation Israel. Likewise, the descendants of Esau formed the nation of Edom, from which comes the term *Edomites.*[81]

WHO ARE THE PALESTINIANS?

Palestinian is the ethnic label tossed about loosely in modern times to identify three primary predominately Arab groups of people: the Palestinians of the Gaza Strip, the Palestinians of the West Bank, and the Palestinian Refugees. These groups inhabit the territories that most closely approach the borders of modern-day Israel, with pocket communities in the surrounding Arab nations. We generally understand that these three groups are comprised of a mixture of peoples who descend from various origins, one of these being traceable back to Esau, father of the Edomites.

Unlike the Jewish people, who all share a common lineage traceable to the biblical patriarchs of Abraham, Isaac, and Jacob, Palestinians have no such common historical lineage specifically linking them biologically to any distinct ethnicity. Their genealogies can be traced back to the Edomites, Egyptians, Assyrians, Philistines, Sidonians, Ammonites, Moabites, Yemenites, Saudi Arabians, Moroccans, Christians from Greece, Muslim Sherkas from Russia, and Muslims from Bosnia, just to name a few.[82]

It is unfortunate that the history books and encyclopedias of our time have generally lost track of the Edomites. However, the fact remains that if the Bible is correct, the Edomites will resurface and they and their former homeland will play parts in future world events. We must remember that when the prophecies of the Bible were written, the peoples and places subject to the prophecies were identified in accordance with their recognized titles at the time. For instance, should any pending prophecies regarding ancient Philistia be fulfilled in modern times, they could be referring to the Palestinians of the Gaza Strip. Likewise, prophecies regarding the Palestinians of the West Bank could find association with the Edomites. As pointed out further in this chapter, many Edomites migrated from Edom into Hebron, which is located in the modern-day West Bank.[83]

Through time, titles often changed as epic events altered the course of ethnic and geographic history. For example, the Romans relabeled Israel the Land of Palaestina in AD 135 when they defeated the Bar Kokhba revolt. There are numerous unfulfilled prophecies in the Bible that concern Philistia, Edom and the Edomites. The Jewish prophets who described them at the time had no Palestinian labels to give further identification as to exactly which of the three Palestinian groups of our day would have specific application. These unfulfilled prophecies are of particular interest in modern times, as knowledgeable students of prophecy suspect that these prophecies will soon find their final fulfillment.

The premise we should now consider is that this ethnic Edomite group never officially ceased to exist; rather, they have apparently been hibernating for many centuries in the Middle East in general and in the land of Israel and Southern Jordan more specifically. Though their identity has been mistaken, we must not overlook their ethnic reality.

Since the Bible predicts future events with 100 percent accuracy, we can recognize that a remnant of the Edomites still exists in some ethnic classification today. Though their identity at present is somewhat obscured, the fulfillment of the predicted events will clearly prove who the Edomites are and have been. As we study the prophecies regarding Edom and the Edomites we are forced to consider their close association with the Palestinians of today.

As you read the following three sections of scripture, you will notice Edom plays a significant role in each of them.

Do not keep silent, O God! Do not hold Your peace, And do not be still, O God!

For behold, Your enemies make a tumult; And those who hate You have lifted up their head. They have taken crafty counsel against Your people, [The Jews] And consulted together against Your sheltered ones. They have said, "Come, and let us cut them off from *being* a nation, That the name of Israel may be remembered no more." For they have consulted together with one consent; They form a confederacy against You: The *tents of Edom* and the Ishmaelites; Moab and the Hagrites; Gebal, Ammon, and Amalek; Philistia with the inhabitants of Tyre; Assyria also has joined with them; They have helped the children of Lot. *Selah* (Psa. 83:1–8, NKJV; emphasis added)

Thus says the LORD GOD: "Because of what *Edom* did against the house of Judah by taking vengeance, and has greatly offended by avenging itself on them," therefore thus says the LORD GOD: "I will also stretch out My hand against *Edom*, cut off man [Palestinian] and beast from it, and make it desolate from Teman; Dedan [Saudi Arabia] shall fall by the sword. I will lay My vengeance on *Edom* by the hand of My people Israel, [The Jews] that they may do in *Edom* according to My anger and according to My fury; and they [Palestinians and the Saudi Arabians by association] shall know My vengeance," says the LORD GOD. (Ezek. 25:12–14, NKJV; emphasis added)

Come near, you nations, to hear; And heed, you people! Let the Earth hear, and all that is in it, The world and all things that come forth from it. For the indignation of the LORD *is* against all nations, And *His* fury against all their armies; [future campaign of Armageddon] He has utterly destroyed them, He has given them over to the slaughter. Also their slain shall be thrown out; Their stench shall rise from their corpses, And the mountains shall be melted with their blood. All the host of heaven shall be dissolved, And the heavens shall be rolled up like a scroll; All their host shall fall down As the leaf falls from the vine, And as *fruit* falling from a fig tree. For My sword shall be bathed in heaven; Indeed it shall come down on *Edom,* And on the people of My curse, for judgment. The sword of the LORD is filled with blood, It is made overflowing with fatness, With the blood of lambs and goats, With the fat of the kidneys of rams. For the LORD has a sacrifice in *Bozrah,* And *a great slaughter* in the land of *Edom.* (Isa. 34:1–6, NKJV; emphasis added)

These scriptures are just a few of the numerous end-time pieces of the prophetic puzzle, and they place either Edom or the Edomite people in the midst of the circumstances. The first piece, the prophecy of Psalm 83, references the "tents of Edom," which if it were fulfilled in modern times would be better translated as the "tents of Palestinians." Tents biblically represent a population assembled in refuge, and/or military encampments. Tent communities housing Palestinians become instrumental to a confederate attempt with the nations of Egypt *(Hagarenes)* Saudi Arabia *(Ishmaelites),* Jordan *(Moab and Ammon, the children of Lot),* Syria *(Assyria),* Lebanon *(Tyre),* and Gaza *(Philistia).*[84] The explicit goal of this confederacy is the destruction of the nation Israel.

They have said, "Come, and let us cut them off from *being* a nation, That the name of Israel may be remembered no more." (Psa. 83:4, NKJV)

Tent communities and military mindsets are well understood among the Palestinians. Presently, the world is witnessing glimpses of the Psalm 83:1–6 confederate scenario in its dangerous beginning stages as these Arab nations lend support to the Palestinians' fight against the nation of Israel. The Palestinians fasten explosives to themselves in a military campaign aimed against Jewish civilian and military targets.

Fig. 1. Dheisha refugee camp, Bethlehem, West Bank 1949. (Reproduced by permission from UNRWA. UNRWA photo, "Palestinian Refugees—Historical Photos," Badil.org, http://www.badil.org/Photos/history/Archive2/Photogallery/photo27847/real.htm [accessed 12/20/07].)

Fig. 2. Baqa'a refugee camp, Jordan, 1969. (Reproduced by permission from UNRWA. UNRWA photo by Jay Nehmeh, "Photo Archive: Refugees' Condition," UN.org., http://www.un.org/unrwa/photos/archive/refugees/jordan.html [Accessed 12/20/07].)

Resulting from this cursed confederate effort, the events of the second prophetic passage above regarding the Israeli Conquest over the "tents of Palestinians" as described in Ezekiel 25:12–14 occurs. This Jewish military effort extends beyond Edom, i.e., Southern Jordan, into at least Dedan, which is located in Northwestern Saudi Arabia. This conquest brings to a conclusion the Psalm 83 war effort and devastates most of what remains of the refugee Palestinian population. Furthermore, it transfers sovereignty of Southern Jordan over to the Jewish people.

This transfer of sovereignty leads to the third prophetic piece previously prescribed in Isaiah 34:1–6. Isaiah describes the "great slaughter in the land of Edom," which regards itself with the return of Jesus Christ to Edom in order to protect the faithful Jewish remnant. This Jewish contingency will be hiding in Bozrah as refugees who temporarily escaped the onslaught of the Antichrist. The Antichrist will be at that time involved in the final extermination attempt of the Jewish people, which climaxes in the campaign of Armageddon.[85]

The Bible predicts two pending judgments destined to occur in the territory of Edom. First the avenging of "My people Israel" against the Palestinians and their confederate member nations, and then subsequently the "great slaughter" by Jesus Christ of the Antichrist and his armies. The emphasis of this book is upon the first of the two pending judgments. The second judgment is entirely unrelated to the "tents of Palestinians."

By now, you are probably wondering about the connection between the Edomites and the Palestinian suicide bombers blowing themselves up in Israel in our modern times. In order to establish such a connection one must trace the migration process of the Edomites into Israel over time, and likewise study the process of the name conversion of the land of "Israel," into the land of "Palestine." Yet even before this, it is important to explore the final fulfillment of two significant prophecies. These two prophecies play a crucial role in understanding how the land in question, developed into its disputed condition of today.

THE TWO PROPHECIES

Presently, the international community desperately seeks to position the Israelis and Palestinians side by side, in a peaceful co-existence. On the table, not yet finalized at the time of the writing of this chapter, is the Roadmap plan, which promotes a "Two State" solution: a Jewish State and a Palestinian State. Did you know that these two groups, the Israelis and the Edomites, once successfully operated in a two-state solution of sorts? However, there were two prophecies written in ancient times that foretold of both Israel's and Edom's national decline, and at the time of the fulfillment of these two prophecies, their operational two-state solution disintegrated.

Hosea issued the first of the two prophecies, and Jeremiah along with Obadiah issued the second. Hosea declared that the Israelites would be declassified from "My people Israel," to "*not My people,*" and Jeremiah and Obadiah predicted that the Edomites would become "*small among the nations.*"

> Now when she weaned Lo-Ruhamah, she conceived and bore a son. Then *God* said: "Call his name Lo-Ammi, For you *are not My people,* And I will not be your *God.*" (Hosea 1:8–9, NKJV; emphasis added)

> I have heard tidings from the LORD, and a messenger has been sent among the nations: "Gather yourselves together and come against her, and rise up for battle!" *For behold, I will make you* [Edom] *small among the nations,* despised among men. (Jer. 49:14–15, RSV; emphasis added)

> The vision of Obadiah. Thus says the LORD GOD concerning *Edom:* "We have heard tidings from the LORD, and a messenger has been sent among the nations: 'Rise up! Let us rise against her for battle!' *Behold, I will make you small among*

the nations, you shall be utterly despised." (Obad. 1:1–2, RSV; emphasis added)

In a twist of fate, the twin brothers, Jacob and Esau, would have their descendants share in a similar divine disciplinary action. The two historically infamous peoples, the Jews and the Edomites, would experience their national decline and at about the same time. Both ethnic groups find themselves conquered by the Roman Empire on or around AD 70 in what turns out to be the final fulfillment of these two important Bible prophecies.

Back then, these two populations co-existed semi-peacefully in a two-state solution of their own. The Jews inhabited Judea, and Samaria, which comprised the Northern and Southern kingdoms of Israel, and the Edomites occupied Idumea, and were known as the Idumeans, which was the Greek word for Edomites. Idumea-Edom encompassed land in Southern Israel, Northeastern Sinai, and Southwestern Jordan. The Jewish capitol was Jerusalem, and the central Idumean city was Hebron approximately 19 miles to the south. At the time of the Roman conquest, the Idumeans and Jews both practiced Judaism, evidencing a common bond between them.[86]

When the Romans conquered Jerusalem and destroyed the second Jewish temple in AD 70, they also fought against the Idumeans. According to the historian Josephus, many Idumeans were either killed, or sold into slavery, and ultimately about 40,000 remaining Idumeans were freed by Caesar to go wherever they desired enabling them to keep their ethnicity in tact.[87] Indeed, by AD 70 the LORD had made Edom/Idumea undeniably "small among the nations."

Maps depicting the layout of the region around AD 135 at the time of the Bar Kokhba Jewish revolt still recognized the existence of the territory of Idumea. As such, one might safely presume that Idumeans still resided in the subject land on or around AD 135.[88] This suggests that at least some of these 40,000 freed Idumeans continued to reside, and repopulate in the territory of Idumea.

To further understand the declassification of the Israelites to "not My people" it is important to read the chapter in this book called *My People Israel*. For now it is important to recognize that the declassification of the Jews into "not My people" began at the rejection by the Jewish leadership of Jesus Christ, and found its final fulfillment in the destruction of Jerusalem and the second Jewish temple in AD 70 at the defeat by the Romans. Lastly, the assumption of the title "not My people" was not prophesied to be a permanent condition, and ultimately the Jews would be reclassified as "My people Israel," and furthermore "sons of the living God."[89]

Back to Edom becoming "made small among the nations," although it found its final fulfillment in AD 70 it will be made clear in this study that as a nation Edom experienced a gradual decline, which led to such a point whereby they slipped as an ethnic group from the pages of history.[90] If it were not for the end-times prophecies contained in the Bible regarding the restored Edomite element, there would be no further cause to remember them. They would be essentially extinguished, however the Bible suggests they have merely been "made small among the nations," and will resurface in that reduced national condition in a final confederate effort aimed at the destruction of the nation Israel.

Herein lies the problem; the Middle East conflict is the derivative of the descendants of these two former nations, attempting to reclaim the land of Israel-Palaestinia. This may seem an over-simplification of the matter; however, it is at the root of the conflict. Both formerly notorious nations who experienced their decline at the same-time and in the same-place, are attempting to pick up where they left off in AD 70. They are seeking to reestablish themselves now, again at the same-time and in the same-place.

When Israel became a nation again in 1948, the Palestinians essentially became a people. They became the refugees of Palestine because of the 1948 Arab-Israeli War. Up until that time, they were generally referred to as the Arabs of Palestine.[91] The surrounding Arab nations protested the reestablishment of the nation Israel, and confederated in a war effort against the returning Jewish people. They instructed the Arabs residing within Israel at the time, to vacate temporarily until the Jewish nation was destroyed, at which time these departing Arabs could return into the land.

Amongst the Arabs who left Israel at the time were those who had descended from Esau, i.e., the Edomites. History reports that the Jewish people were victorious, and these Edomites became numbered among the refugees of Palestine. Hence, at the time they became refugees residing in tents. The Edomites were essentially at the time the "tents of Palestine," or as they are called today, the Palestinian people. (See bottom photo on page 93)

The present plight of the Palestinians is, in large part, the result of the failed Arab war against Israel, and therefore primarily the responsibility of the surrounding Arab nations. These Arab nations have done little to absorb and assimilate them into their lands, but have done much to use them as pawns against the developing nation of Israel. Hence, you have Israel aspiring to become "My people Israel" again, which is prophesied to successfully occur, and Edom wanting to become greater than the tents of Palestine, which will likely never occur!

Edom will never be great among the nations, as they were permanently "made small among the nations," and that is the best condition they will ever experience. In fact, because of their present attempt to curse the developing nation of Israel, the Edomites will be extinguished as a people. In other words, the Palestinians of today will likely never nationally ascend much beyond a refugee condition. Listen to what the Psalmist labeled them as in the coming Arab war against the Jews, which is still to find its final fulfillment.

They have said, "Come, and let us cut them off from *being* a nation, That the name of Israel may be remembered no more." For they have consulted together with one consent;

They form a confederacy against You: The *tents of Edom* [Palestinians] and the Ishmaelites; Moab and the Hagrites; (Psa. 83:4–6, NKJV; emphasis added)

THE MIGRATION OF THE EDOMITES

The Edomites, later known as the Idumeans, became assimilated into the so-called Palestinians of today. This section studies the migratory path of the Edomites out of ancient Edom (present day Southern Jordan), into Southern Israel. It also explains the reasons for the migration, and in the end establishes the intelligent presumption that though history has lost sight of the Edomites ethnically, the Bible student can identify them today prophetically. They are an integral part of the present Palestinian population.

The ascent of the Edomites into the land of Israel officially began in 586 BC, which coincided with the destruction of Jerusalem by the Babylonians. At that time, the Edomites began to trespass into the land of Israel in large numbers, and began their homestead of the Holy Land with little to no Jewish, Philistian, Chaldean or Babylonian restriction. Hebron, which is located 19 miles south of Jerusalem, became their popular new frontier. Unlike Jerusalem, which was destroyed at the time, much of Hebron was still left in tact. Standing approximately 3,040 feet above sea level, and having been established as a city over 1,500 years earlier, it was considered prime property for the taking.

Coincidentally, about the same time a nomadic tribe known as the Nabateans began to migrate out of Arabia into Edom. They began to establish themselves alongside the Edomites, causing cultural and territorial conflicts, which played an instrumental part in this first wave of Edomite migration into Israel. Israel was the logical destination of Edomite relocation for the following reasons. First, it was directly to the west of Edom with established routes of passage making it easy to enter. Second it was historically a more prosperous and resourceful land than Edom, which was primarily a place filled with unfertile deserts and jagged mountains. Thirdly, it was a land that the Edomites bore brotherly association with, in that their patriarch Esau was the twin brother of Jacob, who later bore the name Israel. They like their ancestral father Esau before them harbored a hatred of Israel and his descendants the Jews and quite possibly felt a form of restitution in their occupation of the land of Israel.[92] Lastly, it was available for the taking, since the Babylonians had exported the Jews off into captivity.

Continued Edomite movement occurred over the fifth and fourth centuries BC into Southern Israel. Then, in 312 BC, the Seleucid King Antigonus, who had come to power when Alexander's empire was divided, conquered Edom. The last of the Edomites still held out in Edom at the time of the advance of Antigonus had to face the possibility of death by defeat or life by fleeing to Israel where they could find refuge with generations of relatives. Many chose to flee making it easier for Antigonus to prevail. This episode in history caused a second major wave of Edomite migration into Hebron and greater Southern Israel. About that time, the Edomites were more commonly referred to by their Greek name, Idumeans. The territory of Southern Israel they inhabited, with its central city of Hebron, had come to be known as Idumea. Ultimately, the Nabateans annihilated Antigonus and his army, when they weighted themselves down with the plunder and booty of Edom, making them to slow to further fight.[93]

Hebron remained under Edomite/Idumean control until Judas Maccabeus retook the city under Jewish control in 164 BC. Thirty-eight years later, in 126 BC, history tells us the Edomites/Idumeans had to be re-conquered by the Jewish army, led by their prince and high priest John Hyrcanus.[94] The Edomites/Idumeans continued to rise up and rebel, causing Hyrcanus to put an end to their insurgency. At that point, the Idumeans were forced to die, flee, or be proselytized into Judaism if they wanted to remain in the territory of Idumea, and/or greater Judea. Many opted to stay rather than move back into their ancient homeland Edom, which still housed many Nabateans.

Then in 47 BC, Julius Caesar promoted the Idumean Antipater
as procurator over Judea, Samaria, and Galilee, which in essence encompassed most all of the remaining Jewish kingdom. Ten years later
in 37 BC, the Romans named Herod as the King over Israel. Herod
was the son of Antipater, an Idumean, and his mother Nabatean. This
evidences the point that the Edomites/Idumeans were well established
in Israel, having over five centuries of prior history in Israel by the
time of the first coming of the Messiah Jesus Christ. Mark 3:8 alludes
to the territory of Idumea, further evidencing that the Idumeans were
still around during the New Testament period.

Josephus the Jewish historian tells us that further Idumean interactions in Israel occurred up to and on through AD 70, at which
time the Romans sacked Jerusalem and destroyed the second Jewish
temple. He identifies them as a "a tumultuous and disorderly nation,
always on the watch upon every motion, delighting in mutations; and
upon your flattering them ever so little, and petitioning them, they
soon take their arms, and put themselves into motion, and make haste
to a battle, as if it were to a feast."[95]

Just prior to the sacking of Jerusalem by the Roman legions,
led by Titus, the Idumeans joined the Jewish rebels led by John the
Zealot, against the Orthodox Jews of the time.[96] All three groups, the
Zealots, Idumeans, and the Orthodox Jews, were in fervor about the
advancing Roman legions throughout the land, and as such, Israel
was in a state of turmoil, which resulted in a civil war. About 20,000
Idumean infantry took part in the slaughter of many Orthodox Jews.[97]
After so doing, they repented and went back to what little, was left of
their Idumean existence.[98] Shortly thereafter, the remaining Jews and
Idumeans banded together against the Roman legions. Josephus goes
on to say that the Idumeans were enlisted alongside the Jews in the
fight.[99] As stated earlier, many Idumeans were either killed, sold into
slavery, or enjoined among the forty thousand set free by Caesar.[100]

These forty thousand Idumeans presumably attempted to reestablish the war torn territory of Idumea. Maps drafted as late as AD

135, at the time of the final Jewish revolt led by Bar Kokhba against the Roman occupation, still displayed Idumea giving it legitimacy as the nation of these Idumeans. Thus, the last traces of the Edomite/Idumean population residing in the land of modern-day Israel were approximately AD 135. From that point forward, further evidence of their ethnic whereabouts becomes scarce. As the next section reveals it was AD 135 when the Romans renamed the Land of Israel the Land of Palaestina, and as such, Idumea disappeared from future map, and the Idumeans fade from history.

THE NAME CONVERSION OF THE LAND

The name Palestine, which is the modern-day translation of the Latin term "Palaestina," the Arabic word "Filastin," and in Hebrew "Pelesheth" or sometimes spelled "Peleset" or "Peleshet," appears eight times in the Old Testament. The Romans renamed the land formerly known as Israel to the land of Palaestina in AD 135.

The original Hebrew word *Pelesheth* referred to the territory on the South West Coast of Israel, which the non-Arab Philistines settled between 1200 and 1100 BC. These people had been driven out of Greece and the Aegean Islands around 1300 BC. They made their way down toward Egypt, and unsuccessfully attempted to invade Egypt around 1200 BC. Because of their defeat, they migrated up to the area generally referred to today as the Gaza Strip.[101] As such, this territory became known as *Philistia*, and was much more limited in landmass, than the Palestine of today. Ancient Philistia became established on territory belonging to the tribe of Judah.

When the Romans ended the Jewish revolt of "Bar Kokhba" around AD 135, they advanced the name "Palaestina" to describe the subject territory. The historical understanding of why the Romans implemented this name change was to blot out any vestiges of residual Jewish identity and interest in connection with the land.

The story is told that "the Roman Procurator in charge of the

Judean-Israel territories was so angry at the Jews for revolting that he called for his historians and asked them who were the worst enemies of the Jews in their past history. The scribes said, 'the Philistines.' Thus, the Procurator declared that Land of Israel would from then forward be called 'Philistia.'"[102] As referenced before, *Palaestina* is the Latin translation of *Philistia*, from which today we derive the word *Palestine*.

Bar Kokhba had about 200,000 men at his command, and in a final Jewish revolt, they recaptured Jerusalem and many strongholds and villages throughout the country.[103] This caused the Emperor Hadrian at the time to call legion upon legion of reinforcements to crush the Jewish insurgents. It is estimated that as many as 580,000 Romans and Jews were slain in this bloody revolt. Some Roman accounts suggest almost that many Jews alone were killed.[104]

This Bar Kokhba revolt was the final straw for the Jews as far as Hadrian was concerned; he purposed to stamp out Jewish nationalism entirely. Jewish traditions like circumcision, the Sabbath, and the reading of the "Mosaic Law" were forbidden. He was determined to convert the war torn city of Jerusalem into a Roman colony. He changed the name from Jerusalem to Aelia Capitolina, and ordered the building of a temple to Jupiter, on the site where the second Jewish temple once stood. Lastly, he forbade any Jew, on pain of death to appear within site of the city.[105]

Though Palaestina was the name the Romans elected to use in AD 135, it was not the only name available to them at the time. *Idumea*, the Greek word for *Edom*, was still on the maps and could have likewise been used. The Idumeans/Edomites, still supported a population in Israel at the time in Hebron, and the surrounding areas near Jerusalem. The most logical explanations why the Romans opted not to name the region Idumea, are first that the Idumeans were most likely still practitioners of Judaism, the religion emperor Hadrian was attempting to vanquish, and secondly as such Idumea did not then rank as one of Israel's greatest historical enemies when compared against Philistia.

Regarding our study the point is not why the Romans chose the name Palaestina at the time; rather, it is the fact that there apparently were still Edomites/Idumeans residing in the land of Israel at the time of the renaming. The Edomites of old still had an ethnic identity well into the first and second centuries. However shortly thereafter they made their way off the pages of any further history.

The Bar Kokhba defeat only compounded the dilemmas of these two ethnic groups, the Jews and Edomites/Idumeans. It offered the necessary certainty that indeed the Jews were no longer the client nation, "My people Israel," and that the Edomites/Idumeans were made even more "small among the nations." Philistia, which had previously been an abandoned territorial name, became reinstated, and Idumea an established identity soon after the revival of Philistia became forgotten.

From that point, the land of Israel commenced to take on an entirely new identity. Around AD 390, the land of Palaestina broadened in scope to include three enlarged units: Prima, Secunda, and Tertia. These three units encompassed Judea, Samaria, the coast of Peraea, the Galilee, lower Jezreel Valley, regions east of the Galilee, Negev, Southern Jordan, and most of the Sinai.[106] The Edomite/Idumean remnant became further absorbed and harder to identify within these three units.

Arab rule over the area began around AD 635, and the Arab rulers back then divided the province into five districts, known as *Junds*, which were tribal corps. This period up to the tenth century was characterized by political upheavals, and several times the boundaries were readjusted. Around the tenth century, the division into Junds began to break down and the establishment of the Latin Kingdom of Jerusalem completed that process. Muslim control was re-established in the twelfth and thirteenth centuries, and the division into districts was reinstated, with boundaries that were frequently rewritten.

Around the end of the thirteenth century, Palestine comprised several of nine kingdoms of Syria, namely the Kingdoms of Gaza,

Karak, Safad, and parts of the Kingdom of Damascus.[107] Then came the Turkish Ottoman Empire, which ruled over the land in question from 1517 to 1917. Their dominance was brought to an end at the conclusion of World War I, which evidenced that nation had begun to come against nation in accordance to the prophecy of Jesus Christ.[108]

Then in 1917, the Balfour Document was drafted which entirely broadened the scope of the land of Palestine. In its original draft, it incorporated most all of the Gaza, Israel, the West Bank, and modern-day Jordan, and this large landmass, approximately 46,000 square miles, was to be devoted to the Jewish State, i.e., Israel. However, by 1948, when the Jewish State became official, the Arabs had convinced the world, that only about 5,591 square miles should be allotted to the returning Jewish people. Annexed out was modern-day Jordan, the West Bank, and the Gaza Strip.[109]

According to Genesis 15:18, the forty-six-thousand square miles would have been more in line with the land mass God promised to Abraham and his descendents, the Jewish people.

On the same day the LORD made a covenant with Abram, saying: "To your descendants I have given this land, from the river of Egypt to the great river, the River Euphrates." (Gen. 15:18, NKJV)

More on the events that shrunk the Balfour Document down through the UN Partition Plan of 1947 to the meager 5,591 square miles committed to the Jewish State in 1948 are documented in the *Isralestine—God's Roadmap Plan To Peace* chapter contained in this book.

SUMMARY

In summary, the land in question during the 1,878 years of Jewish dispersion out of Israel and into the nations of the world, changed hands on several occasions. It experienced Roman, Christian, Arab, Turkish, and British rule, and the name Palestine, which Rome implemented in AD 135 was tossed, turned, shrank, and stretched in whichever way the dominant political influence decided at the time of its respective sovereignty. It went from the scope of ancient Philistia (Gaza Strip), down through the Sinai, up to Damascus, over to the River Euphrates, and then in 1948 came back down in size to about 8,000 square miles which encompasses, Gaza, Israel, and the West Bank as defined today.

Palestine was essentially never officially recognized as a state or a nation; the terms were generally used loosely through the centuries to describe a territory with grossly undefined borders. However, in these times, the movement is to declare such a Palestinian state. This is because now there is a population group known as the Palestinians, and they have convinced the international community that they are deserving of such a state.

Today this population has definitely attained for themselves an ethnic identity, and as such have become a force to be reckoned with. Their general identity is founded in association with their refugee condition, and in that condition, they depict themselves, unlike "rebels without a cause," as "terrorists with a cause." Their movement is generally supported by the Muslim international influence, but is intrinsically lifted up by those Arab countries that most closely border the nation of Israel today. These Arab countries are the very same nations listed alongside the Palestinians in the forthcoming Psalm 83 confederacy. As stated in the beginning of this chapter, this confederacy is committed to the destruction of Israel and will surface in the end-times.

Perhaps we can glean a prophetic insight into the connection between the Edomites, later identified as the Idumeans, who today in many respects resemble the Palestinians and their tactics of terror.

"*The terror you* [Edomites–Idumeans–Palestinians] *inspire*
and the pride of your heart have deceived you, you who live

in the clefts of the rocks, who occupy the heights of the hill. Though you build your nest as high as the eagle's, from there I will bring you down," declares the LORD. "Edom will become an object of horror; all who pass by will be appalled and will scoff because of all its wounds." (Jer. 49:16–17 NIV; emphasis added)

The prophet Jeremiah speaks in the context of the end-times judgment predicted to come against Edom. Edom will become an "object of horror" due to the terror the Edomite population inspires. The word Jeremiah uses in the Hebrew is tiphletseth, and it is translated as a shuddering, horrific terror.[110] This gripping term is uniquely utilized only in this single instance in the entire Bible, yet it is the most descriptive word available in the ancient Hebrew language to identify the recently fashioned terrorism plaguing the nation Israel today. Back in Jeremiah's day there was warfare, ambush, and murder without cause, however Israel's enemies back then did not have the shuddering, horrific ability to strap explosives to themselves and take out not only themselves, but also large groups of Jews and/or Jewish supporters in one attempt.

The crimes of terror that were enacted on 9/11/2001 against America by the pro-Palestinian group Al-Qaeda put the world on alert that terrorism had become a bona fide method of warfare. What began in its fledgling stages in the Middle East had expanded its dangerous reach well into the international arena.

Presently, the world witnesses the "War on Terror" being waged against terrorist groups and the nations that sponsor them. The sizeable nations of Afghanistan and Iraq were promptly overturned for their sponsorship of terrorism. Their defeat evidences the international concern over the seriousness of the tiphletseth Jeremiah described. It is indeed a shuddering and horrific terror inspired by the Palestinians.

As this study suggests, the Edomites have a descendant population within the modern-day Palestinians. Therefore, this present behavior of the Palestinians, who inspire tactics of terror against the Jews in order to prevail over the land in question, is destined for judgment. This judgment is foretold to be delivered through the "exceedingly great army" of the nation Israel, and is described in Ezekiel 25:12–14 and Obadiah 1:18![111]

So then, is there any question today as to who the Edomites are? The Palestinians in part represent the Edomites in modern times. The terror that grips the Middle East is the result of their inspiration. It became a reality after the three conventional military attempts to destroy the nation Israel by the surrounding Arab nations in 1948, 1967, and 1973 failed. Terror is their relatively recently adopted attempt to accomplish the same aim, which is the destruction of the nation Israel.

They have said, "Come, and let us cut them off from *being* a nation, That the name of Israel may be remembered no more." (Psa. 83:4, NKJV)

Terrorism will eventually give way to the fulfillment of the Psalm 83 prophecy, whereby the "Plight of the Palestinians," i.e., the "tents of Edom," in their final attempt to be made more than "small among the nations" causes them to confederate with the surrounding Arab nations that support their cause. One last Arab-Israeli war results, however this time, they will meet with the formidable "exceedingly great army" of Israel spoken of in Ezekiel 37:10. It is this great army that finally brings to conclusion the present conflict in the Middle East.

All political attempts presently on the table that struggle to resolve the tension between the Arabs and the Jews are at best a temporary salve, designed to make Israel less of a nation and the Palestinians into a nation. This goes against the grain of God, Who has previously decided that Israel will again be called "My people Israel," and that Edom has been permanently "made small among the nations"!

10

OLAM EBAH

The Ancient Arab Hatred of the Jews

The present hostilities experienced in the Middle East between the Arabs and Jews, can be traced to a disposition of hatred originating almost four thousand years ago. It was about that time, that the God of the Old Testament, made an unconditional covenant with the Jewish Patriarch Abraham.[112] Due to the inherent blessings contained within this covenant, the infamous Bible characters Hagar, Ishmael, Esau, Moab, and Ammon coveted the contents of this covenant. These jealous individuals and their descendants that followed came to hate the Hebrews, who were the heirs of this blessed covenant.

Throughout time, the neighboring Gentile peoples of the region found it advantageous to embrace rather than resist this adversarial disposition. Ultimately, it evolved into a cleverly conceived religious package giving it license to unleash itself in a holy war. The *Jihad*, as it is often labeled, presently underway in the Middle East, finds its justification in Islam, but its roots in this longstanding hatred.

The Bible describes this disposition as an ancient hatred or in some translations a perpetual enmity. The two Hebrew words are *olam ebah*, and when used together they describe a condition stemming back long ago in ancient times, perpetuated throughout time, manifesting into hostility with no apparent end in sight.[113] They are only paired together in the entire Bible in the two passages listed below:

> Because you have had an ancient [olam] hatred [ebah], and have shed the blood of the children of Israel by the power of the sword at the time of their calamity, when their iniquity came to an end. (Ezek. 35:5, NKJV)

> Thus says the LORD GOD: "Because the Philistines dealt vengefully and took vengeance with a spiteful heart, to destroy because of the old [olam] hatred [ebah]." (Ezek. 25:15, NKJV)

The first passage refers contextually to Mount Seir located in Edom, which is the territory of Esau.[114] Today this area is known as Southern Jordan. In the Ezekiel 35:5 passage, we see that the hatred *was had* in the territory most closely associated with Esau. In the second passage of Ezekiel 25:5 we find that the Philistines embraced what was already preconditioned in Edom by Esau. Today what was formerly known as Philistia, the land of the Philistines, is now referred to as the Gaza Strip. In both scriptures, it is an enmity exhibited exclusively against the Jewish people.

The Bible teaches that this continuous and contagious disposition of hatred will evidence itself in a final showdown. It predicts a major war in the Middle East between those Arab nations that have refused to abandon the angered ancient attitude of their ancestors, and the Jews.[115] It amounts to the final contest over the blessed contents contained within the Abrahamic covenant! The victor is finally exalted as the true heir apparent!

This study explores the roots of the hatred through biblical accounts centered on the main patriarchs of the modern-day Middle Eastern peoples. Much of the population in the region has their decent traceable back to the patriarchs contained within this study. These ancestors were notable characters on the world scene, from which several historical nations were born. These individuals were involved in significant events relative to the plan of God intended for the benefit of man. Therefore, their interactions proved to be consequential in the history and development of the Middle East. Their attitudes have remained alive in the region throughout time immemorial.

SARAH VS. HAGAR (THE ROOT OF THE HATRED)

> So he [Abraham, father of the Jews] went in to Hagar [Egyptian], and she conceived. And when she saw that she had conceived, her mistress [Sarah, mother of the Jews] became despised in her [Hagar's] eyes. Then Sarah said to Abram, "My wrong *be* upon you! I gave my maid into your embrace; and when she saw that she had conceived, I became despised in her eyes. The LORD judge between you and me." (Gen. 16:4–5, NKJV)

Sarah knew that God had previously promised Abraham a son, through whom a multitude of descendants would follow.[116] Genesis 16:2 informs us that Sarah possessed a barren womb. Because of her barrenness, she concluded that the promised heir would not come from her womb. In Genesis 16:3 we are told that Sarah in accordance with the legal custom of her day, gave her maidservant Hagar to Abraham to be his substitute wife in order that the child could be conceived, and the Abrahamic covenant advanced.

"In the legal custom of that day a barren woman could give her maid to her husband as a wife, and the child born of that union was regarded as the first wife's child. If the husband said to the slave-wife's son, 'You are my son,' then he was the adopted son and heir. So Sarah's suggestion was unobjectionable according to the customs of that time."[117]

Abraham likewise concluded it could not be Sarah's barren womb through which his descendants would come, and therefore acted in accordance with the legal custom of his day and took Hagar as a surrogate wife. Upon Hagar's conception, she became contemptuous toward Sarah. This contempt was in violation of Abraham and Sarah's plan. Hagar was merely to be a surrogate mother and was scheduled to forfeit her son to Sarah, the first wife.

Hagar's response from the human perspective of our day is understandable, however at the time much more was at stake. The covenant God had previously made with Abraham may very well be what caused Hagar to despise Sarah. Hagar most probably understood the significance of Abraham, and therefore the purpose of her surrogacy in relationship to the covenant his God made with him.

Hagar should have understood that Abraham, as the recipient of the covenant, was promised a land, a nation, and the most prominent stature among men upon the Earth. God's foreign policy toward all other peoples residing upon the Earth was directly connected to their relationship with Abraham and his descendants. It is quite likely that Hagar's contempt toward Sarah was rooted in her coveting of the contents of the covenant.

No matter her motivation, the scripture goes on to tell that Abraham was clear on the custom of his day, and the covenant of his God.

So Abram said to Sarah, "Indeed your maid *is* in your hand;
do to her as you please." And when Sarah dealt harshly with
her [Hagar], she fled from her presence. (Gen. 16:6, NKJV)

Sarah dealt harshly with Hagar with the permission of Abraham, because of Hagar's contempt for the covenant of God, the legal custom of their day, and her disdain toward Sarah her mistress. The severity of the harsh treatment caused Hagar to flee from Sarah's presence.

When we ponder the significance of this entire episode, we can conclude that the roots of the ancient hatred may well begin here. Furthermore, these roots are likely grounded in a jealous attitude toward the Abrahamic Covenant, as advanced by Hagar.

Though Abraham and Sarah laughed at the prospect of Sarah ever conceiving a child out from her barren womb, this episode with Hagar was no laughing matter.[118] Abraham and Sarah were esteemed as the respondents to the covenant God made for the benefit of humankind. As such, the consequences of their actions relative to all of the contents of the covenant had the potential to cause disturbance within all of humanity, then and now.

Certainly, it was an unconditional covenant; however, Abraham and Sarah were its critical components. Similarly was the historical case of Adam and Eve in their Garden of Eden episode. Their mistake injected the sin nature into all of humanity. Abraham and Sarah's mistake involving Hagar appears to have injected the ancient hatred into the Middle East.

Due to the mistake by Adam, Jesus Christ "the Jew" was crucified to rectify the sin problem. Unfortunately, because of the ancient hatred, the Jews are being killed in the land of Israel today. Those Arabs terrorizing the Jews in Israel, whether consciously or unconsciously are in essence exhibiting the same attitude of coveting the contents of the Covenant, i.e., the land and prominence promised to Abraham and his Jewish descendants.

Scripture and history tells us that Hagar returned in submission to Sarah, but there is no evidence that her hatred toward Sarah was ever reversed. Abraham had paternal instincts of high regard for Hagar's son Ishmael, but it does not appear that Abraham ever officially accepted Ishmael in accordance with the legal custom as heir to the covenant.[119] Furthermore, many years later after the birth of Isaac out of Sarah's womb, at the time of his weaning we are told that this Ishmael scoffed at Isaac. Isaac was the true heir of the covenant in contrast to Ishmael.

So the child [Isaac] grew and was weaned. And Abraham made a great feast on the same day that Isaac was weaned. And Sarah saw the son [Ishmael] of Hagar the Egyptian, whom she had borne to Abraham, scoffing. (Gen. 21:8–9, NKJV)

Again there arises a significant episode involving Sarah and Hagar revolving around the Abrahamic Covenant. For Ishmael to scoff at the miraculously born Isaac, who had come out of the formerly barren womb of the aged Sarah, indicated that there still existed an attitude of animosity over the contents of the covenant. Perhaps Ishmael exhibited an exclusive adversarial attitude toward Isaac; however, both Hagar and Ishmael were immediately forced to leave.

Therefore she [Sarah] said to Abraham, "Cast out this bondwoman [Hagar] and her son [Ishmael]; for the son of this bondwoman shall not be heir with my son, *namely* with Isaac." (Gen. 21:10, NKJV)

What Sarah recognized was the enmity exhibited by Hagar, passed on through to her son Ishmael. Likewise, God confirmed this disposition developed in Ishmael.

But God said to Abraham, "Do not let it be displeasing in your sight because of the lad or because of your bondwoman. Whatever Sarah has said to you, *listen to her* voice; for in Isaac your seed shall be called." (Gen. 21:12, NKJV; emphasis added)

God said to listen to her voice and "*Cast out* this bondwoman [Hagar] and her son [Ishmael]; for the son of this bondwoman shall not be heir with my son, namely with Isaac." These are the harshest of words, and represent Sarah and God's recognition of the severity of Ishmael's jealous attitude. This takes us back to the rightful atti-

tude of Sarah in Genesis 16:6 at the time of the conception of Ishmael, whereby she dealt harshly with Hagar for this same adversarial
attitude.

> So Abraham rose early in the morning, and took bread and
> a skin of water; and putting *it* on her shoulder, he gave *it*
> and the boy to Hagar, and sent her away. Then she departed
> and wandered in the Wilderness of Beersheba. (Gen. 21:14,
> NKJV)

God and Sarah told Abraham to cast out Hagar and Ishmael, so
in obedience Abraham rose early and sent them away. Hagar wanders
off into the wilderness and has her second divine encounter, this time
with her son Ishmael present.[120] Ultimately, Hagar, an Egyptian, took
for Ishmael an Egyptian bride.[121]

Thus, we see two powerful episodes whereby Sarah and Hagar
are at odds with each other over the rightful heir to the Abrahamic
Covenant. This argument still rages on between the three prominent
religions of our time: Christianity, Judaism, and Islam. Christians and
Jews believe that the covenant was passed on through Abraham, Isaac,
and Jacob, whereas the Islamic holy book known as the Koran memo-
rializes Ishmael in first position over Isaac.[122]

ISAAC VS. ISHMAEL

As previously stated, Isaac became the true heir of Abraham. This
disqualified Ishmael, Abraham's first-born son, who according to the
legal custom of that day should have been the rightful heir. The thing
of greatest value to the rightful heir of Abraham was his covenant
made by God between them.

Imagine the conditions of the first fourteen years of Ishmael's life,
after which time Isaac arrived on the scene. Ishmael in his formative years was probably caught in this triangle of powerful emotions.

Abraham exhibited paternal love to Ishmael his firstborn son, Hagar exhibited envy toward Sarah her mistress, and Sarah viewed Ishmael as her mistake for meddling with the Abrahamic Covenant. Is it any wonder that Ishmael scoffed at the weaning of Isaac? But scoffed indeed he did, and at a most important time in Isaac's life, his weaning. This scoffing was much more significant than a sibling squabble; otherwise, a simple disciplining would have been in order, rather than a casting-out.

Hagar and Ishmael, for a lack of a better descriptions, were players at that time on the world scene. They were elevated in stature due to their unique relationships with Abraham. The leadership of Egypt certainly knew of Abraham due to his previous encounter with Pharaoh, recorded in Genesis 12:10–20. Nine other most prominent kings in the region must also have come to know and revere Abraham.[123]

Therefore, the point to understand is that through Hagar and Ishmael this attitude of hatred was likely being spread among the elite circles in the region. The arguments against the rightful heir and the contents of the covenant were reaching foreign soil. After all Hagar and Ishmael could proudly boast that they were also involved in a covenant of their own personal interest. Ishmael was to be a "great nation!"

Then the Angel of the LORD said to her, "I will multiply your [Hagar] descendants exceedingly, so that they shall not be counted for multitude." And the Angel of the LORD said to her: "Behold, you *are* with child, And you shall bear a son. You shall call his name Ishmael, Because the LORD has heard your affliction. He shall be a wild man; His hand *shall be* against every man, And every man's hand against him. And he shall dwell in the presence of all his brethren." (Gen. 16:10–12, NKJV)

And as for Ishmael, I have heard you [Abraham]. Behold, I have blessed him, and will make him fruitful, and will multiply him exceedingly. He shall beget twelve princes, and *I will make him a great nation.* (Gen. 17:20, NKJV, emphasis added)

And God heard the voice of the lad. Then the angel of God called to Hagar out of heaven, and said to her, "What ails you, Hagar? Fear not, for God has heard the voice of the lad where he *is.* [18]Arise, lift up the lad and hold him with your hand, for *I will make him* [Ishmael] *a great nation.*" (Gen. 21:17–18, NKJV, emphasis added)

Ishmael went on to father twelve sons; he and his sons predominately settled in the Arabian territories. Thus, God fulfills this prophecy of the great nation in the manifestation of the nation of modern-day Saudi Arabia. The Psalm 83 confederacy section refers to them as the Ishmaelites.[124]

JACOB VS. ESAU

By the time Isaac and Rebecca had their twins Esau and Jacob, the disposition of hatred was advancing and infecting the Middle East region through the exploits of Hagar and Ishmael. The environment was a powerful incubator for the hatred Esau ultimately displayed toward his younger twin brother Jacob.

So *Esau hated Jacob* because of the blessing with which his father blessed him [Jacob], and Esau said in his heart, "The days of mourning for my father are at hand; then *I will kill my brother Jacob.*" (Gen. 27:41, NKJV, emphasis added)

"Esau hated Jacob." This hatred was akin to the attitude already advanced by Uncle Ishmael and step-grandmother Hagar. Esau likewise came to covet the contents of the covenant. As the firstborn, it was his birthright to be the heir of the Abrahamic Covenant, not his twin brother Jacob. In Esau's estimation, the line of command was to be Abraham, Isaac, and Esau. A study of the interactions between Esau and Jacob give understanding into the development of Esau's hatred toward Jacob.

> Now Jacob cooked a stew; and Esau came in from the field, and he was weary. And Esau said to Jacob, "Please feed me with that same red stew, for I am weary." Therefore his name was called Edom. But Jacob said, "Sell me your birthright as of this day." And Esau said, "Look, I am about to die; so what is this birthright to me?" Then Jacob said, "Swear to me as of this day." So he swore to him, and sold his birthright to Jacob. And Jacob gave Esau bread and stew of lentils; then he ate and drank, arose, and went his way. Thus Esau despised *his* birthright. (Gen. 25:29–34, NKJV)

On the road to his hatred of Jacob, Esau first gave up his birthright for a short order of food. This episode evidenced his contempt for the contents of the covenant at the time. Ultimately, his nickname became Edom, which means red, in association with the red stew for which he sold his birthright to Jacob. Thus, "Esau despised *his* birthright." The Hebrew word for despised is *bazah*, a primitive root meaning to disesteem, despise, disdain, contemptible, think to scorn, or vile person.[125] At the time, Esau disesteemed the significance of the Abrahamic Covenant, which evidenced his lack of reverence for the God of his father Isaac, and his grandfather Abraham.[126]

By way of review, let us remember that the Abrahamic Covenant is the source of blessings toward all humankind.

> To Abraham and his descendants this promise was made; I will bless those who bless you, And I will curse him who curses you; And in you all the families of the Earth shall be blessed." (Gen. 12:13, NKJV)

Thus, Esau's disrespect for the contents of the covenant was an ultimate display of his disregard for humankind, its benefactor. As a consequence, the prophets Jeremiah and Obadiah would prophecy centuries later that the descendants of Esau would likewise in reversal be despised by men.

For indeed, I will make you [Edom] small among nations, Despised [bazah] among men. (Jer. 49:15, NKJV)

Behold, I will make you [Edom] small among the nations; You shall be greatly despised [bazah]. (Obad. 1:2, NKJV)

The prophets use the Hebrew word *bazah* to describe the attitude among men toward the descendants of Esau. This prophecy likely depicts that Esau's disposition of enmity toward the contents of the covenant, was forwarded on through his descendants, as one would not expect God arbitrarily to advance a judgment well into the future generations without a cause.

Things go from bad to worse as the story goes regarding these brothers; before we study further it is important to preface the next event with the understanding that not only was Esau the firstborn, he was the preferred son of Isaac.

So the boys grew. And Esau was a skillful hunter, a man of the field; but Jacob was a mild man, dwelling in tents. And Isaac loved Esau because he ate *of his* game, but Rebekah loved Jacob. (Gen. 25:27–28, NKJV)

This favoritism being displayed by Isaac toward Esau was in conflict with a prophecy that Rebekah had received from God. Rebekah realized that Jacob was destined to be the heir to the Abrahamic Covenant.

> But the children struggled together within her; and she said, "If *all is* well, why *am I like* this?" So she went to inquire of the LORD. And the LORD said to her: "Two nations *are* in your womb, Two peoples shall be separated from your body; *One* people shall be stronger than the other, And the older shall serve the younger." (Gen. 25:22–23, NKJV)

As Isaac's death drew near he was about to mistakenly pass on the blessings of the Abrahamic covenant to his firstborn Esau, rather than the appropriate recipient, Jacob.

> Now it came to pass, when Isaac was old and his eyes were so dim that he could not see, that he called Esau his older son and said to him, "My son." And he answered him, "Here I am." Then he said, "Behold now, I am old. I do not know the day of my death. Now therefore, please take your weapons, your quiver and your bow, and go out to the field and hunt game for me. And make me savory food, such as I love, and bring *it* to me that I may eat, that my soul may bless you before I die." (Gen. 27:1–4, NKJV)

However, Rebekah convinced Jacob to deceive Isaac by impersonating Esau. It was her intent that the blessings would flow through Jacob, which was in line with the prophecy she had received from God that "the older shall serve the younger." Genesis 27 records the details of their conspiracy.

Most commentaries tend to exaggerate the point that this mother-son collaboration was a bit on the sinister side; however, the fact is that Isaac was already deceived as to whom the rightful recipient of the blessings should be. Isaac was about to bestow the blessings of the covenant to his preferred choice Esau the older, rather than Jacob the younger, God's chosen child. This would have been an enormous mistake, and therefore due to the severity of Isaac's foolishness in this matter, Rebekah and Jacob felt compelled to conspire in the manner that they did.

Centuries later, the Jewish prophet Malachi reinforced the fact that Rebekah was right-minded in her thinking. The contents of the Abrahamic covenant were indeed intended to flow through the loins of Jacob and his descendants. God preferred Jacob over Esau:

The burden of the word of the LORD to Israel by Malachi. "I have loved you," says the LORD. "Yet you say, 'In what way have You loved us?' *Was* not Esau Jacob's brother?" Says the LORD. "Yet Jacob I have loved; But Esau I have hated, And laid waste his mountains and his heritage For the jackals of the wilderness." (Malachi 1:1–3, NKJV)

There is little doubt that Rebekah had previously informed Isaac of her prophecy that "the older shall serve the younger." Isaac should have recognized that it was Jacob and not Esau, who was to receive the blessings. Furthermore, one can suspect that Isaac had also been informed that Esau had previously sold his birthright to Jacob for a bowl of red (Edom) stew. In light of this information, it can be considered foolish for Isaac even to consider Esau, who had blatantly expressed his disregard toward the contents of the covenant, as the rightful heir to these all-important blessings.

Because of their successful collaboration, Jacob rightfully became the recipient of the blessings. As such, Esau came to hate Jacob and wanted to murder him. Harboring this attitude against Jacob, again displayed Esau's disrespect for the contents of the covenant, and his disregard for humankind. Like his uncle Ishmael before him, Esau likewise exhibited contempt toward the plan of God for the benefit of man.

So Esau hated Jacob because of the blessing with which his father blessed him [Jacob], and Esau said in his heart, "The days of mourning for my father are at hand; then I will kill my brother Jacob." (Gen. 27:41, NKJV)

The above passage declares that Esau hated Jacob because of the blessing, which concluded in:

Let peoples serve you [Jacob], And nations bow down to you. Be master over your brethren, And let your mother's sons [including Esau] bow down to you. Cursed *be* everyone who curses you, And blessed *be* those who bless you! (Gen. 27:29, NKJV)

Far from being excited about the prospects for his brother Jacob, the heir apparent as chosen by God to carry the torch of the Abrahamic Covenant, we are informed that:

When Esau heard the words of his father, he cried with an exceedingly great and bitter cry, and said to his father, "Bless me—me also, O my father!" (Gen. 27:34, NKJV)

At this point we see Esau begin to covet the contents of the covenant: "Bless me—me also, O my father!"

Then Isaac answered and said to Esau, "Indeed I have made him [Jacob] your master, and all his brethren I have given to him as servants; with grain and wine I have sustained him. What shall I do now for you, my son?" And Esau said to his father, "Have you only one blessing, my father? Bless me—me also, O my father!" And Esau lifted up his voice and wept. Then Isaac his father answered and said to him: "Behold, your dwelling shall be of the fatness of the Earth, And of the dew of heaven from above. By your sword you shall live, And you shall serve your brother; [Jacob] And it shall come to pass, when you become restless, That you shall break his yoke from your neck." So Esau hated Jacob because of the blessing with which his father blessed him, and Esau said in his heart, "The days of mourning for my father are at hand; then I will kill my brother Jacob." (Gen. 27:37–41, NKJV)

Isaac instructed Esau to serve Jacob, not to hate and desire to kill him. However, Esau, who had cried with "an exceedingly great and bitter cry," decided to deviate from the plan. In so doing, he evidence his lack of fellowship with the God of his father Isaac and his grandfather Abraham.

In his embittered state Esau goes to the clan of Ishmael and marries a daughter of Ishmael named Mahalath. Commentaries are mixed as to whether Esau did this in an attempt to please his father Isaac, or if he intended to be spiteful. Regardless of the motivation, the fact is that in so doing he entered into hostile territory, whereby the hatred harbored by Ishmael and his offspring was presumably well established. Esau married the daughter of a powerful figure, with a well-known dislike for Isaac. It is probable that Mahalath fueled rather than extinguished the flame of Esau's bitterness toward his brother Jacob.

Esau saw that Isaac had blessed Jacob and sent him away to Padan Aram to take himself a wife from there, *and that* as he blessed him he gave him a charge, saying, "You shall not take a wife from the daughters of Canaan," and that Jacob had obeyed his father and his mother and had gone to Padan Aram. Also Esau saw that the daughters of Canaan did not please his father Isaac. So Esau went to Ishmael and took Mahalath the daughter of Ishmael, Abraham's son, the sister of Nebajoth, to be his wife in addition to the wives he had. (Gen. 28:6–9, NKJV)

Esau, like Ishmael, was also a big name on the Middle Eastern scene at the time. In accordance with the prophecy given to his mother Rebekah ("Two nations are in your womb"), a nation arose out from him, also.[127] Modern-day Southern Jordan, was formerly called Edom. This was the territory settled by Esau, and Edom became the nation that grew out of him.[128] Jacob, as heir to the Abrahamic Covenant which also promised the rise of a nation, became the nation Israel.

Hence, you have these three family members forming nations that border each other. As Ishmael (Saudi Arabia) and Esau (Edom/ Southern Jordan) formed their nations, they infused their hatred toward Jacob (Israel) into their cultures and descendants. As the nation of Edom formed, it advanced many aggressions against the Jewish people. For more detail, read the chapter in this book called *The Final Palestinian Farewell.*

MOAB AND AMMON: THE CHILDREN OF ABRAHAM VS. THE CHILDREN OF LOT

The animosity that developed between Moab and Ammon, the children of Lot, toward the Jewish people can be understood, but its roots are more difficult to trace.[129] Unlike their relatives Hagar, Ishmael, and Esau, Moab and Ammon are not noted in the Bible as having any negative personal encounter with Abraham, Isaac, or Jacob. Though the lives of Moab and Ammon paralleled Ishmael and Isaac on the timeline, most of the adversarial activities between the Moabites and Ammonites in relationship to the Jews were manifested through their descendant's centuries after the deaths of Moab and Ammon.

There are several presumptions we can consider regarding the awareness of both Moab and Ammon:

1. They were familiar with the land boundaries Abraham appropriated to their father Lot (we study this episode later in this section).

2. They were familiar with the Abrahamic Covenant.
3. They were familiar with their kinship with Ishmael and Isaac, and knew them, or at least knew of them personally.
4. They had heard of the rivalries between Hagar and Sarah and Ishmael and Isaac.
5. They were familiar with the hatred (*ebah*) developing in the entire region.
6. They were also notable characters on the world scene during their time.

In time, the ancient hatred permeated into the Moabite and Ammonite cultures, and in Psalm 83 we are told that their descendants ultimately align themselves with the final Arab confederacy to be formed in the future against Israel.[130] Furthermore, biblical accounts often find the descendants of Moab and Ammon acting out the *olam ebah* antagonistically toward the nation Israel. Interactions between the Moabites and Ammonites against the Jews often depict a dispute over the possession of certain parts of the Promised Land.[131] Considering the presumptions above, the historical biblical accounts, and the Psalm 83 prophecy, let us explore the development of the region in relationship to the land appropriated to Lot, which later formed into the territories named after his children, Moab and Ammon.

The tribal boundaries of Israel were established approximately four to five hundred years after the territories of Moab and Ammon became settled. These tribal boundaries of Israel penetrated eastward of the Jordan River, and abutted up to the previously established borders of Moab and Ammon.

THE CHAIN OF TITLE

Perhaps a biblical search into the chain of title of these lands is a good starting point. The initial conveyance of the Land was to Abraham, and it was recorded in the Abrahamic Covenant.

Now the LORD had said to Abraham: "Get out of your country, From your family and from your father's house, To a land that I will show you. I will make you a great nation; I will bless you And make your name great; And you shall be a blessing. I will bless those who bless you, And I will curse him who curses you; And in you all the families of the Earth shall be blessed." (Gen. 12:1–3, NKJV)

The land in question at this point lacked description. Abraham, then known as Abram, moved in the direction of Canaan, which gives us our first clue as to the vicinity of the land promised to him.[132] Ultimately it was identified as the land between the River of Egypt and the River Euphrates.[133] However, beforehand, while the land was yet generally unidentified, a significant dispute, which is recorded in Genesis 13: 5-7, arose regarding the land between the herdsmen of Abram and the herdsmen of Lot, Abram's Nephew.[134]

So Abram said to Lot, "Please let there be no *strife* between you and me, and between my herdsmen and your herdsmen; for we *are* brethren. *Is* not the whole land before you? Please *separate* from me. If *you take* the left, then I will go to the right; or, if *you go* to the right, then I will go to the left." And Lot lifted his eyes and saw all the plain of Jordan, that it *was* well watered everywhere (before the LORD destroyed Sodom and Gomorrah) like the garden of the LORD, like the land of Egypt as you go toward Zoar. Then Lot chose for himself all the plain of Jordan, and Lot journeyed east. And they separated from each other. (Gen. 13:8-11, NKJV)

Abraham granted Lot the area eastward of Canann, referred to in the above passages as the plain of Jordan. This land later came to be known as Moab, and Ammon, named after the direct descendants of Lot. Today this territory best represents modern day Central and Northern Jordan.

Abram dwelt in the land of Canaan, and Lot dwelt in the cities of the plain and pitched *his* tent even as far as Sodom. But the men of Sodom *were* exceedingly wicked and sinful against the LORD. And the LORD said to Abram, after Lot had separated from him: "Lift your eyes now and look from the place where you are—northward, southward, eastward, and westward; for all the land which you see I give to you and your descendants forever." (Gen. 13:12–15, NKJV)

God told Abram to lift his eyes and look panoramically about him, and that all the surrounding land would become his and his descendants forever. Lot, apparently possessing the same panoramic view as Abram also lifted his eyes, and turned his focus to the fertile soil to the East of where they stood. This land, presumably also in the scope of Abram's view, was thus Abram's to keep or convey. Abram opted to appropriate this land to Lot and his herdsmen.

The territories that today best represent most of modern-day Israel and Northern and Central Jordan were then available at the discretion of Abram to be distributed. This ability of Abram to distribute the land evidenced that at least those subject portions were part of the Promised Land; otherwise, he would have lacked the ability to convey appropriately the title between the two of them.

So it was that Abraham settled west of the Jordan River (Israel), and Lot settled east of the Jordan (Northern and Central Jordan). Southern Jordan was eventually developed by Abraham's grandson Esau and became known as Edom. Historically, Central Jordan was territorially developed by the descendants of Moab, Lot's firstborn son, and Northern Jordan likewise developed by the descendants of his second son Ben Ammi.[135] The territory was identified as Ammon. Thus, the children of lot are better known biblically as Moab and Ammon.

This event gives the first official description of the Promised Land,

and in the same instance depicts the first contest over the Promised Land in question. As stated previously in Genesis 13:7–8, "there was strife" between the herdsmen of Abram's livestock and the herdsmen of Lot's livestock. So Abram said to Lot, "Please let there be no strife between you and me and between my herdsmen and your herdsmen; for we *are* brethren."

In order to avoid further strife between them and their herdsmen over the coveted covenanted Promised Land, Abraham requests that Lot and his herdsmen depart.

> *Is* not the whole land before you? Please separate from me. If *you take* the left, then I will go to the right; or, if *you go* to the right, then I will go to the left. (Gen. 13:9, NKJV)

The second encounter of significant proportion was between the Hebrews and the Moabites, whereby the Jews were making their way out of Egypt back into the Promised Land via the Exodus route through Edom, Moab, and Ammon (modern-day Jordan). The Moabites were concerned that the Hebrews would overtake the territory of Moab and reclaim it back into their promised land.[136]

By this point, it was understood that this land, which was situated between the River of Egypt and the river Euphrates, had in Genesis 15:18 (over four hundred years prior) been given by God back to Abraham and his Hebrew descendants. This meant the Hebrews returning to their Promised Land could reclaim Moab and Ammon.

The Hebrews in power exited Egypt and the leadership of Moab sought to curse them.[137] Thus, early on we see the descendents of Moab already harbored hostility toward the children of Abraham.

Whereas the people of Moab harbored hatred toward the Jews, the Jews were taught early on that they were not to harm the land appropriated to the descendents of Lot. This respect for the land chosen by Lot caused the Hebrews to remember their history. They would be responsible to recall the dispute between the herdsmen of Abraham, and herdsmen of Lot, which eventuated in the separation of the land.[138]

> Then the LORD said to me [Moses], "Do not harass Moab, nor contend with them in battle, for I will not give you *any* of their land *as* a possession, because I have given Ar to the descendants of Lot *as* a possession." (Deut. 2:9, NKJV)

> And *when* you come near the people of Ammon, do not harass them or meddle with them, for I will not give you *any* of the land of the people of Ammon *as* a possession, because I have given it to the descendants of Lot *as* a possession.'" (Deut. 2:19, NKJV)

The next historical interaction between the children of Lot and the children of Israel was a story of conflict. Subsequently Moab and Ammon confederated in war against Israel and defeated it. Israel was under the sovereignty of Moab for approximately eighteen years.[139] Israel later regained their own sovereignty by defeating Moab, their enemy, killing about 10,000 of the stout men of Moab.[140]

The Bible records numerous conflicts that continued throughout time between Moab and Ammon against Israel. These encounters prove that early on the precedent had been clearly established; Moab and Ammon chose to embrace the ancient hatred spreading rampantly in the region. For the most part, Moab and Ammon considered Israel their enemy. They chose to serve their gods, rather than Jehovah, God of the Jews, the God who gave their patriarch Lot their prescribed lands.

The map below portrays the point that the Jewish people became surrounded by the ancient hatred. The nations that formed from all the patriarchs listed in this chapter embraced a jealousy of something very Jewish—the Abrahamic Covenant. Additionally the *olam ebah* engulfed the region and was easily embraced by the Philistines of

Philistia, which today is generally synonymous with the Gaza Strip. As quoted in Ezekiel 25:15, "the Philistines dealt vengefully and took vengeance with a spiteful heart, to destroy because of the old (olam) hatred (ebah)."

By association, the map displays: Hagar of Egypt, Ishmael patriarch of Saudi Arabia, Esau founder of Southern Jordan, Moab patriarch of Central Jordan, and Ammon patriarch of Northern Jordan. The location of ancient Philistia is also displayed on this map.

Fig. 3. Map by Lani Harmony, www.gallery3nine.com.

Also contributing to the ancient hatred in the region were the plagues that came against Egypt, represented by the lightening bolt imposed upon the map. This devastating period in Egyptian history eventually led to the Hebrew Exodus out of Egypt and into the Promised Land. These plagues cemented the ancient hatred firmly in place in Egypt. The Egyptians were already prone to hate the Hebrews from the disposition Hagar had introduced to them about five hundred years prior. This map further helps to illustrate the fact that Israel is held hostage by the ancient hatred, which comes at them from all sides. In the present day nothing has changed, the Middle East conflict pinning Arab against Jew, is an echo out of the annals of history.

"Because you have had an ancient [olam] hatred [ebah], and have shed the blood of the children of Israel by the power of the sword at the time of their calamity, when their iniquity came to an end, therefore, *as* I live," says the LORD GOD, "I will prepare you for blood, and blood shall pursue you; since you have not hated blood, therefore blood shall pursue you. Thus I will make Mount Seir most desolate, and cut off from it the one who leaves and the one who returns." (Ezek 35:5–7, NKJV)

This prophecy of Ezekiel tells the story. It points out that when the iniquity of the Jewish people had run its due course, those who harbored the ancient hatred still persisted in shedding Jewish blood. For this, those who persisted in the shedding of Jewish blood well beyond that point in time when the Jewish "iniquity came to an end" will see their own blood shed.

The inference is as follows: The iniquity of the Jews was the rejection of Jesus Christ; this evidenced their total apostasy as the client nation of their God Jehovah, i.e., "My people Israel." Subsequently, in AD 70 they were dispersed out of Israel into the nations of the world at large. This Jewish judgment "came to an end" as evidenced by the Holocaust episode in world history. In the aftermath, the Jewish people began to make their way back to their homeland Israel, and immediately met with "the power of the sword" upon their return. This hostile welcoming committee exhibited the "ancient hatred" (olam ebah).

It was not part of the prophetic program that upon the restoration of the nation Israel, whereby the Jewish people would return into their homeland, that the Arabs should shed Jewish blood. Therefore, in accordance with the curse for curse in kind clause contained within the Genesis 12:3 clause of the Abrahamic Covenant, these Arabs will experience the shedding of their own blood.

Though the Arabs who harbor the "ancient hatred" have made several confederate attempts in modern history to destroy the restored nation Israel, the one that issues the final farewell is described in Psalm 83. The confederate effort, expected to occur in the not-so-distant future, will finally provoke God to judge the "ancient hatred."

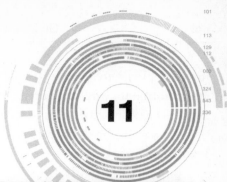

THE FINAL PALESTINIAN FAREWELL

The Reprisal of Edom

D id you know the Bible has foretold for us the events that must occur in order to make an end of the present Israeli-Palestinian conflict? It predicted the arrival of the present Middle East predicament, and in keeping with its sovereign authority as the holy Word of God, dared to forecast its finality. This study focuses upon the reprisal of Edom, the expanse of which abruptly brings to a conclusion the ongoing Arab-Israeli conflict.

> For the day of the LORD upon all the nations is near; As you have done, it shall be done to you; *Your reprisal shall return upon your own head.* (Obad. 1:15, NKJV; emphasis added)

This key passage, written by the Jewish prophet Obadiah, speaks of a reprisal which returns upon the head of the descendants of Esau. Esau's descendants presently share ethnical representation within the Palestinians. This head blow knocks them down to the canvas and out for the count. It results in the final Palestinian farewell.

Though the world continues to cough up attempts at a political solution to the conflict, the Bible describes its end coming from events of an entirely different nature. "As you have done, it shall be done to you," alludes to a curse-for-curse-in-kind response. "Your reprisal shall return upon your own head," presents a boomerang affect, sending a blow back to the point of its origin.

By way of brief review, at this point you should recall the following:

1. Esau was the twin brother of Jewish patriarch Jacob.[141]
2. Esau was the founder of Edom, making him the father of the Edomites.[142]
3. The Edomites initially inhabited what we today call Southern Jordan.
4. They eventually migrated into Israel, maintaining a population in both places.
5. They later assumed the Greek name Idumeans.
6. A remnant of Esau's descendants resides within the Palestinians of today.

Digesting these facts, we can discern that Obadiah describes a judgment destined to debilitate the Palestinian people. Their mistreatment of the Jewish people, results in their own ethnical demise. It matters not what the world envisions, rather what has been written, is that which will indeed occur!

I cannot emphasize enough that God established His foreign policy toward the Gentile nations long ago in Genesis 12:1–3. Whether or not the Gentile would be blessed or cursed was directly related to his or her treatment, then and now, of Abraham and/or his descendants, the Jews. Though Abraham fathered several children, the context of the blessing or cursing clause finds its application through the patriarchal lineage of Abraham, Isaac, and Jacob, from who the Hebrew people came.[143]

Now the LORD had said to Abram: "Get out of your country, From your family

And from your father's house, To a land that I will show you. I will make you a great nation; I will bless you And make your name great; And you shall be a blessing. I will bless those who bless you, And I will curse him who curses you; And in you all the families of the Earth shall be blessed." (Gen. 12:1–3, NKJV; emphasis added)

In essence, what Genesis 12:3 declares is "As you have done, (to Abraham or his descendants) it shall be done to you." Your reprisal, translated "your reward" in the King James Version, "shall return upon thine own head." This reprisal comes in strict accordance with the curse-for-curse-in-kind clause contained within the Abrahamic Covenant formulated approximately 4000 years ago. Unfortunately, Esau and his descendants, including the Palestinians, opted for the curse.

Before Obadiah issues the reprisal edict in Obadiah 1:15, he lists the crimes committed against Israel, by the Edomites, in Obadiah 1:10–14. We find a detailed explanation of these crimes in the *Obadiah's Mysterious Vision* chapter of this book.

Obadiah concludes in verse 15 with a devastating uppercut to the jawbone of the Palestinians: "As you have done, it shall be done to you; Your reprisal shall return upon your own head." This dreadful declaration is actually preceded by "For the day of the LORD upon all the nations is near;" which gives indication of the timing of the reprisal. The knockout punch to the Palestinians occurs prior to the "day of the LORD upon all the nations." This means the Arab-Israeli conflict will be concluded prior to the infamous seven-year Tribulation Period, otherwise known as Daniel's Seventieth Week.

As if the crimes committed in Obadiah 1:10–14 against the Jews, which occurred prior to the Holocaust, weren't horrific enough, the descendants of Esau picked up where they left off upon the return of the Jews back into the land of Israel, which commenced on May 14, 1948.[144] Ezekiel saw this subsequent misbehavior well in advance. He declares:

"Because you [descendants of Esau] have had an ancient hatred, and have shed *the blood of* the children of Israel [the Jews] by the power of the sword at the time of their calamity, *when* their iniquity *came to an* end, [subsequent to the Holocaust] therefore, *as* I live," says the LORD GOD, "I will prepare you for blood, and blood shall pursue you; since you have not hated [the spilt Jewish] blood, therefore [the spilt Jewish] blood shall pursue you." (Ezek. 35:5–6, NKJV)

The international community continually complicates and confounds foreign policy, though God formatted it centuries ago in an utterly simplistic manner. How one interacts with the descendants of Abraham determines whether he or she is blessed or cursed. The world has no ability to override God's will in this matter. The descendants of Esau opted to curse the Jews by antagonizing them upon their restoration back into the land of Israel, thereby provoking upon themselves divine longstanding foreign policy of a similar negative nature.

The return of the Jews back into the land of Israel was not an unknown prophetic phenomenon; many Jewish prophets had predicted its occurrence. Among them Ezekiel actually foretold the condition from which the restoration would occur. He stated that they would come back into the land only after they, the Jews, would go through the horrifically grave conditions of the Holocaust.

Then He said to me, "Son of man, these bones are *the whole house of Israel.* They indeed say, '*Our bones are dry, our hope is lost, and we ourselves are cut off.*' Therefore prophesy and say to them, 'Thus says the LORD GOD: "Behold, O My people, I will open your graves and *cause you to come up from your graves, and bring you into the land of Israel.* Then you shall know that I *am* the LORD, when I have opened your graves, O My people, and brought you up from your graves."'" (Ezek. 37:11–13, NKJV; emphasis added)

Imagine experiencing these grave events and then returning to your ancient homeland, only to be greeted with continued hostility. Indeed, that is what occurred; the descendants of Esau, alongside the other ancient Arab enemies of Israel, immediately protested the return of the Jews. In 1948, Egypt, Jordan, Syria, Lebanon, Saudi Arabia, and Iraq attacked the tiny Jewish state.[145] More of the same followed in 1956, 1967, and 1973 as the Arabs continued to war against the reformation of the nation Israel. Meanwhile, the descendants of Esau diminished into a refugee condition, out from which Palestinian guerilla forces arose to engage in various stages of the conflict.

Can this behavior be excused and continue without a reprisal? According to Obadiah, it will not be excused but be brought to an end! He declares that a great price will be extracted for the punishment the Palestinians, and their Arab cohorts continue to inflict upon the Jewish people.

THE TWO JUDGMENTS UPON EDOM

Throughout this book, we reference the two judgments that come upon Edom. These two judgments are episodes extremely relevant to the understanding of end-times Bible prophecy. Because of these two judgments, Edom finds itself desolated, a wilderness unsuitable for human habitation.

The reprisal of Edom referenced by Obadiah regards itself with the first of the two. Though the reprisal brings a degree of damage to the territory of Edom, which is modern-day Southern Jordan, it is primarily a military campaign regarded with bringing a cessation to the perpetual enmity forwarded against the Jewish people by the Edomite descendants of Esau.

The reprisal of Edom extends beyond the ethnical boundaries of the Edomites and encompasses even those Arab cohorts who, throughout time, have embraced this enmity established long ago.

Collectively these populations will confederate in one final and massive Arab attempt to destroy the nation Israel.

> They have said, "Come, and let us cut them off from *being* a nation, That the name of Israel may be remembered no more." For they have consulted together with one consent; They form a confederacy against You: The *tents of Edom* and the Ishmaelites; Moab and the Hagrites; Gebal, Ammon, and Amalek; Philistia with the inhabitants of Tyre; Assyria also has joined with them; They have helped the children of Lot. *Selah* (Psa. 83:4–8, NKJV; emphasis added)

This confederacy will have for its lead member the "tents of Edom," thereby making them one, if not the primary, representative of this coalition.[146] Therefore, we can understand scriptures associated with the first judgment of Edom in the broader context of their collective effect upon the surrounding Arab nations assembled in the Psalm 83 confederacy. In direct correlation to this confederate effort aimed entirely at Israel's annihilation comes the issuance of the divine response, which of course is the reprisal. Not withstanding, numerous scriptures specifically target individual judgments at these Arab nations that occur concurrently during the time of the reprisal of Edom.

What needs to be recognized is that the descendants of Esau known as the Edomites have throughout time never thoroughly abandoned the enmity established long ago by Esau toward his twin brother Jacob, patriarch of the Jewish people. In fact, this ancient hatred quoted earlier from Ezekiel 35:5 is at the center of the Arab-Israeli conflict. The primary nations listed in Psalm 83:6–8 that will confederate alongside the tents of Edom, are Saudi Arabia, Jordan, Egypt, Lebanon, and Syria.

This is how this prophetic information translates in real-time application. The Edomites of old have a remnant of descendants amalgamated within the so-called Palestinians. Therefore, when the Bible speaks of the Edomites in reference to unfulfilled prophecy, it finds its closest association with their modern-day equivalent, the Palestinians. Thus, the "tents of Edom" are none other than the tent-like communities occupied by the Palestinians.

The Bible uses tents descriptively to represent either refugee communities or military encampments. Today both scenarios find application—there are millions of displaced Palestinian refugees, and contained therein are millions opposed to the restoration of the Jewish nation of Israel. This opposition has developed a military mindset and has manifested into the ongoing struggle the world witnesses daily in the Middle East.

The plight of the Palestinians, whereby they seek to antagonize the restoration of the Jewish nation Israel, has become endearing to the surrounding Arab nations listed in Psalm 83:6–8. Their Arab ancestors, much like the Edomites, have harbored hatred toward the Jewish people throughout time. The plight of the Palestinians banners their common concerns regarding the restoration of the nation Israel as the Jewish state.

The fulfillment of Psalm 83 looms somewhere in the not-so-distant prophetic future, at which point the reprisal of Edom will result. This animosity toward the restoration of the nation Israel as the Jewish state, spearheaded by the Palestinians and applauded by the Arabs, will not subside, as it is too deeply rooted in its ancient origins. It will rear its ugly head in fulfillment of Psalm 83, at which time all the dastardly deeds of the Edomites throughout time immemorial will receive their reward! "Your reprisal shall return upon your own head."

Hence, we have the first of the two final judgments regarding the territory of Edom. The first judgment is executed via the means of the "exceedingly great army" of Israel.[147] The world is witnessing the emergence of this army in these present times. This is the promise of reward to Edom that God made through the prophets:

> For the day of the LORD upon all the nations *is* near; As you have done, it shall be done to you; Your reprisal shall return upon your own head…The house of Jacob shall be a fire, And the house of Joseph a flame; But the house of Esau *shall be* stubble; They shall kindle them and devour them, And no survivor shall *remain* of the house of Esau," [The Final Palestinian Farewell] For the LORD has spoken. (Obad. 1:15, NKJV; Obad; 1:18, NKJV)

> "I will lay My vengeance on Edom by the hand of My people Israel, that they may do in Edom according to My anger and according to My fury; and they shall know My vengeance," says the LORD GOD. (Ezek. 25:14, NKJV)

Edom can look forward to experiencing first hand the vengeance of God. It will become very familiar with His anger and fury, and ultimately "no survivor shall remain of the house of Esau!" This will be a catastrophic reprisal, and will essentially decimate the Palestinians at the time. As stated earlier, the expanse of the devastation extends deep into the collaborating Arab populations.

Whereas the Jewish people are instrumental in the execution of the first judgment destined for Edom, the second judgment concerns an entirely different campaign and is not delivered by the Jewish people, but by the Jewish individual Jesus Christ!

> For My [the Messianic person's] sword shall be bathed in heaven; Indeed it shall come down on Edom, And on the people of My curse, for judgment. [Antichrist and his armies] The sword of the LORD is filled with blood, It is made over-

flowing with fatness, With the blood of lambs and goats, With the fat of the kidneys of rams. For the LORD has a sacrifice in Bozrah, And a great slaughter in the land of Edom. (Isa. 34:5–6, NKJV)

Who *is* this who comes from Edom, With dyed garments from Bozrah. This *One who is* glorious in His apparel, Traveling in the greatness of His strength? "I who speak in righteousness, mighty to save." [the Messianic person] Why *is* Your apparel red, And Your garments like one who treads in the winepress? "I have trodden the winepress alone, And from the peoples no one *was* with Me. [single handedly] For I have trodden them in My anger, And trampled them in My fury; Their blood is sprinkled upon My garments, And I have stained all My robes." (Isa. 63:1–3, NKJV)

These two sections of scripture quoted from Isaiah evidence that Edom will be the site of the final blood bath between Jesus Christ and the Antichrist and his armies. He single handedly conquers this enemy group in its entirety, trodding over them like one "who treads in the winepress." Edom will be the location of "a great slaughter."

The second judgment has nothing to do with the Palestinians per se, but has everything to do with the second coming of Jesus Christ. The Palestinian issue will have been resolved because of the reprisal of Edom prior to the second coming of Christ! Remember that the first judgment of Edom occurs when "the day of the LORD upon all the nations *is* near!"[148] The second judgment occurs subsequently when the day of the LORD upon all the nations is here.

For *it is* the day of the LORD'S vengeance, The year of recompense for the cause of Zion. (Isa. 34:8, NKJV)

For the day of vengeance *is* in My heart, And the year of My
redeemed has come [recompense for the cause of Zion]. (Isa.
63:4, NKJV)

These passages from Isaiah 34 and 63 inform us that the timing
of the Messiah, who comes to Edom and treads the winepress and
gets blood sprinkled upon His garments at the time of the sacrifice in
Bozrah, also referred to as the great slaughter in the land of Edom, is
not when the day of the LORD is near, but rather when the day of the
LORD has come. "It is the day of the LORD'S vengeance!"

This distinction is important in that it helps to clear up the common confusion taught from many prophetic pulpits, that the seven-
year peace treaty between the Antichrist and the Jewish people has
something to do with the current Arab-Israeli conflict in the Middle
East. The seven-year pact made between the Jews and the Antichrist
has absolutely nothing to do with the plight of the Palestinians. That
conflict concludes in advance of the day of the LORD. The Jews will
have already conquered the Arabs, who will be generally subservient
under Israeli sovereignty.

It is not Arabs and Jews who make the seven-year treaty, but it
is Antichrist and Jews, with the explicit purpose of neutralizing the
strengthening empowerment of the nation Israel. The Jews will have
conquered the Psalm 83 confederacy, expanded their borders and sovereignty well into Arab territory, and become regionally superior as a
result. Additionally, they will have become further esteemed by the
events described in Ezekiel 38 and 39, whereby God divinely devastates the larger coalition of Russia, Iran, Libya, Ethiopia, and others.
It is the episode that God has ordained through the Jewish people to
uphold once again His Holy Name.

And I will send fire on Magog [Russia] and on those who live
in security in the coastlands [The Russian-Iranian Coalition].
Then they shall know that I *am* the LORD.[7] "So I will make

My holy name known in the midst of My people Israel, and I will not *let them* profane My holy name anymore. Then the nations shall know that *I am* the LORD, the Holy One in Israel. Surely it is coming, and it shall be done," says the Lord GOD. "This *is* the day of which I have spoken." (Ezek. 39:6–8 NKJV)

By the time the Antichrist drums up the seven-year treaty proposal, the Jewish people and the land of Israel will be operating from a position of extreme empowerment. This treaty has nothing to do with stopping Palestinian terrorism and bringing peace to the Middle East, as we think of it these days. The Antichrist forwards this treaty in an attempt to neutralize the stature of the Jewish people, and their God, Who has once again made His holy name known through the client nation Israel, or "My people Israel."

The Antichrist at the time will be furthering his rise to world power and ultimately his bid toward world worship. The Jewish system of political power and religious worship will be in competition with the Antichrist systems of the same. Remember that the prophet Daniel foretold of the intentions of this crazed individual:

Then the king [Antichrist] shall do according to his own will: he shall exalt and magnify himself above every god, shall speak blasphemies against the God of gods, and shall prosper till the wrath has been accomplished; for what has been determined shall be done. He shall regard neither the God of his fathers nor the desire of women, nor regard any god; for he shall exalt himself above *them* all. (Dan. 11:36–37, NKJV)

The first judgment of Edom is handed down to make and end of the enmity of the Arabs toward the Jews, and the second comes to make an end of the enmity of the Antichrist and his system of worship apart from Jesus Christ.

THE RESULTS OF THE TWO JUDGMENTS UPON EDOM

Scripture does not lack adequate description of the devastation resulting from the two judgments upon Edom. Below are numerous passages we can identify with either the first or the second judgment. The territory of ancient Edom (Southern Jordan), will witness some of the worst destruction the world has ever known.

As you read the following passages, you can generally determine whether the judgment is associated with the first or second judgment. The first judgment primarily affects the Palestinian people and some general war-torn territory in ancient Edom, whereas the second has little or nothing to do with the Edomites, but everything to do with the ancient territory of Edom. The second judgment permanently adversely affects the land of Southern Jordan.

The burden of the word of the LORD to Israel by Malachi [Malachi 450 BC].[149]

"I have loved you," says the LORD. "Yet you say, 'In what way have You loved us?'

Was not Esau Jacob's brother?" [Esau and Jacob were twin brothers] Says the LORD.

"Yet Jacob I have loved; [Jacob fathered the Jewish nation] But Esau I have hated, [Esau fathered the Edomites represented by the Palestinians] And laid waste his mountains and his heritage For the jackals of the wilderness."[150] Even though Edom has said, "We have been impoverished, [in fulfillment of Bible prophecy][151] But we will return and build the desolate places," Thus says the LORD of hosts: "They may build, but I will throw down [The Reprisal of Edom] They shall be called the Territory of Wickedness, And the people against whom the LORD will have indignation forever. Your eyes shall see, And you shall say, 'The LORD is magnified beyond the border of Israel.'" (Malachi 1:1–5 NKJV; footnotes added)

Egypt shall be a desolation, And Edom a desolate wilderness, Because of violence *against* the people of Judah, For they have shed innocent blood in their land. But Judah shall abide forever, And Jerusalem from generation to generation. (Joel 3:19–20, NKJV)

Flee, turn back, dwell in the depths, O inhabitants of Dedan! [Saudi Arabia] For I will bring the calamity of Esau upon him, The time *that* I will punish him. [The Reprisal of Edom] If grape-gatherers came to you, Would they not leave *some* gleaning grapes? If thieves by night, Would they not destroy until they have enough? But I have made Esau bare; I have uncovered his secret places, And he shall not be able to hide himself. His descendants are plundered, [Palestinians] His brethren and his neighbors, [Surrounding Arab Nations] And he *is* no more [The "Final Palestinian Farewell" resulting from the first judgment]. (Jer. 49:8–10, NKJV; emphasis added)

"Will I not in that day," says the LORD, "Even destroy the wise *men* from Edom, And understanding from the mountains of Esau? Then your mighty men, O Teman, shall be dismayed, To the end that everyone from the mountains of Esau May be cut off by slaughter. [The Reprisal of Edom] For violence against your brother Jacob, [As you have done it shall be done to you] Shame shall cover you, [Your reprisal shall return upon your own head.] And you shall be cut off forever." (Obad. 1:8–10 NKJV; emphasis added)

Therefore hear the counsel of the LORD that He has taken against Edom, And His purposes that He has proposed against the inhabitants of Teman: Surely the least of the flock shall draw them out; Surely He shall make their dwelling places desolate with them. The Earth shakes at the noise of their fall; [The noise and shaking result from the war] At the cry its noise is heard at the Red Sea. [The battle cry extends to the Red Sea] Behold, He shall come up and fly like the eagle, And spread His wings over Bozrah; The heart of the mighty men of Edom in that day shall be Like the heart of a woman in birth pangs. [Resulting from the first judgment] (Jer. 49:20–22, NKJV)

"I see Him, but not now; I behold Him, but not near; A Star [Messianic Person] shall come out of Jacob; A Scepter shall rise out of Israel, And batter the brow of Moab [Central Jordan], And destroy all the sons of tumult. "And Edom shall be a possession [Israel expands its borders and sovereignty]; Seir [Southern Jordan] also, his enemies, shall be a possession [resulting from the first judgment], While Israel does valiantly. Out of Jacob One shall have dominion, And destroy the remains of the city. (Num. 24:17–19, NKJV; emphasis added)

Its [Edom's] streams shall be turned into pitch [resulting from the second judgment], And its dust into brimstone; Its land shall become burning pitch. It shall not be quenched night or day; Its smoke shall ascend forever. From generation to generation it shall lie waste; No one shall pass through it [Southern Jordan] forever and ever. But the pelican and the porcupine shall possess it, Also the owl and the raven shall dwell in it. And He shall stretch out over it. The line of confusion and the stones of emptiness. They shall call its nobles to the kingdom, But none *shall be* there, and all its princes shall be nothing. And thorns shall come up in its palaces, Nettles and brambles in its fortresses; It shall be a habitation of jackals, A courtyard for ostriches. The wild beasts of the desert shall also meet with the jackals, And the wild goat shall bleat to its companion;

Also the night creature shall rest there, And find for herself a place of rest. (Isa. 34:9–14, NKJV; emphasis added)

"Edom also shall be an astonishment; Everyone who goes by it will be astonished And will hiss at all its plagues. As in the overthrow of Sodom and Gomorrah And their neighbors," says the LORD, "No one shall remain there, Nor shall a son of man dwell in it." (Jer. 49:17–18, NKJV)

Thus says the LORD GOD: "The whole Earth will rejoice when I make you desolate. As you rejoiced because the inheritance of the house of Israel was desolate, so I will do to you; you shall be desolate, O Mount Seir, as well as all of Edom—all of it! Then they shall know that I *am* the LORD.: (Ezek. 35:14–15, NKJV; emphasis added)

Therefore thus says the LORD GOD: "I have raised My hand in an oath that surely the nations [Psalm 83 confederates] that *are* around you [Israel] shall bear their own shame. [Resulting from the first judgment] (Ezek. 36:7, NKJV; emphasis added)

Thus says the LORD: "For three transgressions of Edom, and for four, I will not turn away its *punishment,* Because he pursued his brother [Israel] with the sword, And cast off all pity; His anger tore perpetually, And he kept his wrath forever. But I will send a fire upon Teman, Which shall devour the palaces of Bozrah [resulting from the first judgment]." (Amos 1:11–12, NKJV; emphasis added)

SUMMARY

God intends the reprisal of Edom to severely affect the Middle East and leave a lasting impression upon all the inhabitants of the world. It will serve in the future as an echo of God's past and present foreign policy. "As you have done it shall be done to you," appropriately describes the curse-for-curse-in-kind clause of the Abrahamic Covenant.

The fact that the timing of the reprisal of Edom occurs when "the day of the LORD upon all the nations is near" is a call to caution for the world population that the end of life on Earth at that time will also be near. It will be a call to remembrance that God blesses and curses in relationship to the treatment or mistreatment of Abraham or his descendants. At the time of the reprisal, the Jewish people will again be classified as "My people Israel," and as such, the Gentiles should carefully consider their behavior toward the nation Israel.

The execution of tremendous fury and vengeance against the Palestinians, leaving none to carry on the lineage of Esau, will demonstrate to the world that if God did not spare the descendants of Jacob's own twin brother Esau, then any who seek to bring harm to the Jewish people will not escape the curse-for-curse-in-kind clause.

It is understandable that the descendants of Esau should be dealt with harshly, in that they among all peoples should have shown brotherly affection toward the Jewish people. After all, Jacob, the patriarch of the Jewish people, was the twin brother of Esau, patriarch of the Edomites.

In contrast to Jacob, who was promised descendants, a homeland, and a King forever, his twin brother Esau will have none of this. The first judgment against Edom eliminates all of Esau's descendants, including any would-be kings, and the second judgment leaves Esau's homeland unsuitable for human habitation. Indeed, one will have to consider the brevity of the Abrahamic Covenant when they think about the contrasting fates of the twin bothers Jacob and Esau.

THE END OF TERROR

Another Bible Prediction

od will judge the terror inspired by the Palestinians and targeted at the Jews—the terror that concerns the international community and is embraced by the Arabs and acclaimed within Islam.

This study explores Jeremiah 49:16 and Obadiah 1:3–4,7 and develops the theme contained therein, in which the Bible foretells the arrival and advance of terrorism. Scripture declares terrorism the inspiration of the Edomites, who have ancestral ties to the Palestinians of modern-day.[152] Furthermore, the Bible depicts the Palestinians in these passages as being deceived into thinking that their god endorses behaviors of terror. As this prophecy unfolds in our day, we have just cause to consider that the prophets Jeremiah and Obadiah were alluding to a link between the Palestinians, Arabs, Allah, Islam, and terrorism.

Certain key understandings must precede this study in order to avoid running the risk of sensationalizing the material and inadvertently rendering it sloppy newspaper exegesis. Additionally, three important Hebrew words will be translated at various points within this study that are germane to the reader's ability to discern what the prophets are declaring. These three words are *tiphletseth, nasha,* and *mazor. Tiphletseth* is translated as a shuddering, horrific act of terror.[153] *Nasha* means to lead astray, beguile, deceive, delude, or come deceitfully.[154] Finally, *mazor* describes "the sense of turning aside from truth; treachery, a plot, or a wound."[155]

KEY UNDERSTANDINGS

Edo-Palestinians

The ancient Edomites later became known by their Greek name Idumeans, and now are best identified as a contingency within the Palestinians. I use "Edo-Palestinians" throughout this study as a bridge term to identify the Edomite remnant within the Palestinian ethnicity. Pending prophetic events regarding Esau, Edom, and/or the Edomites will find their final fulfillment through the Palestinians. More can be found on this in the chapter called *Who-domites?: Who Are the Edomites Today?*

Terrorism is a Method of Warfare

The world has come to know terrorism as a bona fide method of warfare. Presently, a segment of the international community is waging war against terror. This war evidences the legitimacy of terror as a method of conducting war. Terrorism in its fledgling stages predominately originated within the ranks of the Palestinians in an effort to antagonize further development of the nation Israel.[156] It quickly gained support from the surrounding Arab nations that most closely border the nation Israel. These countries had waged four unsuccessful conventional military attempts against Israel in 1948, 1956, 1967, and 1973. Because of these failed attempts, these Arab nations adopted and generally embraced the unconventional means of terrorism as a method of conducting war.

God Will Judge Terrorism

This study will demonstrate that terrorism is the inspiration of a particular ethnic group formerly known as the Edomites. Although today it has international implications, terrorism in general is the recently adopted method of unconventional warfare targeted against the nation Israel. Today, the Palestinians best represent the Edomites. This terror, inspired by the Palestinians, provokes upon itself the curse-for-curse-in-kind clause contained with the Abrahamic Covenant.[157] Thus, through this ancient covenant established centuries ago as God's foreign policy plan for humanity, terrorism will and must pay a divine price.

The Two Judgments of Edom

Two judgments occur against Edom in the end-times. I further describe them in the chapter of this book entitled *The Final Palestinian Farewell*. This study on terrorism regards itself only with the first of the two, which is carried out against the Palestinians and their confederating Arab allies described in Psalm 83:6–8 by the "exceedingly great army" of Israel.[158]

Esau and Jacob were Brothers

These two notable biblical characters were twin brothers. Esau was the father of the ethnic group known as the Edomites, who have a remnant constituency residing today within the overall Palestinian contingency.[159] Jacob was later renamed Israel, and hence along with Abraham can be considered a patriarch of the Jewish people.[160]

The Arab Confederacy

Psalm 83 prophesies of an Arab confederacy that will soon emerge and have as its lead member the "tents of Edom." This is a reference to the Palestinians in a refugee or military condition or both.[161] This study points out how the Palestinians' involvement within this confederacy deceives them through the arrogance of their hearts into thinking they are divinely exalted and supported in their terrorist attacks against Israel.

The Exceedingly Great Army of Israel

Ezekiel 37 foretold a time when the Jewish people would be scattered among the nations of the world, and would ultimately end up in a horrific grave-like condition. He then declared that from that point they would be brought back as a people into the land of Israel. Of course, we know that prophecy was fulfilled through the events of the Holocaust, and subsequently on May 14, 1948 with the reformation of the nation Israel. However, most interestingly, Ezekiel 37:10 further states that from this terrible Holocaust condition the Jewish people will emerge into an "Exceedingly great army." The LORD utilizes this army as the critical tool in the first of two judgments destined to come against Edom.

Jeremiah and Obadiah on Terrorism

The prophetic passages are listed below with certain key terms and phrases highlighted. They are then cross-correlated and paraphrased, in order to explore the possibility of their modern-day, real-time application:

> "*The terror [tiphletseth] you inspire and the pride of your heart have deceived [nasha] you, you who live in the clefts of the rock, who hold the height of the hill.*
>
> *Although you make your nest as high as the eagle's, from there I will bring you down," says the LORD.* [162] (Jer. 49:16, NRSV; emphasis added)

"The pride of your heart has deceived you, *You* who dwell in the clefts of the rock, Whose habitation is high; *You* who say in your heart, 'Who will bring me down to the ground?' Though you ascend *as* high as the eagle, And though you set

your nest among the stars, From there I will bring you down,"
says the LORD. (Obad. 1:3–4, NKJV; emphasis added)

The prophet Jeremiah speaks of inspired terror coming from the
ethnic group formerly known as the Edomites. What is left of the
Edomites today is a small group of Bedouins residing in Southern
Jordan, and a larger remnant somewhat obscured within the modern-
day Palestinian contingency. The Hebrew word Jeremiah uses is tiphletseth, translated as "a shuddering, horror; -terror."[163] This gripping
term is uniquely utilized within the entire Bible only in this single
instance, yet it is possibly the most descriptive word available in the
ancient Hebrew language to identify the relatively recently fashioned
terrorism plaguing the nation Israel today.

By cross—correlating and paraphrasing these two prophetic passages we discover the interesting possibility of a link between the Palestinians, terror, Islam, and Allah.

The *terror* you (Palestinians) *inspire* and the pride (arrogance)
of your heart have *deceived* (mislead) you, you who live in the
clefts of the rock… (spiritual covering)[164]

Though *you ascend as high as the eagle,* (religious thinking)[165]
And though you set your *nest among the stars* (angelic typology)[166], From there *I will bring you down," says the LORD* (divine judgment).

Terrorism is the inspiration of a deceived group. Their deception
is caused by their misguided theology. They are under the allusion
that they are nestled among the stars, which in Bible typology is a
reference to the angelic host. Their deception is rooted in their per-
ception that from their vantage point they believe themselves to be
divinely justified to inspire terror, and therefore protected from its
consequence.

The problem for this specific type of terrorism, however, is that it is primarily targeted at the Jewish people, through whom the Abrahamic Covenant is in force. This covenant formatted approximately 4000 years ago between God Jehovah and Abraham the patriarchal father of the Jewish people, is still operable and in good standing.[167] It specifically calls for a curse-for-curse-in kind reaction to all terrible treatment targeted at Abraham or his descendants.[168] This is where the pride of their heart has deceived them ("them" being the Edo-Palestinians).[169] It has misled them into thinking their Islamic faith has the ability to override this critical curse component contained in the Abrahamic covenant.

Analyzing these pertinent scriptures causes us to consider their potential for more than a literal interpretation. Phrases like "you ascend as high as the eagle," "you set your nest among the stars," and "you live in the clefts of the rock" make it difficult to limit our thinking to airplanes, bird nests, and cave dwellers. Fortunately, all of these phraseologies have biblical typologies from which we can perhaps draw better conclusions as to what the prophets Jeremiah and Obadiah were describing.

As we single these passages out and break them down for their possible typological translations, we must not lose sight of the overall theme, which is curse-for-curse-in kind. The terror inspired by the Palestinians results in a judgment from God. "I will bring you down," says the LORD." The passages we are translating when studied in their entire prophetic content allude to the Edo-Palestinians cursing the Jews. It is for this misbehavior that the Palestinians are brought down by the LORD. This judgment is the first of the two judgments referenced in the *Key Understandings* at the onset of this chapter.

For violence against your brother Jacob [Jews], Shame shall cover you [Edo-Palestinians], And you shall be cut off forever. (Obad. 1:10, NKJV)

The house of Jacob [Jews] shall be a fire, And the house of Joseph [Jews] a flame; But the house of Esau [Edo-Palestinians] *shall be* stubble; They [Jews] shall kindle them [Edo-Palestinians] and devour them, And no [Edo-Palestinian] survivor shall *remain* of the house of Esau," For the LORD has spoken. (Obad. 1:18, NKJV; emphasis added)

"From there I will bring you (Edo-Palestinians) down," says the LORD.[170]

"From there," the Edo-Palestinians will be brought down, meaning from the high point where "you (Edo-Palestinian) ascend as high as the eagle," "you (Edo-Palestinian) set your nest among the stars," and "you (Edo-Palestinian) live in the clefts of the rock." Allah becomes the wind beneath their wings as they ascend to the highest point of their Islamic theology, whereby they conclude that they are justified in the acts of terror they commit against the Jewish people, the client nation of God, "My people Israel." Though they think they are protected in the clefts of the rock, it is from there that the God of the nation of Israel promises to bring them down.

What the prophets Jeremiah and Obadiah portray is a bird of prey nested in a cave in the rugged high cliffs of Mount Seir in ancient Edom. It is a place extremely inaccessible to a hunter of ordinary means. Remember that at the time of these writings there were no helicopter drops, high-powered rifles, or bunker-buster bombs. Back then, all a hunter had at his disposal to reach such a lofty target was his bow and arrow, horse, rope, and his own two feet. In this example, the nest of the target is among the stars, evidencing the utter impossibility of an ordinary hunter to make this kill.

From its high position, this bird of prey commits horrific acts that terrorize the neighboring community below, and that population has no natural means of bringing this bad bird down. This particular population needs extraordinary assistance in order to put an end to this eagle's escapades. The eagle is the Edo-Palestinian; the community is the Jewish population of Israel, and the horrific acts committed; the *tiphletseth*, or modern-day terrorism described by Jeremiah. The *tiphletseth* is specifically fashioned by the Palestinians to bring harm to the Jew. It therefore provokes the enactment of the curse-for-curse-in kind clause contained in the Abrahamic Covenant. As such, the result will be "From there I will bring you down."

However, at the time, there were no normal means from which to bring this bad bird down. The actual time of the fulfillment of the *tiphletseth*-terror is now; presently the Jewish community has the military means to put an end to this eagle's mischief. Because of terror, Arab assault, Allah, and Islam, the gathering of the Jew back into the land of Israel has caused the creation of the Israeli Defense Force. Ezekiel foretold of its emergence.

> So I prophesied as He commanded me, and breath came into them, [the Jewish people] and they lived, and stood upon their feet, an exceedingly great army. (Ezek. 37:10, NKJV)

The mechanism by which this bad bird will be brought down from its high point is the army of Israel.

> Thus says the LORD GOD: "Because of what Edom [Edo-Palestinians] did against the house of Judah [the Jews] by taking vengeance, and has greatly offended by avenging itself on them," therefore thus says the LORD GOD: "I will also stretch out My hand against Edom, cut off man [Edo-Palestinians] and beast from it, and make it desolate from Teman; Dedan shall fall by the sword. I will lay My vengeance on Edom by the hand of My people Israel, that they may do in Edom according to My anger and according to My fury; and they [Edo-Palestinians] shall know My vengeance," says the LORD GOD. (Ezek 25:12–14, NKJV)

Although the army of Israel will devastate the Edo-Palestinians, they can do so only by divine orchestration. It is their God Jehovah that equips them for the fight, which eventuates in the conquest. Hence, you have the "exceedingly great" characteristic incorporated into the "exceedingly great army." This conquest goes well beyond the Palestinian population, and is expounded upon further in the chapter The Exceedingly Great Army. All of this, of course, is designed in accordance with the curse-for-curse-in kind clause contained in the Abrahamic Covenant. The Edo-Palestinians terrorize the Jews, and in return, the Jews are appropriately equipped and empowered to retaliate. This war ultimately results from the Palestinians enjoining the Arab Confederacy referenced at the beginning of this chapter as a key understanding.

"YOU WHO LIVE IN THE CLEFTS OF THE ROCK"

This phrase, along with "you ascend as high as the eagle" and "you set your nest among the stars," begins with the pronoun "you." This "you" identifies the subject(s) of the prophecy. It is the Edomites, the ethnic group, whose habitation was the land of Edom. The connection as to who they were and have now become is found in the *Who-domites?* chapter.

Understanding who the Edomites were helps in part to explain "you who live in the clefts of the rock," in that their ancient homeland Edom was the location of the mountains of Seir. These mountains range from 600 to 6,000 feet high.[171] At certain points, these mountains are almost impassable due to treacherous terrain.[172] Thus, the Edomites had, at least historically, some of its population resembling cave dwellers residing in the "clefts of the rock."

The problem with limiting this phrase to its literal historical and geographical interpretation is that it emphasizes who the Edomites were and not who they are at present. Furthermore, it does not contextually fit in with the other two phrases, "you ascend as high as the eagle," and "you set your nest among the stars," which obviously cannot be understood literally, as who can ascend as high as an eagle and dwell in a nest in the stars? Therefore, in addition to the literal interpretation, which adequately identifies those among the "clefts of the rock" as Edo-Palestinians, let us also explore the theme of typological translation.

We can trace the Edomites primarily to their modern-day equivalents, the Palestinians. They are at least a contingency contained therein and, when spoken of prophetically, duly represent the Palestinian ethnicity. At the time of these prophetic writings, there were no such Palestinian peoples in existence; therefore, the prophets wrote of future peoples, places, and events as formatted in the customary and identifiable terms of their times.

One possible typology applicable to "you who live in the clefts of the rock" is that the "clefts of the rock" exemplify a place of protection whereby the Palestinians feel covered spiritually by their god. The example refers to the time of Moses in Exodus 33:22, when Moses requests to see the glory of his God and is placed in "the cleft of the rock," from where he is able to experience the presence of God.

> And he said, "Please, show me [Moses] Your glory." Then He said, "I will make all My goodness pass before you, and I will proclaim the name of the LORD before you. I will be gracious to whom I will be gracious, and I will have compassion on whom I will have compassion." But He said, "You cannot see My face; for no man shall see Me, and live." And the LORD said, "Here is a place by Me, and you shall stand *on the rock*. So it shall be, while My glory passes by, that I will put you in the *cleft of the rock*, and will cover you with My hand while I pass by. Then I will take away My hand, and you shall see My back; but My face shall not be seen." (Exod. 33:18–23, NKJV; emphasis added)

This episode informs us that it was the goal of Moses to see the glory of his God. His God put Moses in a safe place, "the cleft of the rock." God then extended His hand out for the protection of Moses. Henceforth divine protection found association with one who sought refuge in the "the cleft of the rock."

Therefore, when both prophets, Jeremiah and Obadiah, undertook the task of describing today's terrorism from the established typologies of their times, they utilized the "cleft of the rock" idiom. They foreknew that far into the future terrorist activities would be spiritually formatted against the Jewish people. By the use of the "cleft of the rock" idiom, they expected our generation, which witnesses the horrific terror *tiphletseth* unfolding before our eyes and television sets, to recognize fully its spiritually spun twist.

Essentially, the terrorism outsourced by the Palestinians aimed at Jewish targets is conducted under the premise that it is accepted under the umbrella of Islam. There is a definite religious association between terrorism and Islam. This is not to say that all Muslims endorse terror as a fundamental tenet of Islam; however, the Islamic terrorist believes inherently in the attack is the acceptance of the attack by Allah. Thus, one could suggest that the plight of the Palestinians falls under the blanket protection of Islam and therefore as an ethnic group the Edo-Palestinians can be considered literally, geographically, and spiritually (Islamically) as "you who live in the clefts of the rock."

"THOUGH YOU ASCEND AS HIGH AS THE EAGLE"

In scripture, the eagle is often analogous with swiftness, divine blessing, protection, or a military campaign.[173] In Jeremiah and Obadiah's usages, the eagle represents both the divine and military aspects. It is a picture of an eagle spreading its wings and yielding to the wind. This enables it to soar upward to the great heights of heaven, whereby it can "nest among the stars." These passages portray the Palestinians as a proud people whose hearts become arrogant by the heights of their spiritual and military achievements, or the terror they inspire.

In the first passage below, the eagle represents faith in typology.

But those who wait on the LORD Shall renew their strength; They shall mount up with wings like eagles, They shall run and not be weary, They shall walk and not faint. (Isa. 40:31, NKJV)

Next, the eagle exemplifies divine blessing.

And Moses went up to God, and the LORD called to him from the mountain, saying, "Thus you shall say to the house of Jacob, and tell the children of Israel: 'You have seen what I did to the Egyptians, and how I bore you on eagles' wings and brought you to Myself.'" (Exo. 19:3–4, NKJV)

Lastly, the following scripture utilizes the eagle in a military analogy.

For thus says the LORD: "Behold, one shall fly like an eagle, And spread his wings over Moab. Kerioth is taken, And the strongholds are surprised; The mighty men's hearts in Moab on that day shall be Like the heart of a woman in birth pangs. And Moab shall be destroyed as a people, Because he exalted himself against the LORD. (Jer. 48:40–42, NKJV)

The eagle example portrays the Palestinian plight, similar to an eagle in flight. They forward terror against the Jews in accordance with their faith in the religion of Islam. They believe that it is acceptable by Allah to antagonize the Jews. Surah [5.51] O you who believe [Muslims]! do not take the Jews and the Christians for friends; they are friends of each other; and whoever amongst you takes them for a friend, then surely he is one of them; surely Allah does not guide the unjust people (suggesting Jews and Christians are the unjust people).[174]

Analogous to this, the prophets describe the Palestinians as being deceived, thinking that divine inspiration propels their terror onward. They feel compelled to carry out a campaign of terror against the Jews under the premise that they have the permission of their god Allah. Jeremiah and Obadiah both confirm, "The pride of your heart has deceived you," describing the terror inspired by the Palestinians as the result of a misguided mindset. In their prideful hearts, they believe that they, like the eagle in flight, are divinely justified in their Palestinian plight. Their religious faith causes them to think the terror they inspire elevates them to the heights of an ascending eagle.

Scripture tells us that the Palestinians will be brought down for terrorizing the Jews, but until that judgment occurs, the terror they inspire continues to gain in momentum. With every successful act of terror comes the deceived mindset that the Palestinian plight is soaring to new Islamic heights. It is generally understood that the greater the act of terror, the greater the support is given by the Arab nations that sponsor terror, to the organization that orchestrated the terror. For example, Saddam Hussein, the former leader of Iraq, was known to offer large sums of money to the families of Palestinian suicide bombers.[175]

Lastly, eagles are known to assemble high above the location of dead carcasses. At the site of a kill, the vultures descend downward in order to feast upon the spoils. The pride of the deceived Palestinian heart is enlarged at the site of dead Jewish carcasses. They believe that with every act of terror, their ethnic plight is further advanced and Allah is greatly pleased. So much so that recently the term "Palestinianism" has been introduced to define the inseparability of the Islamic spiritual connection with the plight of the Palestinians.[176] It appears as though the struggle between the Jews and Palestinians has become labeled Zionism verses Palestinianism.

"YOU SET YOUR NEST AMONG THE STARS"

In scripture, "stars" can sometimes be interpreted as a reference to the angelic or heavenly realm. In certain passages, they are clearly representative of angels. Listed below are several scriptures that evidence this point.

> When the morning stars sang together, And all the sons of God [angels] shouted for joy? (Job 38:7, NKJV)

> The mystery of the seven stars which you saw in My right hand, and the seven golden lampstands: The seven stars are the angels of the seven churches, and the seven lampstands which you saw are the seven churches. (Rev 1:20, NKJV)

> And another sign appeared in heaven: behold, a great, fiery red dragon [the devil] having seven heads and ten horns, and seven diadems on his heads. His tail drew a third of the stars of heaven [fallen angels] and threw them to the Earth. And the dragon stood before the woman [Israel] who was ready to give birth, to devour her Child as soon as it was born. (Rev 12:3–4, NKJV)

In keeping with the theme of typological translation, "you set your nest among the stars" becomes a reference to the Palestinian plight being securely established in the "Heavenly Haven." Their nest represents their place of residence, and the Edo-Palestinians have set it among the stars. This is not wishful thinking on the part of the Palestinians; the prophet Obadiah acknowledges that their campaign of terror ultimately reaches its religious plateau.

> "Though you ascend as high as the eagle, And though you set your nest among the stars, From there I will bring you down," says the LORD. (Obad. 1:4, NKJV)

It is from the highest point of their religiously driven campaign that the LORD brings them down as an ethnic group. This gives credibility to the possibility that a certain segment of the angelic host embraces and supports their hostility toward the Jewish people. This would position Allah as the high ranking being placed in charge of the supervision of their war efforts against the nation Israel, or more specifically the Jewish people and their Zionism.

Who do the renegade Palestinians believe in? For the most part, they believe in Allah. So then who might Allah be? In order to answer this question it is necessary to search out what the scriptures say regarding angels. The first point of recognition is that angels are not a figment of ones imagination, but are spoken of frequently in scripture. They are intelligent beings considered to be of a higher order than man.

What is man that You are mindful of him, And the son of man that You visit him?

For You have made him [man] a little lower than the angels, And You have crowned him with glory and honor.[177] (Psa.8:4–5, NKJV)

At least one of their primary functions is that they are to serve as ministering spirits to the men and women who will inherit salvation.

But to which of the angels has He ever said: *"Sit at My right hand, Till I make Your enemies Your footstool?"* Are they [angels] not all ministering spirits sent forth to minister for those [men and woman] who will inherit salvation? (Heb. 1:13–14, NKJV; emphasis added)

Though all the angels were appointed to benevolent service toward humanity, not all angels complied with the will of God in this matter. They, like man, were capable of missing the righteous mark of God, which is the essence of sin. The following two scriptures inform us that a segment of the angels deserted their primary post and sinned.

> For if God did not spare the angels who sinned, but cast *them* down to hell and delivered *them* into chains of darkness, to be reserved for judgment; (Peter 2:4, NKJV; emphasis added)

> And angels that kept not their own principality, but left their proper habitation, he hath kept in everlasting bonds under darkness unto the judgment of the great day. (Jude 1:6, ASV)

From scriptures like these, most Bible scholars understand that a condition of disorder was manifested in the principalities of the heavenly realm. This created a conflict among the angelic beings, causing a disruption in their service toward man. In Ephesians, the apostle Paul instructs man to be always on the alert regarding this angelic conflict. Those angels that elected not to serve as ministering spirits toward the benevolence of man became spiritual hosts of wickedness. Having left their own principle and proper habitation, they roam about powerfully and freely creating havoc toward those men and woman, who they were otherwise destined to minister in favor of.

> Put on the whole armor of God, that you may be able to stand against the wiles of the devil. For we do not wrestle against flesh and blood, but against principalities, against powers, against the rulers of the darkness of this age, against spiritual *hosts* of wickedness in the heavenly *places.* (Eph. 6:11–12, NKJV; emphasis added)

Scripture ascribes princes to these principalities referenced in the previous passages. For instance, Michael the archangel is the benevolent prince over the Jewish people.[178]

At that time Michael shall stand up, The great prince who stands *watch* over the sons of your people [The Jews]; And there shall be a time of trouble, Such as never was since there was a nation, *Even* to that time. And at that time your people shall be delivered, Every one who is found written in the book. (Dan. 12:1, NKJV; emphasis added)

During the time of the Babylonian captivity of the Jewish people, the prophet Daniel records an episode that occurred because of this angelic conflict. The angelic princes of the then-developing empires of Persia and Greece positioned themselves in opposition to the great prince Michael the archangel, "who—having never left his proper post of habitation—still stands watch over" the Jewish people.

Then he said to me, "Do not fear, Daniel, for from the first day that you set your heart to understand, and to humble yourself before your God, your words were heard; and I have come because of your words." But the prince of the kingdom of Persia withstood me twenty-one days; and behold, Michael [the archangel], one of the chief princes, came to help me, for I had been left alone there with the kings of Persia. (Dan. 10:12–13, NKJV)

Then he said, "Do you know why I have come to you? And now I must return to fight with the prince of Persia; and when I have gone forth, indeed the prince of Greece will come. But I will tell you what is noted in the Scripture of Truth. No one upholds me against these, except Michael [the archangel] your prince." (Dan. 10:20–21, NKJV)

Scripture describes for us the ministry of "Prince" Michael the archangel, but Allah gained his notoriety on the world scene about the time of the inception of the religion of Islam around the seventh century. Therefore, there are no biblical inscriptions available to describe him or his ascent to his present "Princely" position over the Islamic empire. However, this Allah, lest he be an enormous figment of the Muslim population's imagination, must be labeled either a god of the Earth or an angelic prince, according to biblical precedent.

If Allah is not a high-ranking angel, then at least Allah can be identified as a "god of the Earth," in that the Muslims worship Allah on the Earth as their god. As such, Allah will fall victim to the judgment of the gods of the Earth as referenced in the book of Zephaniah.[179]

> The LORD *will be* awesome to them, For He will reduce to nothing all the gods of the Earth; *People* shall worship Him, Each one from his place, Indeed all the shores of the nations. (Zeph 2:11, NKJV; emphasis added)

Hence, the Palestinian plight appears to be nested in the religious realm of the angelic conflict. Allah, the head figure of the Islamic empire, much like the angelic forerunners the Prince of Persia, and the Prince of Greece, spoken of by Daniel the prophet, likewise stands in opposition to Michael the archangel "who stands watch over" the Jewish people.

Some would argue that Allah does not stand in opposition to the Jewish people. However, the majority of his congregants in the world, and especially in the Middle East, evidenced by their actions, believe otherwise. Unmistakably, the Palestinian plight has ascended, in flight on the wings of Islam to the heights of the stars, where those principalities opposed to the restoration of the nation Israel have embraced it.

Unfortunately, this creates an intolerable situation, as the restoration of the Jewish nation resides within the will of God. As such, the Palestinians will be caught in the crossfire. They have become victims of their own divisiveness.

> The terror you [Palestinians] inspire and the pride of your heart have deceived you. (Jer. 49:16, NKJV)

"Though you [Palestinians] ascend as high as the eagle, And though you set your nest among the stars, [principalities, powers, and spiritual hosts of wickedness in the heavenly places]. From there [the religious platform] I will bring you down," says the LORD (Obad. 1:4, NKJV)

THE PALESTINIAN DECEPTION

Up to this point, this study has pointed out that the Edomites, represented today by the Palestinians, are guilty of two things: they inspire terror and have prideful hearts. As such, they find themselves in the unfortunate predicament of being deceived. This deceit is *nasha* in the Hebrew language and it is translated as "to lead astray, beguile, deceive, delude, or come deceitfully." The *nasha* of the Palestinians is likewise described in Obadiah 1:7 as Edom's dilemma relative to its role in the upcoming Arab confederacy.

All the men in your confederacy [Psalm 83:1–8] Shall force you to the border [of Israel]; The men at peace with you Shall deceive [*nasha*] you and prevail against you.

Those who eat your bread shall lay a trap [*mazor*] for you. No one is aware of it. (Obad. 1:7, NKJV)

The Edomites, represented by their modern-day equivalents the Palestinians, through the arrogance of their hearts allow themselves to become mesmerized by their allies. The word for trap in Hebrew is *mazor*, and it is only used this one time in all of the Old Testament. The definition of the word when translated is "the sense of turning aside from truth; treachery, that is, a plot: wound."[180] Furthermore *mazor* appears to be a derivative of the root Hebrew word *zur*,[181] which means "to turn aside, foreigner, or strange."

So then, to what could Obadiah be alluding? He appears to be suggesting that the Palestinians, i.e., the tents of Edom, turn aside or otherwise become estranged to their brotherly relationship with Israel by allowing themselves to become deceived.[182] Remember, one of the key understandings is that Esau, father of the Edomites, and Jacob, the Jewish patriarch, were twin brothers. The Edomite contingency within the Palestinians becomes ensnared *mazor* by the men at peace with them, those who eat bread with them. This could refer to all the men in the Arab confederacy.[183]

Those at peace with the Palestinians are the surrounding Arab nations in favor of the Palestinian plight and its tactics of terror. Those who eat bread with them, probably refer to the allegiance of those Arab nations to Palestinianism. They are all the men that become members of the Psalm 83 confederacy.[184] As Esau was a brother to Israel, his descendants the Palestinians should be in support of the reformation of the nation Israel as the Jewish State. However do to their deceived terror inspiring condition, which is endorsed by their Arab allies they have turned aside *mazor* from their obligations toward brotherly love.

This deceit arises through their prideful arrogant hearts as described in Jeremiah 49:16 and is easily manipulated by the confederate Arab-Islamic nations with which they align themselves. These nations are listed in Psalm 83:6–8. They are the surrounding Arab nations that most closely border the nation of Israel today. Ultimately, these nations will confederate against the Jewish state of Israel. This confederacy is bent upon the destruction of the nation Israel, "that the name Israel may be remembered no more."[185] It would appear that, like some of the angelic hosts, these surrounding Arab nations have embraced the plight of the Palestinians.

SUMMARY

The Palestinians of modern-day find themselves in the most unenviable position. They essentially have become puppets not only of the surrounding Arab nations that most closely border Israel, but also of the angelic conflict. They have been reduced to pawns in the overall power play of opposition to the restoration of the nation Israel as the Jewish State. These two groups, the Islamic Arabs, and the fallen angels, are generally antagonistic toward the Jewish people.

The Islamic Arabs seek to stop the spread of Zionism in the world, and of democracy in the Middle East. The fallen Angels seek to kill all Jews, thus making the God of the Jews out to be a liar. They seek to justify their departure from their primary posts of proper habitation as referenced earlier, by discrediting the covenant making ability of God. God promised Abraham that he would never cease to have descendents. These descendents of Abraham are the Jewish people. The fallen angels think that the destruction of the last Jew on Earth evidences that God is a liar. If God is a liar, then these angels were justified in departing from His so-called perfect plan.

The Palestinians offer both groups the tangible ability to accomplish their dirty work with clean hands. The terror they inspire against the Jewish people receives dual endorsements. The Arabs provide political propaganda and monetary and military means; the fallen angels spiritualize their plight. Thus, you have Palestinianism or the plight of the Palestinians. Palestinianism is in essence the embodiment of the collective efforts aimed at antagonizing the restoration of Israel as the Jewish State. Islamic propaganda has persuaded the international community for the most part to take its eyes off the true Palestinian agenda, but when the lies are uncovered, what becomes evident to the naked eye is that the Jews and their reforming state of Israel are being antagonized.

Therefore, the Palestinians push their plight forward in arrogance, thinking they have the support of both Allah and the Arabs. As such, they are deceived (*nasha*) into thinking that the terror (*tiphletseth*) they inspire is justified. They believe that their acts of terror have legitimized their ethnic existence within the international community, which presently favors the establishment of a Palestinian State. In essence, they believe that the terror they have inspired has been successful.

Ultimately, the surrounding Arab nations inclusive of the Palestinians will formulate a final confederate effort with the aim of destroying Israel "that the name Israel may be remembered no more." At that point, the Palestinians will be brought down as an ethnic group. They, along with the other confederating nations, will experience defeat at the hands of the "exceedingly great army" of Israel. Likewise, Allah will begin his descent toward the god-reduction process in fulfillment of Zephaniah's prophecy:

The LORD will be awesome to them, For He will reduce to nothing all the gods of the Earth; People shall worship Him, Each one from his place, Indeed, all the shores of the nations. (Zeph. 2:11, NKJV)

THE PSALM 83 REPORT

Psalm 83 imparts invaluable information of utmost relevance in the twenty-first century. It contains prophecy that should find its final fulfillment therein on the Earth's timeline. It predicts the unification of an Arab confederacy comprised of those nations that most closely border the modern-day nation of Israel. This confederacy will consult together and form a consensus among them; they will unite in the sentiment that the nation Israel must be destroyed.

> They have said, Come, and let us cut them off from being a nation; That the name of Israel may be no more in remembrance. (Psa. 83:4, NKJV)

We see evidence of this mindset already firmly established within the predominant Middle Eastern terrorist organizations like Hamas, Hizbollah, and Al-Qaeda, to name a few. These groups and others like them receive sponsorship presently, be it directly or indirectly, from Lebanon, Syria, Saudi Arabia, and Egypt.[186] These nations are among those referenced by Asaph, author of Psalm 83. At some point, these Arab nations will no longer hide behind the terrorists, but will boldly declare their collective disdain for Israel. At that point, the fulfillment of the world's most dreaded event will occur: war in the Middle East!

171

The *Psalm 83 Report* is an attempt to find out what God intends to do about this desperate effort by the Arabs. It is justifiable to presume that God will not sit by idly and watch the Jewish people meet with their bitter end. After all, if every Jew were destroyed and there were no more nation Israel, then God could understandably be considered a liar. This God made an unconditional covenant with Abraham promising him that he would have descendants throughout eternity.[187] These descendants are the Jews, and they are the intended targets of the Psalm 83 conspiracy campaign.

To preface the assertion that we can count on the fact that the God of the Jews will issue a report on the subject matter, let me quote what the Jewish prophet Amos said about 2,760 years ago:

Surely the LORD GOD does nothing, Unless He reveals His secret to His servants the prophets. (Amos 3:7, NKJV)

From this declaration, we can be certain that an event of the magnitude of the Psalm 83 scenario will not go without a report. If God intends to do something to stop this Arab brigade, He will certainly reference His plans somewhere through the writing of "His servants the prophets."

Although there are many instances found in scripture where a prophet's petition is promptly followed by a divine report, in Asaph's case no such report was recorded. This causes the need to search elsewhere within the writings of "His servants the prophets" to identify the divine response to this forthcoming radical confederate effort of the Arabs.

Before we study the divine report, which is primarily delivered in Jeremiah 49:1–27, and Obadiah 1:1–21, let us read and analyze the opening petitions of Asaph's prophetic Psalm 83.

Do not keep silent, O God! Do not hold Your peace, And do not be still, O God! (Psa. 83:1, NKJV)

In essence, Asaph is petitioning God as follows:

Do not keep silent, O God! Issue a report! (*shemuah* in Hebrew)
> Do not hold Your peace! Issue a declaration of war!
> Do not be still, O God! Issue a conquest!

This petition for the issuance of a report, a declaration of war, and ultimate victory, arises out of the following concerns:

For behold, Your *enemies* make a *tumult*; And those *who hate You* have lifted up their head. (Psa. 83:2, NKJV; emphasis added)

At that time, these nations will best be identified as those "who hate" God. This certainly will distinguish between Allah, the god of the Arabs, and Jehovah, God of the Jews. These Arabs will demonstrate their hatred towards Jehovah, the God of the Jews. Presently it is common to hear Muslims preach in their mosques that their god is the same god as that of the Jews and Christians. However, this nonsensical preaching will be extinguished at the time that the Arabs come against the Jews in Psalm 83.

Asaph declares, "those (Arab nations) who hate You (Jehovah) have lifted up their head." These are neither Atheists nor Agnostics; rather they are Allah-worshipping Arabs! If, as they teach, Allah and Jehovah are indeed one, then they could be classified at that time as those who hate Allah. The possibility that they will ever turn against Allah is extremely preposterous. Therefore, from the minor premise we can conclude the major premise. The minor premise is that the Arabs will worship Allah but will hate Jehovah; therefore, the major premise is Allah the Arab god and Jehovah the Jewish God are not the same!

Furthermore, they will declare themselves enemies of Jehovah. As a result, the two-way street of peace will no longer be an option to God in this irreverent matter. Is it not interesting that the world today thinks a lasting peace can be achieved with the nations who will prove in this century that they are the very enemies of the God of the Jews?

These adversaries "have lifted up their head," and furthermore they "make a tumult." Perhaps by using the word "tumult," Asaph identifies for us the associated modernized and heavily publicized Arabic terms *Jihad* and *Intifada*.[188] Since these enemies will no longer be operating peacefully, rather they will move in aggression, it would not be wise for God to "be still" at the time of this assault.

> They have taken crafty counsel against Your people, And consulted together against Your sheltered ones. They have said, "Come, and let us cut them off from *being* a nation,
>
> That the name of Israel may be remembered no more." For they have consulted together with one consent; They form a confederacy against You: (Psa. 83:3–5, NKJV; emphasis added)

Silence can no longer be the golden rule in this matter. "They have said" certain things that will force God to "keep silent" no longer. They will concoct specific strategies that will force God to issue a report.

The Psalmist goes on to list these enemies (Palestinians, Lebanese, Syrians, Jordanians, Saudi Arabians, and Egyptians) and the historical biblical examples that he would like God to follow in His conquest over these enemies. Now let us proceed to locate, introduce, and study the "report" (*shemuah*) that God issues in response to the Asaph's petition. Segments of the report are scattered in the chapters of several different prophets, but as stated earlier the main components of the report were delivered through Jeremiah and Obadiah.

> I have heard a message [*shemuah*] from the LORD, And an ambassador has been sent to the nations: "Gather together, come against her, And rise up to battle!" (Jer. 49:14, NKJV)

The vision of Obadiah. Thus says the LORD GOD concerning Edom (We have heard a report [*shemuah*] from the LORD, And a messenger has been sent among the nations, saying, "Arise, and let us rise up against her for battle"). (Obad. 1:1, NKJV)

Comprehensive studies of Jeremiah 49:1–27, and Obadiah 1:1–21 are critical to the understanding of the Psalm 83 Report. These studies further develop the theme of the Israeli Conquest over these confederate nations. This study picks up in Jeremiah 49:7 and regards itself with Edom, the apparent lead member of the confederacy. Edom is the first member mentioned in Psalm 83:6–8 of the ten-member alliance.

Similar to the credits at the end of a movie, whereby the star's name is displayed before the supporting cast and crew, whenever a nation is listed first in the Bible it often identifies it as the star of the show. Furthermore, information delivered through the prophets about the lead member is generally understood to find some correlation with the other enjoining member nations. In Edom's case, this principle applies. Unfortunately, this star of the show turns out to be the villain rather than the victor.

In this instance, Edom is referred to as "the tents of Edom."[189] This implies that at the time of the fulfillment of the Psalm 83 prophecy, Edom will resemble an assemblage of refugees in tents, a military encampment, or both. For our purposes, we will intelligently presume the both scenario. Upon entering into the Arab confederacy, Edom will be refugees, who have assembled themselves into a militia.

Here is how this is to be understood in the twenty-first century: "the tents of Edom," labeled as such by Asaph centuries before there were ever Palestinian refugees, are indeed these refugees.[190] These Palestinian refugees are the stars of the show! The plight of these refugees becomes the thread that unites these Arab nations and ignites them into the ten-member confederacy of Psalm 83.

Palestinianism is an emerging term, which represents the common brotherhood that continues to develop between the Palestinians and those Islamic nations that support their struggle for autonomy. The term was coined by Egyptian-born author Bat Yeor, a pioneer in the study of Dhimmitude and Jihadist tactics.[191] Bat Yeor defined Palestinianism in her book *Eurabia: The Euro-Arab Axis* as follows:

> Palestinianism condenses jihadist values. It promotes the destruction of Israel, the denial of Hebrew biblical history and hence Christianity. It preaches Islamic replacement theology and the Arabization and Islamization of the Holy Land's biblical archeology.

Throughout history, these Arabs often fought each other, yet in this century, their empathy for the Palestinian refugees has served to unite them in the common cause of Palestinianism. This also evidences their collective hatred of Zionism. Remember that the battle cry of the Psalm 83 confederacy is the destruction of the nation Israel.

ZIONISM[192]

Movement founded by the Viennese Jewish journalist Theodor Herzl, who argued in his 1896 book *Der Judenstaat* (The Jewish State) that the best way of avoiding anti-Semitism in Europe was to create an independent Jewish state in Palestine. Zionism was named after Mount Zion in Jerusalem, a symbol of the Jewish homeland in Palestine since the Babylonian captivity in the sixth century BC. The movement culminated in the birth of the state of Israel in 1948.

PALESTINIANISM VS. ZIONISM

Palestinianism paired with Zionism becomes a recipe for disaster. These two philosophies cannot coexist in the Middle East. Zionism calls for a Jewish state and Palestinianism promotes the denial and ultimate destruction of any such state. The Jews feel compelled to migrate into Israel because of Zionism, and the Arabs attempt to deny them that right.

The makings for the coming Middle East War come down to Palestinianism verses Zionism. The tents of Edom get their Arab cohorts to sympathize with the continuing saga of their prolonged refugee status. One of the reasons they feel sorry for these Palestinian souls is that the Arabs never appropriately assimilated these displaced refugees back into their respective lands. These Palestinians were instructed by the surrounding Arab nations temporarily to vacate Israel in 1948, under the premise that the Arabs would destroy the newly forming Jewish state. The Arabs lost, and their miscalculation created the Palestinian refugees, also known as "tents of Edom."[193]

The pages of history advocate adversities amongst these Arabs. At no time in the past were all ten members of Psalm 83:6–8 ever sincerely united in a common cause. However, this trend began to change with the invention of Islam in the seventh century. Islam served to unite the Arabs ideologically. They began to embrace similar holy days, places, and practices, and slowly the longstanding issues that once divided them started to erode.

Probably the most notable attempt at Arab unity came in 1945 with the formation of the Arab League. They married up together for two primary purposes; first to promote independence for Arab States, and secondly to prevent the formation of an independent Jewish State. They achieved their first goal of becoming autonomous Arab States promptly, as the British and French began to relinquish their sovereignty in the rebellious region. Their success in this area led them to believe that they would have similar success in their second cause, which was the prevention of the restoration of the Jewish state of Israel.

Immediately upon the formation of the Jewish state in 1948, the surrounding Arab nations of Egypt, Jordan, Iraq, Syria, and Lebanon, supported by other Arabs, attacked the Jewish nation. They lost and the tents of Edom became a startling reality.

Fig. 4. Palestinian refugee camp, 1949. (Reproduced by permission from UNRWA. UNRWA photo, "Palestinian Refugees—Historical Photos," Badil.org, http://www.badil. org/Photos/history/Archive1/Photogallery/photo9757/real.htm [accessed 12/20/07].)

Fig. 5. Palestinian refugee camp, 1949. (Reproduced by permission from UNRWA. UNRWA photo, "Palestinian Refugees—Historical Photos," Badil.org, http://www.badil. org/Photos/history/Archive1/Photogallery/photo9757/real.htm [accessed 03/10/08].)

The twenty-first century stands upon this unsettled soil. The surrounding Arab nations empathize predominately with the Palestinian disposition of hatred for the reforming nation of Israel. Failed conventional Arab wars against the Jews have evolved into unconventional terrorist entities. These terrorists have extended their reach out of the region and into the international community. The world ponders the predicament, and proposes political solutions aimed at resolving this conflict.

The world cries out "heaven forbid" that a major war breaks out in the Middle East between the Arabs and Jews, but heaven foreknows that it will happen! War is prophesied to occur, as these Arabs will settle for nothing less than exclusive title to the fertile riches of the Promised Land.

THE REPORT

We begin with Jeremiah's assessment against Edom, which parallels closely that of Obadiah. Both prophets talk about the final judgments determined by God against Edom. There are two judgments that come against the territory of Edom in the latter years. The first is by the Jews against the Palestinians and their confederate neighbors, and the other is by the Jew, Jesus Christ, against the Armageddonites (the armies assembled in the campaign of Armageddon allied with the Antichrist).

Both judgments will extend into and thereby adversely affect the geography of Edom, which is modern-day Southern Jordan. Jeremiah and Obadiah chronicle both judgments with more emphasis on the first of these two judgments.[194]

> Against Edom. Thus says the LORD of hosts: "Is wisdom no more in Teman? Has counsel perished from the prudent? Has their wisdom vanished? (Jer. 49:7, NKJV)

Since "the tents of Edom" references the lead member of the Psalm 83 confederacy, we will begin at Jeremiah 49:7, whereby the prophet declares, "Thus says the LORD of hosts" and then fires out three rhetorical questions "Against Edom."[195] To decipher the significance of these three questions, one must first look at the context in which they apply, and secondly understand the history of the Edomites.[196]

The context is the coming confederate war effort of the Arabs to destroy the nation Israel. In essence, the God of the Jews is asking the Edomite descendants, who can be linked to a contingency residing within the Palestinians of today, "What on Earth are you thinking? Is wisdom no more in Teman?" Teman was the grandson of Esau, and the Temanites who came from his loins were renowned in ancient times for their wisdom.[197]

Teman understood from his grandfather Esau, who is the father of the Edomites that the birthrights to the Abrahamic covenant, passed through to Isaac who was Esau's father.[198] Furthermore, he was taught that this birthright passed over Esau and was afforded to Jacob, Esau's younger twin brother. Therefore when God has Jeremiah ask, "Is wisdom no more in Teman?" we are to glean the fact that what was understandably the most foundational understanding of Teman has been overlooked by his descendants currently existing within the Palestinians.

The God of Teman's great-great-grandfather Abraham made an everlasting, unconditional covenant that guaranteed the survival of the very people that the descendants of Teman are attempting to annihilate. Esau's twin brother is Jacob, Jacob is Israel, and his descendants are the Jews![199]

Has counsel perished from the prudent? Apparently. Asaph informs us of the following: For they have consulted together with one consent; They form a confederacy against You: The tents of Edom and the Ishmaelites; Moab and the Hagrites; Gebal, Ammon, and Amalek; Philistia with the inhabitants of

Tyre; Assyria also has joined with them; They have helped the children of Lot. *Selah.* (Psa. 83:5–8 NKJV)

Due to the fact that the wisdom of the Abrahamic covenant no longer exists within Teman's descendants, the counsel advanced by their contingency within the Palestinians at this future final Arab summit, whereby they all consult "together with one consent," is void of any reference to this eternal covenant. As such, in the absence of any such rhetoric, these rhetorical questions asked by Jeremiah against the Palestinians, are astoundingly rudimentary! "Has their wisdom vanished?" Indeed, it has vanished. It has disappeared somewhere between their turbans and Allah's nostrils.

The answers to the three questions directed at Edom are given at the time of Edom's first judgment. Yes, wisdom is no more in Teman! Yes, counsel has perished from the prudent! Yes, wisdom has vanished! Obadiah 1:8–9 tells us that the vanishing of wisdom results in the military slaughtering of Edom.

The three questions above follow in line with the theme of rhetorical questioning throughout Jeremiah chapter 49.

1. Against the Ammonites [Northern Jordanians] Thus says the LORD: "Has Israel no sons? Has he no heir? Why *then* does Milcom inherit Gad, And his people dwell in its cities?" (Jer. 49:1, NKJV; emphasis added)
2. Why is the city of praise [Jerusalem], the city of My joy, not deserted? (Jer. 49:25, NKJV) This question is directed at Damascus, Syria.

In Ammon's case (Jer. 49:1) it is the inheritance of the land that is fore fronted. In Edom's case (Jer. 49:7) it is the wisdom of the birthright of Jacob and his descendants, right to exist in fulfillment of the Abrahamic Covenant. In Damascus's case (Jer. 49:25) it is the eternal throne to be established in Jerusalem its appropriate place, "the city of My joy."

What is being highlighted by this sequence of rhetorical questions in Jeremiah 49:1,7,25 is the Abrahamic Covenant. At the time of the Psalm 83 war effort, Ammon, represented by Northern Jordan, will be encroaching upon the Holy Land allotted to Israel. The descendant Jewish heirs of Abraham will come under attack by Edom, represented by Southern Jordan and the Palestinians[200] the eternal city of Jerusalem will come under threat by Damascus.[201]

THE REPORT CONTINUED

Flee, turn back, dwell in the depths, O inhabitants of Dedan!
For I will bring the calamity of Esau upon him, The time *that*
I will punish him. (Jer. 49:8, NKJV; emphasis added)

This is a warning to the Saudis to disengage from their confederate allegiance with the Palestinians. They are instructed to flee from the slaughter back into the depths of Saudi Arabia. The historical location of "Dedan" was in Northwest Saudi Arabia. Ezekiel tells us below that the Saudis do not heed Jeremiah's warning.

Therefore thus says the LORD GOD: "I will also stretch out
My hand against Edom, cut off man and beast from it, and
make it desolate from Teman; *Dedan* shall fall by the sword."
(Ezek. 25:13, NKJV; emphasis added)

This reference to Dedan, Arabia offers a connection to the confederacy of Esau/Edom found in Psalm 83:4–8 and Obadiah 1:7. In Psalm 83:6, the Saudi's are represented by their ancestor Ishmael, and are labeled as the "Ishmaelites." Esau is Edom, according to Genesis 36:1, much like his twin brother Jacob is also called Israel Genesis 32:28.

If grape-gatherers came to you, Would they not leave *some*
gleaning grapes? If thieves by night, Would they not destroy

until they have enough? I have uncovered his secret places, And he shall not be able to hide himself. His descendants are plundered, His brethren and his neighbors, And he *is* no more. (Jer. 49:9–10, NKJV; emphasis added)

The descendants of Esau ultimately align themselves with their Arab neighbors in a confederate effort to come against Israel. Psalm 83:1–8. Israel defeats this confederacy, and thus "His descendants are plundered, His brethren and his neighbors." This theme of severe judgment is echoed by Obadiah 1:5–7. The plundering, which is the result of a military defeat, extends beyond Edom's borders into the borders of "his neighbors." One of the neighbors has already been identified in verse 8 as Saudi Arabia (Dedan). The others are Gaza, Jordan, Egypt, Lebanon, and Syria, all of which are enlisted members of the confederacy of Esau. This defeat brings an end to Esau and all his enmity that was harbored by his descendants throughout the centuries "he *is* no more."

Leave your fatherless children, I will preserve *them* alive; And let your widows trust in Me." (Jer. 49:11, NKJV; emphasis added)

The refugees left behind are the fatherless and the widows. The "mighty men" (soldiers) as they are called in Obadiah 1:9 are slaughtered in defeat, and the refugees left behind are instructed to trust in the LORD.

Then your *mighty men*, O Teman, shall be dismayed, To the end *that everyone* from the mountains of Esau May *be cut off by slaughter*. (Obad. 1:9, NKJV; emphasis added)

According to Obadiah, these fatherless children and widows are transported to internment camps.

The captives of this host of the children of Israel Shall possess
the land of the Canaanites [Israel] As far as Zarephath [South-
west Lebanon]. (Obad. 1:20, NKJV)

For thus says the LORD: "Behold, those whose judgment *was*
not to drink of the cup have assuredly drunk. And *are* you the
one who will altogether go unpunished? You shall not go unpunished, but you shall surely drink *of it*." (Jer. 49:12, NKJV;
emphasis added)

In this passage, we get the first hint as to why the first of the two
judgments against Edom is necessary. Edom and its confederacy are
guilty of the unauthorized oppression of the Jewish people. The Jews
had already adequately been served the cup of judgment as evidenced
by the Holocaust for their apostate condition, which long ago had led
to their rejection of Christ at His first coming. Ezekiel tells us that they
were to be scattered and judged for their mistaken ways and misdeeds.

So I scattered them among the nations, and they were dispersed throughout the countries; *I judged them* according
to their *ways* and their *deeds*. (Ezek. 36:19, NKJV; emphasis
added)

The dry bones vision of Ezekiel 37:1–13 pointed to the grave-
like conditions of the Holocaust that would bring to end this Jewish
judgment sequence. Thus when Jeremiah says "Behold, those whose
judgment *was* not to drink of the cup have assuredly drunk, he is
referencing the Jews being subsequently oppressed by the Palestinians
and their Arab confederacy. They are operating "in Excess" of what
was determined as the just judgment of the Jewish people for their rejection of Messiah. They are forcing another "cup" of judgment down
the throat of the Jewish people. God has not prescribed this "cup" of
bad medicine.

This causes Jeremiah to forewarn Esau as follows: "You shall not go unpunished, but you shall surely drink *of it.*" Obadiah 1:16 also references this cup of judgment from which Esau and his Arab neighbors shall surely drink.

> For as you (Esau) *drank* on My holy mountain, *So* shall all the nations *drink* continually;
>   Yes, they shall drink, and swallow, And they shall be as though they had never been. (Obad. 1:16, NKJV; emphasis added)

Obadiah's passage is useful in that it connects Esau's judgment with Israel ("My holy mountain") and that it determines the timing of this judgment as occurring before "all the nations drink." The judgment of all the nations of the world occurs at the second coming of Christ. Therefore, the judgment of Esau concludes sometime before the second coming of Christ. "For as you (Esau) *drank*, *So* shall all the nations *drink.*" Obadiah further depicts the timing to be before the "day of the LORD."

> For the day of the LORD upon all the nations *is* near; [not yet] As you have done, it shall be done to you; Your reprisal shall return upon your own head. (Obad. 1:15, NKJV; emphasis added)

The reprisal against the Palestinian refugees and their Arab partners occurs before the day of the LORD comes. It happens in the end-times, just before the final seven years of tribulation on the Earth. The reprisal against the Psalm 83 confederates is to be fashioned in the similar method as their oppression against Israel: "As you (Arab confederates) have done (to the Jews), it shall be done to you." This prescription is in alignment with the curse-for-curse-in-kind clause contained in the Genesis 12:3 clause of the Abrahamic Covenant.[202]

THE REPORT

> "For I have sworn by Myself," says the LORD, "that Bozrah shall become a desolation, a reproach, a waste, and a curse. And all its cities shall be perpetual wastes." (Jer. 49:13, NKJV)

To emphasize further the scope of the pending judgments Jeremiah declares that the LORD personally has sworn that Bozrah, which is located in ancient Edom, will "become a desolation, a reproach, a waste, and a curse. And all its cities shall be perpetual wastes." This is a result of the two judgments destined to befall Edom: one by the Jews and the final by the Jew Jesus Christ at His Second Coming.

The first judgment executed by the Jews is the cup of judgment served to Esau and his neighbors, who "shall surely drink of it" for their violent confederate attempt to destroy the nation Israel.[203] The second judgment, executed by Jesus Christ at His second coming, is against the nations of the world who assemble with the Antichrist in his Armageddon campaign. ("So shall all the nations drink"). These nations are judged in Edom because that is where they arrive in their attempt to destroy the faithful Jewish remnant, which at that time will have fled to the area of Bozrah/Petra in Southern Jordan, which is located in ancient Edom.

It is important to make this distinction in order to disassociate any connections between these two judgments. The first judgment destroys the Arab confederacy listed in Psalm 83:6–8, comprised of Palestinians, Lebanese, Syrians, Jordanians, Saudi Arabians, and Egyptians. This is a result of the Israeli Conquest at the hands of the exceedingly great army of the Jewish people prophesied about in Ezekiel 37:10. The second judgment destroys the Armageddon confederacy comprised of all the remaining nations of the world, conducted single handedly by the exceedingly great one-man army of Messiah Jesus Christ Himself. Isaiah puts it this way:

Who *is* this who comes from Edom, With dyed garments from Bozrah, This *One who is* glorious in His apparel, Traveling in the greatness of His strength? "I who speak in righteousness, mighty to save." Why *is* Your apparel red, And Your garments like one who treads in the winepress? "I have trodden the winepress alone, And from the peoples no one *was* with Me." (Isa. 63:1–3, NKJV; emphasis added)

THE REPORT

I have heard a message [*shemuah*] from the LORD, *And* an ambassador has been sent to the nations: Gather together, come against her, And rise up to battle! (Jer. 49:14, NKJV; emphasis added)

Jeremiah makes two statements. He first declares he has "heard a message from the LORD," then makes the announcement that "an ambassador has been sent to the nations." The report Jeremiah has heard, also heard by Obadiah, is the response by God to the message that the ambassador sends out "to the nations." The nations rally around the battle cry "Gather together, come against her." Jeremiah uses the Hebrew word *goy* which can mean Gentiles, nations, heathen, or Gentile nations. In this context, it refers to the Gentile Arab nations assembling against Israel in fulfillment of Psalm 83:1–8.

Some commentaries suggest that the message Jeremiah and Obadiah receive from the LORD is that "an ambassador has been sent to or among the nations" and that "the nations" confederate together to "come against her," alluding to Edom. However, for the following four reasons it is more likely that Jeremiah is identifying Israel as "her."

And an ambassador has been sent to the (Arab) nations: "Gather together (confederate), come against her (Israel), And rise up to battle (fulfilling Psalm 83)!"

1. Edom is referred to as "her" only one time in the entire Bible, in Ezekiel 32:29, whereas Israel is referred to in the feminine context over 100 times in the Old and New Testaments.[204]

2. According to Jeremiah 49:15 and Obadiah 1:2, Edom is among the nations the "ambassador" rallys into a confederacy. As such, it would not make sense that the members of this confederacy, which are assembled to destroy Israel, would "rise up to battle" to attack one of their own members.

3. The brief study of the history of Edom and the Edomites that follows illustrates that at no time since the prophecies of Jeremiah, which spanned from approximately 627 BC to 587 BC and up until the present, has any confederacy of nations come against them.

4. The Bible only references two end-time judgments against Edom and the Edomites, and neither involves a confederacy of nations. The exceedingly great army of Israel against the Psalm 83 Arab confederacy executes the first judgment.[205] Jesus Christ delivers the second judgment at the time of His return to the Earth. As previously stated, the second judgment serves to defeat the Antichrist and his armies assembled in the campaign of Armageddon.

EDOM'S DECLINE

The history of Edom's decline began around 586 BC as the nomadic tribe named the Nabateans trespassed into Edom. Then around 312 BC the Seleucid King Antigonus, who had come into power when Alexander's empire was divided, conquered Edom. Then in 164 BC, Judas Maccabeus of the Jews overtook the Edomites, who were then called Idumeans, and what Judas overtook was primarily Idumea. Idumea was formerly part of the tribal territories of Judah and Simeon, but was subtly annexed from the land of Israel through several waves of Edomite migration into the tribal territories. In essence, the Edomites fled Edom and homesteaded the Holy Land.

In 126 BC, a similar conquest over the Edomites (Idumeans) occurred by the Jewish prince and high priest John Hyrcanus. Lastly, around AD 70 the Romans conquered Israel and Idumea, at which point Edom was clearly "made small among the nations" in fulfillment of the prophecies contained in Jeremiah 49:15 and Obadiah 1:2.

This history lesson illustrates the point that Edom's decline did not occur by any contemporary group of confederating nations; rather, it occurred chronologically by individual tribes, nations or empires. This would mean that a confederate assault against Edom would have to be fulfilled in the future.

As identified as reason four above, the Bible only references two end-times judgments against Edom and the Edomites, and they are not from a confederacy of nations, rather they result first from the "exceedingly great army" of the Jews, and secondly from Jesus Christ upon His return.

Conversely, "The Report" Jeremiah heard from the LORD is most likely that "an ambassador has been sent to the nations" to "rise up to battle against her," Israel. The Bible does speak of a time when such a confederacy will form, against Israel. Their battle cry is:

They have said, "Come, and let us cut them off from being a nation; That the name of Israel may be no more in remembrance." (Psa. 83:4, NKJV; emphasis added)

The confederacy is described in Psalm 83:5–8, and it is inclusive of Palestinians, Saudi Arabians, Jordanians, Egyptians, and Lebanese. Jeremiah 49 previews these nations in Jeremiah 49:1–6 (Ammon), Jeremiah 49:7 (Edom), Jeremiah 49:8 (Dedan/Saudi Arabia), Jeremiah 49:10 (Neighbors) Jeremiah 49:23–27 (Damascus, Syria).[206]

For I will make you [Edom] least among the nations, despised by humankind [mankind]. (Jer. 49:15, NRSV)

Jeremiah announces a provision contained within "The Report" he has heard from the LORD that Edom will be made "least or small among the nations, despised by Mankind."[207] The brief history lesson included in this chapter depicted the decline of Edom in fulfillment of this prophecy. Through the process of time, Edom was indeed made "small among the nations." Today there is no acknowledged Edomite existence, apart from some Bedouins residing in the Southern Jordan area; however, if you follow the migratory path of the Edomites, they end up primarily in Israel. Contained amongst the Palestinians of modern times resides a remnant of the Edomites.[208]

The reference to the Palestinians in Psalm 83:6 as those assembled as the "tents of Edom," informs us that at the time the Arabs confederate to come against Israel, the descendants of Esau, who through time were "made small among the nations" will be the "least among the nations," referring to the Palestinians as the smallest in stature among the confederacy. None of the other confederating members is identified with the "tents of" condition.

Today we see this is the case, as the Palestinian refugees are without their own Arab state. Although the Arab League succeeded quickly in legitimizing autonomy for member nations like Saudi Arabia, Iraq, Lebanon, Syria, and Jordan, the Palestinians are still recognized by the international community as refugees. The world community is hard at work attempting to establish a Palestinian state; however, at the time of the authoring of this book, the Palestinians are yet stateless. Therefore, if the Psalm 83 prophecy were to be fulfilled in advance of the establishment of a Palestinian state, the most suitable title for the Palestinians would be "the tents of Edom," reflecting the current condition of the Palestinian refugees.

The Palestinian refugees enjoined within the Arab confederacy, as the star of the show, is the least in stature among them. This is because through time, they were "made small among the nations." However, Jeremiah further prophesies that they will also become, "despised by humankind." This results from the next events described in "The Report."

"The terror you [Palestinians] inspire and the pride of your heart have deceived you, you who live in the clefts of the rock, who hold the height of the hill. Although you make your nest as high as the eagle's, from there I will bring you down," says the LORD. (Jer. 49:16, NIV)

The Palestinians are guilty of inspiring terror! This terror has become a mushroom cloud, extending over the international community. As such, it is beginning to concern all of mankind. Terror as we understand it today is mainly associated with the Middle East. It is the unconventional method of warfare inspired by Arab nations coincidentally listed in the Psalm 83:6–8.

This method of warfare was primarily introduced to the world scene after Israel became a nation in 1948. More specifically, it was the result of the recognition by these Arab nations that conventional methods of warfare were no match against the developing army of Israel. This reality dawned on them in the aftermath of the Six-Day War of 1967. This fact was further driven home at the defeat of the war at the time of Yom Kippur in 1973.

Terrorist entities like Hezbollah, Hamas, Al-Qaeda, and Islamic Jihad have several things in common: Islamic faith, Middle-Eastern origins, combative attitudes toward Israel, and encouragement from the Palestinian struggle for Arab statehood. Therefore, when Jeremiah declares of the Edomite descendants of Esau, the "terror you inspire," we can prophetically credit the world's newfound foe terrorism to its inspirational source, the Palestinians. A detailed prophetic study of the terror inspired by the Palestinians is contained in the chapter within this book called *The End of Terror: Another Bible Prediction.*

"The pride of your heart has deceived you." The Palestinian refugees are deceived through prideful hearts into thinking that their plight is a worthy cause. The Hebrew word for deceived is *nasha,* which is also used in Obadiah 1:7. The Obadiah usage portrays the Palestinians as a beguiled member among their Arab allies.

> All your allies have deceived [*nasha*] you, they have driven
> you to the border [of Israel]; your confederates have prevailed
> against you; your trusted friends have set a trap under you—
> there is no understanding of it. (Obad. 1:7, RSV)

What Obadiah 1:7, in connection with Jeremiah 49:16, describes
for us today in real-world application, is that the Palestinian refugees
are beguiled by the pride of their hearts into thinking Palestinianism
can become reality. This thinking enables their Arab allies strategically
to keep them deployed at the borders of Israel in lieu of assimilating
them into their own national borders. Collectively, the other confederate members of Psalm 83 have successfully convinced the Palestinian refugees into thinking they ultimately belong inside the borders of
Israel, in full possession of the Holy Land.

Obadiah further discloses, "your trusted friends have set a trap
under you."[209] It will prove a grave mistake for the Palestinian refugees
to conclude in their prideful hearts that they will someday inherit the
Holy Land of Israel. These Edomite descendants of Esau elevate their
cause of Palestinianism into the embrace of their Arab allies, who in
turn ensnare them at the borders of Israel.

Obadiah says, "There is no understanding of it." This statement
alludes to the underlying dangerous misconception that incites the
Arabs to unite, and ultimately will ignite the Arabs to fight in fulfillment of Psalm 83. Whereas Zionism has become a reality, Palestinianism will prove to be frivolity, a trap that ensnares the "tents of Edom"
and their Arab cohorts.

"Though you make your nest as high as the eagle." Hand-in-hand
with this inspired terror is the religious thinking that convinces Esau
that his fierceness is invincible. Edom, inspiring terror supported by
its confederate partners, believing itself invincible, is brought down
from that deceived condition by the LORD. "I will bring you down
from there," says the LORD.

THE REPORT

> "Edom also shall be an astonishment; Everyone who goes by it will be astonished And will hiss at all its plagues. As in the overthrow of Sodom and Gomorrah And their neighbors," says the LORD, "No one shall remain there, Nor shall a son of man dwell in it." (Jer. 49:17–18, NKJV)

The result of the two judgments against Edom leaves it uninhabitable for humans. It will astonish everyone in the Messianic Kingdom that goes by it. It will serve as a reminder to them of the severe judgment that came against Sodom and Gomorrah, and their neighbors.

The Bible suggests it will be only suitable for the habitation of the demons, and or fallen angels of Revelation 12:9. They are cast out of heaven with Satan and team up with the Antichrist in the campaign of Armageddon. Scripture tells us that the Antichrist and the false prophet end up in the Lake of Fire described in Revelation . Revelation 20:1–13 declares that Satan ends up in chains years, returns to Earth, and ends up in the Lake of Fire. Furth ore, unsaved men and women end up in Hades for 1000 years until the White Throne Judgment, at which point they too are sent to the Lake of Fire. However, it does not specifically reference the whereabouts of the fallen angels.

Isaiah 34:1–17 and Isaiah 13:19–22, in association with Revelation 18:2, tells us that Babylon and most probably Edom will be their places of confinement during the kingdom period. The fallen angels are thought to possess the creatures that inhabit those areas during the Messianic Kingdom.

> Behold, he shall come up like a lion from the *floodplain of the Jordan* Against the dwelling place of the strong; But I will suddenly make him [Esau] run away from her [Israel]. And who

is a chosen *man that* I may appoint over her [Israel]? For who *is* like Me? Who will arraign Me? And who *is* that shepherd Who will withstand Me?" (Jer.49:19, NKJV; emphasis added)

We must compare Jeremiah 49:19–22 to the counterpart passages found in Jeremiah 50:43–46. The depiction in both cases is a military effort staged at the "floodplain of the Jordan" against the Jews. The first campaign is by the Psalm 83 confederacy led by Edom, and the second is the campaign of Armageddon, led by the Antichrist. In both instances, the motivation is to destroy the client nation Israel.

The genocide of the Jewish people is a paramount goal of Satan within the angelic conflict. This is a topic for a different book; however, the point is that if there is no Jewish remnant to beckon the return of Christ, the word of God is breached. Hosea 5:15 tells us that Christ returns when the Jewish remnant seeking refuge in Edom pleads for Him to come rescue them.

I will return again to My place Till they [the Nation Israel] acknowledge their offense. Then they will seek My face; In their affliction they will earnestly seek Me. (Hosea 5:15, NKJV)

Both assaults against the Jews fail and the LORD causes the enemies to flee. As a result of the Jewish victory over the first assault, four rhetorical questions are asked.

1. *Who is a chosen man that I may appoint over her?* This question causes the reader to remember that it is the LORD who sets up and takes down kings (Dan. 2:21). Whenever God used the Gentiles to discipline the Jewish people, it was because God empowered those Gentile nations to do so. In neither of these instances has God authorized the Psalm 83 confederacy or the Antichrist and his armies to commit genocide on the Jewish people.

2. *For who is like Me?* This question emphasizes the sovereignty of God.

3. *Who will arraign Me?* As the client nation, the Jewish people are likened to the apple of God's eye (Zech. 2:9, Deut. 32:10). Matthew 25:40,45 depicts the same concept, that whatever they do to the least of them, they do to Him, Christ.

4. *Who is that shepherd Who will withstand Me?* God has reserved the role of shepherding for Christ (Isa. 40:10–11, Ezek. 34:12–16, Matt. 2:6, John 10:11,14, Heb. 13:20, 1 Peter 5:4, Rev. 7:17). In the Messianic Kingdom, Christ will delegate this responsibility to the resurrected King David (Ezek. 34:23, 37:34). No other shepherds will withstand the Messiah, Jesus Christ!

Therefore hear the counsel of the LORD that He has taken against Edom, And His purposes that He has proposed against the inhabitants of Teman: Surely the least of the flock shall draw them out; Surely He shall make their dwelling places desolate with them. (Jer. 49:20, NKJV)

By now, "wisdom was no more in Teman," and good counsel had "perished from the prudent" (Jer. 49:7), so therefore Teman and the prudent of Edom will receive "the counsel of the LORD." This counsel is contained within "The Report" Jeremiah and Obadiah jointly heard from the LORD (Jer. 49:14, and Obad. 1:1).

"Surely the least of the flock shall draw them out" refers to the complete and exacting victory of Israel's exceedingly great army over the Psalm 83 Confederacy. There will be no mighty men left in Teman (Obad. 1:9), There will be no grapes to glean (Obad. 1:5, Jeremiah 49:9), Esau will be left bare (Jer. 49:10). The shepherd theme was introduced in Jeremiah 49:19, so the "least of the flock" would be all Jews.

To "draw them out," probably references the Jewish taking of Arab prisoners of war. This occurs in the aftermath of the first judgment against Edom. "Surely, He shall make their dwelling places desolate with them." Ultimately, after the return of Christ, He will make the entire territory of Edom desolate. This occurs in the aftermath of the second judgment in Edom.

"The Earth shakes at the noise of their fall; At the cry, its noise is heard at the Red Sea" (Jer. 49:21, NKJV). The whole Earth is shaken by the soundness of the defeat of the Psalm 83 confederacy. The defeat itself extends to the Red Sea.

The implication is that the confederate nations of Jordan, Egypt, and Saudi Arabia, which border the Red Sea, are also soundly defeated.

> Behold, He shall come up and fly like the eagle, And spread
> His wings over Bozrah; The heart of the mighty men of Edom
> in that day shall be Like the heart of a woman in birth pangs.
> (Jer. 49:22, NKJV)

The emphasis here is on the first judgment of Edom, which the prophet Ezekiel declares will be fashioned in this format: "I will lay My vengeance on Edom by the hand of My people Israel, that they may do in Edom according to My anger and according to My fury; and they shall know My vengeance," (Ezek. 25:14, NKJV).

The point here is that the exceedingly great army of Israel is divinely empowered by the LORD. It is likened to the spreading of the wings of an eagle over the prey, causing an alarming fear to the mighty men of the confederacy, particularly the mighty men of Teman Obadiah 1:9. The theme of a woman in birth pangs or fear is referenced in other passages relative to this defeat (Isa. 19:16, Egypt; Jer. 48:41, Moab; Jer. 49:24, Damascus). This study picks up again in the chapter *Obadiah's Mysterious Vision*.

14

OBADIAH'S MYSTERIOUS VISION

The Jewish prophet Obadiah receives a mysterious vision, the contents of which I outline and describe in this important chapter. In order to understand better his vision, it is important for the reader to review the chapters in this book entitled *The Who-domites?* and *The Psalm 83 Report.* These chapters contain the introductory content necessary to understand comprehensively Obadiah's mysterious vision.

To preface this chapter, remember that Obadiah identifies historical and future names, places and events using the Hebrew vernacular of his day. Furthermore, he presumes that his readers possess a basic understanding of Hebrew history at the time that his vision becomes discerned. Since this vision is to be deciphered in these present times, this historical consideration is inclusive of their exodus out of Egypt, the Babylonian captivity, their centuries of worldwide dispersion, on past the rebirth of the nation Israel in 1948, and on into these modern times. The most important facts to note as his mysterious vision opens up are:

1. Esau settled in the territory of ancient Edom, which is modern-day Southern Jordan, and is the patriarchal father of the Edomite peoples.

2. A remnant contingency of the Edomite population can be located within the modern-day Palestinians.

This Palestinian generation will be judged for the historical crimes their Edomite fathers previously committed and the current crimes they presently perpetrate against the Jewish people. The execution of this judgment upon the Palestinians will be delivered through the military might of the nation Israel.

> The vision of Obadiah. Thus says the LORD GOD concerning Edom (We have heard a report from the LORD, *And* a messenger has been sent among the nations, *saying,*
> "Arise, and let us rise up against her for battle." (Obad. 1:1 NKJV; emphasis added)

Two things are declared in verse 1. First, the prophets (plural) have heard "a report from the LORD." Second, "a messenger has been sent among the nations." Note that the "report from the LORD" is not necessarily the message sent to the nations; rather, the message to the nations dictates the need for the report. The report is given through the prophets so that the Jewish people will know God's response to the battle-stirring message "sent among the nations."

We know what the message says: "And rise up to battle" (Jer. 49:14, NKJV). But who are the "We" to whom the report is given? Who are the nations "among the nations" to which the messenger has been sent? Lastly, who is "her" that these nations will attack?

The prophets are Obadiah and Jeremiah. "We," Obadiah and Jeremiah, "have heard a report from the LORD." Obadiah echoes a report first heard by Jeremiah: "I have heard a message from the LORD, And an ambassador has been sent to the nations: 'Gather together, come against her, And rise up to battle!'" (Jer. 49:14, NKJV).

Who are the nations "among the nations?" There are three key ways to determine what nations are "among the nations." First, in verse 2 we are told that Edom is among these nations:

Behold, I will make you [Edom] small *among the* [confederating] *nations;* You shall be greatly despised. (Obad. 1:2, NKJV; emphasis added)

Secondly, in verse 7 the other nations, in addition to Edom, are assembled along with these Edomites in a confederacy:

All the men in *your confederacy* Shall force you [Palestinians] to the border; The men at peace with you Shall deceive you *and* prevail against you. (Obad. 1:7, NKJV; abbreviated with emphasis added)

Lastly, in verse 1 the mandate of the confederacy is to rise up to battle against some nation referred to as "her." Is Edom this "her?" Scripture generally references Edom or Esau as "him" or "he," rather than "her" or "she." In addition, how could Edom be a member of a confederacy that was against him? Though verse 7 depicts Edom as a deceived member within the confederacy, he is still a known member of the confederacy. It is not probable that the Edomites, who are linked to the modern-day Palestinians, would rise up to battle among the confederating nations, with the nations, to extinguish their own existence.

More importantly, however, is to note that the report Obadiah hears concerns the final judgment against the Edomite peoples. Scripture points to the final judgment against the Palestinians as being leveled by one single nation—that nation is Israel.[210] There is no scriptural basis to assume that the final destruction of the Edomite people will be at the hands of Edom itself, assembled with a multiplicity of nations.

Presently residing within the modern-day Palestinian refugees is a contingency of Edomite descendants.[211] Therefore, this yet unfulfilled prophecy is destined to find its association with a pending judgment against the Palestinians and their neighboring Arab cohorts that support them. These nations are identified further on in this study.

So then, who is the "her" of verse 1 destined to be attacked? She comes under attack by a group of confederating nations. Since Edom is among these attacking nations, "her" must be someone the Palestinians want to destroy. Obadiah 1:10–14 tells us it is Israel that Edom antagonizes. Psalm 83:1–8 tells us that the Palestinians involve themselves in a confederacy for rising up to battle against Israel. In addition, Israel is referred to as "her" within the Bible more times than any other nation.

Thus, in summary, God gives the Jewish people through their prophets, predominately Jeremiah and Obadiah, as prescribed in the prophetic formula of Amos 3:7 an important report, the contents of which will be spelled out in Obadiah 1:1–20 and Jeremiah 49:7–22. This report from the LORD serves as God's response to the petition of the Psalmist Asaph in Psalm 83.

Surely, the LORD GOD does nothing, Unless He reveals (reports) His secret to (through) His servants the prophets. (Amos 3:7, NKJV)

Secondly, "a messenger has been sent among the nations." Though it singles out Edom, this response also incorporates the Psalm 83:6–8 confederated member nations of Lebanon, Syria, Jordan, Saudi Arabia, and Egypt, and the Gaza; Edom is only one member "among the nations." We can restrict the "among the nations" grouping to those members who in Obadiah 1:7 are aligned in a confederacy with Edom.

"Arise, and let us rise up against her for battle." Among the confederated nations, the call to battle has sounded in Obadiah's vision of the future. The time has come for the Psalm 83:6–8 members to rise up against her, the nation Israel, for battle. The intent:

They have said, "Come, and *let us cut them off from being a nation*, That the name of Israel may be remembered no more." (Psa. 83:4, NKJV; emphasis added)

ONWARD WITH OBADIAH'S VISION

Behold, I will make you [Edom] *small among the* [confederate] *nations*; You shall be greatly despised. (Obad. 1:2, NKJV; emphasis added)

The report from the LORD begins by making two prophetic assertions in verse 2 regarding Edom. First, they will be reduced in national stature among the nations, and secondly they will be greatly despised.

Among the confederate nations, Edom will be the least in stature. This condition is emphasized in Psalm 83:6, whereby the Palestinians are identified as "the tents of Edom." By the time the call to battle among the confederate nations arises, "Edom" will be "small among the nations." The Palestinians are identified as tent dwellers, likely referring to them as a displaced population, perhaps a people without their own state. biblically, "the tents of" refers to refugees, military encampments, or both.[212]

Many consider Obadiah to be a contemporary of Jeremiah, which means his prophetic ministry flourished about the time of the Babylonian captivity.[213] A study of the history of Edom from the time of the Babylonian captivity illustrates the process of the national reduction of Edom, i.e., "Behold, I will make you small among the nations." From the *International Standard Bible Encyclopedia:*

They [the Edomites] gave what help they could to Nebuchad-nezzar, and exulted in the destruction of Jerusalem, stirring the bitterest indignation in the hearts of the Jews (Lam. 4:21; Ezek. 25:12; 35:3ff; Ob. 1:10ff). The Edomites pressed into the then evacuated lands in the South of Judah. In 300 BC, Mt. Seir with its capital Petra fell into the hands of the Nabateans.

West of the Arabah the country they occupied came to be known by the Greek name Idumea, and the people as Idumeans. Hebron, their chief city, was taken by Judas Mac-cabeus in 165 BC (1 Macc 4:29, 61; 5:65). In 126 BC, the country was subdued by John Hyrcanus, who compelled the people to become Jews and to submit to circumcision. Anti-pater, governor of Idumaea, was made procurator of Judea, Samaria and Galilee by Julius Caesar. He paved the way to the throne for his son Herod the Great. With the fall of Judah under the Romans, Idumaea disappears from history.

Presently, there is a group of displaced Arabs in the region fight-ing for a homeland. They have become a state within a state. They are commonly called Palestinians. Over the past one hundred years, the in-ternational community has at various times encouraged them to resettle into their ancestral Arab lands away from what is known as modern-day Israel. However, to date these peoples are still predominately residing as refugees and are generally unable to resettle in the Arab nations.

There are numerous Palestinian refugee camps located at vari-ous locations inside the borders of Israel and her neighboring Arab countries. These countries have generally refused to assimilate these refugees into their citizenry. These displaced peoples, at least in part, likely find their ancestry traceable to the ethnic group known as the Edomites. We might infer that these displaced peoples, i.e., this state within a state consisting of Palestinians and numerous refugees, have been "made small among the nations."

ONWARD WITH OBADIAH'S VISION

"The pride of your heart has deceived you, *You* who dwell in the clefts of the rock, Whose habitation is high; *You* who say in your heart, 'Who will bring me down to the ground?' Though you ascend *as* high as the eagle, And though you set your nest among the stars, From there I will bring you down," says the LORD. (Obad. 1:3–4, NKJV)

Though they are the least among the member nations of the confederacy, they are under the illusion that they are invincible. This is the result of their deluded religious thinking, "you ascend *as* high as the eagle; you set your nest among the stars." By his usage of "stars," Obadiah prompts us to recognize the Bible typology of angels. Numerous passages in the scriptures associate the angelic realm with the stars. Thus, there is a possible connection to be made between the deluded condition of the Palestinians, and their religious Islamic mindset.

Notice the decline of Edom. First they are reduced nationally in Obadiah 1:2, and then they are to be brought down spiritually in Obadiah 1:4. It is important to recognize the role of Islam as the embodiment of all the ancient hatred passed down through the ages, throughout the region, against Israel.[214] Islam tends to encourage violence against the Jewish people.[215]

The Islamic suicide bomber usually utters the chant "Allah Akbar" just before he or she blows up their intended Israeli target. This chant means Allah, their Islamic god, is greater than everything. Furthermore, remember that the predominant attitude of the Arab countries in the Middle East is to hinder the worship of Jehovah, the Old Testament God of the Jews. They generally prohibit the establishment of Jewish synagogues on Arab soil.

ONWARD WITH OBADIAH'S VISION

> If thieves had come to you, If robbers by night—Oh, how
> you will be cut off!—Would they not have stolen till they had
> enough? If grape-gatherers had come to you, Would they not
> have left *some* gleanings? Oh, how Esau shall be searched out!
> *How* his hidden treasures shall be sought after! (Obad. 1:5–6,
> NKJV; emphasis added)

Up to verse 5, Edom has been described as a confederate member
"among the nations," that would become "made small among them
(the nations)," and "greatly despised," but now in verse 5–6 Edom
"will be cut off," and "his (Esau's) hidden treasures shall be sought
after." Obadiah warns of the severest form of judgment, thieves taking everything, grape-gatherers leaving no gleanings, and even hidden
treasures sought after.

The prophet Amos tells us that there is a point whereby Edom's
punishment cannot be postponed.

> Thus says the LORD: "For three transgressions of Edom,
> and for four, I will not turn away its *punishment*, Because he
> pursued his brother [Israel] with the sword, And cast off all
> pity; *His anger tore perpetually, And he kept his wrath forever."*
> (Amos 1:11, NKJV; emphasis added)

Amos alludes to the historical hatred of the Jews by their Edomite
brothers with "His anger tore perpetually," and informs us that it
continued through the ages: "And he kept his wrath forever." From
generation to generation, an enmity toward the Jews tore at the very
core of Edomite existence. They never abandoned this feeling, which
perpetuates even today through the Edomite remnant contingency
residing within the modern-day Palestinians.

It is important to note that God does not levy punishment upon

Gentile nations randomly. He judges Edom specifically for their continual assaults against the Jews. As such, they will provoke upon themselves the Genesis 12:3 clause contained within the Abrahamic Covenant, i.e., the curse-for-curse-in-kind.

I will bless those who bless you, And *I will curse him who curses you*; And in you all the families of the Earth shall be blessed. (Gen. 12:3, NKJV; emphasis added)

The "him" that curses you has individual, national, and international applications. All who individually or collectively come against Israel beyond that point determined by God as acceptable will provoke the curse-for-curse-in-kind clause upon themselves.

There is a point whereby God used Gentile nations, such as in the Babylonian captivity, to serve out judgment against the Jews, and in these instances, those nations were "in exempt." However, the minute those nations crossed beyond the acceptable point and persecuted the Jews, they were determined to be operating "in contempt" or "in excess," and they provoked this clause upon themselves.

All the men in your confederacy Shall force you to the border; The men at peace with you Shall deceive you *and* prevail against you. *Those who eat* your bread shall lay a trap for you. No one is aware of it. (Obad. 1:7, NKJV; emphasis added)

In verse 7 we gain the recognition that Edom, made small among the nations and greatly despised, is involved in a confederate effort, which is most likely the same confederacy described in Psalm 83:5–8.[216]

For they have consulted together with one consent; They form a confederacy against You: The tents of Edom [Palestinians] and the Ishmaelites [Saudi Arabians]; Moab [Central Jorda-

nians] and the Hagrites [Egyptians]; Gebal [Northern Leba-
nese], Ammon [Northern Jordanians], and Amalek; Philistia
[Gaza Strip Hamas] with the inhabitants of Tyre [Southern
Lebanese]; Assyria [Syrians] also has joined with them; They
have helped the children of Lot. *Selah* (Psa. 83:5–8, NKJV)

These nations, supposedly having pledged a peaceful allegiance
with the Edomites in support of the Palestinians plight, actually
"force" them "to the border" (of Israel). Because the Edomites have
their minds set upon their religious invincibility "Though you ascend
as high as the eagle, And though you set your nest among the stars,"
the Palestinians become deceived. The deception encourages them
toward the border of Israel, and serves the other nations purposes to
use them as their pawns. This diabolical scheme uses the Palestinians
as insulation between Israel and the other confederate nations listed
above.

This deception predominately started in 1967 because of the Arab
defeat in the Six-Day War. At that point, the Jews expanded their borders and the Arab leaders realized they could not cut off the nation
Israel militarily. Henceforth, the Arab leaders in the region adopted
the unconventional strategies of terror and propaganda.

Terror enabled them to conduct an ongoing war against Israel,
aimed at the continued disruption of Israel's national sovereignty. Terror also gave these Arab nations the ability to conduct this dirty war
with clean hands. They found the displaced Palestinians to be great
foot soldiers and human land mines, yet the Jewish blood would not
appear as stains upon their national hands.

These nations opted to keep these displaced peoples deceptively
deployed within the Gaza Strip, West Bank, and various border lying
refugee camps. Note that all of these locations above are nearby the
border of Israel. These Palestinians now breed profusely in these bor-
der-lying communities, and from their moment of birth are taught in
textbooks to hate Israel.

With apparently clean hands, these nations go about the dirty business of promoting Palestinian propaganda within the international community. The three main issues that fuel the unrest in the Middle East are: Israel's right to exist as a sovereign nation, a Palestinian state within the borders of Israel, and the rights of the Arab-Palestinian refugees at the borders of Israel to return to Israel. What to do about Jerusalem is a byproduct of these three issues. These Arab nations refuse Israel the right to exist, they demand a state for the displaced Arabs—but only within the borders of Israel—and they demand the refugees be assimilated within the borders of Israel.

Numerous studies have shown that the Arab refugees could be easily assimilated into these bordering Arab nations, but these nations make it difficult for the refugees to become citizens. All of these issues are only issues, because these Arab nations are poised to confederate in an attempt to disturb and destroy the nation Israel.

> They have said, "Come, and let us cut them off from *being* a nation, *That the name of Israel may be remembered no more.*" (Psa. 83:4, NKJV; emphasis added)

This confederacy is rising into formation for the specific purposes referenced in Obadiah 1:1: "Arise, and let us rise up against her for battle." They confederate to destroy Israel. They encourage the Palestinians toward the borders of Israel as their front line offensive, while they themselves protect their own borders.

Is this not the case today, with the Palestinians and the many refugee camps along the borders of Israel? These Palestinians have a plight, and their so-called Arab partners have fully propagandized it to their favor. They discourage the thought that Israel has any right to exist, and encourage the thought that the Palestinians and refugees belong in Israel. They do not assimilate these peoples into their borders; rather, they promote the thought that they all belong in the land of Israel. They have encouraged the myth that Israel is the homeland of the Palestinians, whereas history suggests no such thing. The trap is that Israel has nowhere else to go and, as such, they have become a great army ready to protect the very borders at which this confederacy forces the Palestinians to remain. As quoted earlier from Obadiah 1:7: "Those who eat your bread shall lay a trap for you." No one is aware of it.

Ultimately, these nations will unite in a conventional military effort to destroy the nation Israel, but the "exceedingly great army" of Israel will decisively defeat these Arab nations.

> So I prophesied as He commanded me, and breath came into them, and they lived, and stood upon their feet, an *exceedingly great army*. (Ezek. 37:10, NKJV; emphasis added)

ONWARD WITH OBADIAH'S VISION

> "Will I not in that day," says the LORD, "Even destroy the wise *men* from Edom, And understanding from the mountains of Esau? Then your *mighty men*, O Teman, *shall be dismayed*, To the end that everyone from the mountains of Esau May be cut off by slaughter." (Obad. 1:8–9, NKJV; emphasis added)

Obadiah has previously stated the severity of the judgment in verse 5–6 to befall Edom, and in v8–9 he extends the scope even further to include the destruction of the "wise" and the "mighty men." These mighty men "shall be dismayed" because of the slaughter that will be inflicted upon them by the exceedingly great army of Israel.

> *For violence against your brother Jacob*, Shame shall cover you, And you shall be cut off forever. (Obad. 1:10, NKJV; emphasis added)

The reason for the slaughter is "For violence against your brother Jacob." As stated previously this behavior provokes upon the persecutor of the Jews the curse-for-curse-in-kind clause of the Abrahamic Covenant as prescribed in Genesis 12:3. Obadiah continues in verses 11 through 14 to outline and identify the historical crimes, whereby Esau's descendants, the Edomites committed "violence against Jacob." Their criminal rap sheet spans the scope of time from the Exodus to the present.

In the day that you stood on the other side. (Obad. 1:11a, NKJV; emphasis added)

The Exodus of the Jews via the route of Edom is referenced in verse 11. The Jews were disallowed by the Edomites to pass through the territory of Edom, as they were making their way into the Promised Land. The Edomite descendants of Esau "stood (their ground) on the other side" in opposition to the request of Moses to harmlessly pass through. This was the first serious offense they committed against the descendants of Jacob.

This was a slap in the face of the God of the Jews, Who had clearly evidenced His favoritism to the Hebrews. Jehovah, their God, had parted the Red Seas and conquered the Egyptian army single-handedly enabling the descendants of Jacob the freedom to migrate toward the Promised Land.

Now Moses sent messengers from Kadesh to the king of Edom. "Thus says your brother Israel: 'You know all the hardship that has befallen us, how our fathers went down to Egypt, and we dwelt in Egypt a long time, and the Egyptians afflicted us and our fathers. When we cried out to the LORD, He heard our voice and sent the Angel and brought us up out of Egypt; now here we are in Kadesh, a city on the edge of your border. Please let us pass through your country. We will not pass through fields or vineyards, nor will we drink water from wells; we will go along the King's Highway; we will not turn aside to the right hand or to the left until we have passed through your territory.'" Then *Edom said to him, "You shall not pass through my land,* lest I come out against you with the sword." Thus *Edom refused to give Israel passage through his territory, so Israel turned away from him.* (Num. 20:14–18, 21, NKJV; emphasis added)

In the day that strangers carried captive his forces, When foreigners entered his gates And cast lots for Jerusalem—Even you were as one of them. (Obad. 1:11b, NKJV; emphasis added)

Obadiah 1:11b is most likely depicting the siege in 845 BC by the Philistines. The Edomites at that time behaved indignantly to the Jews, much like the Philistines did. "Even you were as one of them."

But you should not have gazed on the day of your brother *In the day of his captivity,* Nor should you have rejoiced over the children of Judah *In the day of their destruction;* Nor should you have spoken proudly *In the day of distress.* (Obad. 1:12, NKJV; emphasis added)

Obadiah 1:12 testifies of the crimes committed by the Edomites during the Babylonian period. Jerusalem and the temple were destroyed, and the Jews were carted off into seventy years of Babylonian captivity. He references three events: "the day of his captivity," "day of their destruction," and "the day of distress." By ordering these episodes chronologically, Obadiah appears to identify for us the three Babylonian sieges that came against the Jewish people.

"The day of his captivity" The Babylonians, led by Nebuchadnezzar, first attacked Judah in 606 BC. This resulted in the first deportation

wave of Jews into captivity. Some royal youths, including the prophet Daniel and some of his companions were relocated into Babylon. Additionally the king and his family along with many notable and skillful Jews were likewise transported out of Judah at this time.[217]

"*The day of their destruction*": In 588 BC there was a second general deportation of Jews by Nebuchadnezzar. Many more principal Jews were moved into Babylon. The first Jewish temple was destroyed, and the Babylonians confiscated many of the holy vessels at this time.

"*The day of distress*": In 582 BC, the last deportation occurred. Many of the heads of families, their wives and children were exiled to Babylon because of this third Babylonian siege. Because of these three deportations, a sizeable Jewish community was established in Babylon.

Ample forewarning of the pending "day of" Esau's twin "brother" Jacob had been given by the prophet Jeremiah, among others. The world was put on notice that the client nation Israel would be disciplined through captivity for a period of seventy years for their idolatrous practices and overall failure to honor and obey their Mosaic Law.[218]

The Edomites "gazed on the day of your brother." The crime of the Edomites was that rather than glean from the mistake of their cousins the Jews; they "gazed" upon them at the time of their first deportation, depicting their severe disdain toward the Jewish people. First, they "gazed" then they "rejoiced" at the events of the second deportation, and lastly they "spoke proudly" at the time of the third Jewish deportation. Furthermore, history tells us at that time that they capitalized on the captivity of the Jews by further migrating into Hebron and the surrounding areas of Israel, further homesteading the Holy Land.

> You should not have entered the gate of My people In *the day of their calamity*. Indeed, you should not have gazed on their affliction In *the day of their calamity*, Nor laid *hands* on their substance In *the day of their calamity*. (Obad. 1:13; NKJV, emphasis added)

Obadiah advances the clock to the time of the Roman Empire. The phrase "day of their calamity," used in this passage three times alludes to a completely calamitous period in Jewish history. Such was the case during the occupation of the Romans in the Holy Land. First the Edomites "entered the gate," as exemplified by Antipater, a full-blooded Idumean (Edomite), who was established by Julius Caesar as the procurator over Judea in 47 BC. Then, Antipater's son, Herod the Great reigned over Israel between 37 BC and 4 BC with the blessings of the Roman Empire.

Subsequently we see that the Edomites are again accused of gazing rather than gleaning: "you should not have gazed on their affliction." They gazed during the Babylonian period, and that led to rejoicing and prideful boasting, Obadiah foretells in the Roman episode, they will likewise gaze, and then possess things of value to the Jews.

One of the things most esteemed by the Jews was their second temple and all of its priestly implements. This temple became known during the Roman era as the "Herodian Temple," named after Herod, who was not even a Jew. He was one-half Edomite, and one-half Nabatean. Herod and his court found themselves in a position to have "laid hands on their (Jewish) substance."

> You should not have stood at the crossroads To cut off those among them who escaped;
>   Nor should you have delivered up those among them who remained In the day of distress. (Obad. 1:14, NKJV)

Obadiah identifies two groups of Jews, those who attempted to escape from the Roman destruction of AD 70 and those who remained in Israel during the destruction, "In the day of distress." In so doing, he concludes his list of historical war crimes committed by the Edomites against their Jewish kindred.

In verse 1:14 he accuses the Edomites of attempting to hinder the prescribed disciplinary dispersion of the Jews out of Israel, into the nations of the world. They "stood at the crossroads to cut off those (Jews) among them who escaped." The Romans destroyed Jerusalem and the second Jewish temple in AD 70. This provoked a majority of the Jewish population to scatter amongst the nations of the world. This dispersion was in fulfillment of numerous Old Testament Bible prophecies.

The irony is that the Edomites as a population were "among them who escaped." At that time, they were identified by their Greek name, the Idumeans. Idumea was a recognized region in Southeastern Israel. The Idumeans "stood at the crossroads to cut off" those Jews attempting to flee from Roman persecution.

A study of Hebrew history between the time of AD 33 to about AD 135 evidences a period of time whereby many Jews began to exit out of Israel into the nations of the world. The Idumeans tended to present themselves more as an obstacle to, rather than a facilitator of, that migration process. Obadiah ranks that episode of Edomite/Idumean history as being comparable to the other war crimes on his lengthy list.

Lastly in Obadiah 1:14, not only did the Idumeans attempt to hinder the exodus of the Jews out of Israel, they "delivered up those among them who remained." This behavior completely evidenced their adversarial attitude against the Jewish people. It served to prove that down through the ages the ancient hatred spawned by Esau against his twin brother Jacob, continued to filter on down through to his descendants, the Edomites, and Idumeans.

The pages of history authenticate and adjudicate Obadiah's accusations. Today it is as if those very damaging pages have been reopened and are being relived through the events of the Arab-Israeli conflict. The Palestinians, who have some traces of Edomite ancestry among their ranks, continue to harbor the same ancient attitude of hatred outlined out of the annals of their history.

The atrocities of their past, combined with the catastrophes of their present seal their fate for the future! They will soon experience their ethnical demise through divine judgment. Although many suggest that the end of the Edomites came in correlation with the conclusion of Obadiah's list of war crimes, Bible prophecy defeats that presumption. The Edomites resurface on numerous pages of end time's prophecy.

Though it would have appeared as though they sealed their judgment from their actions in the past, that judgment has not been officially executed as of yet. The Judgment of the Edomites, who became called the Idumeans, and can now be best referred to as the Palestinians, will be judged in the fashion described in Ezekiel 25:14 and Obadiah 1:18.

> "I will lay My vengeance on Edom by the hand of My people Israel, that they may do in Edom according to My anger and according to My fury; and they shall know My vengeance," says the LORD GOD. (Ezek. 25:14, NKJV)

> "The house of Jacob shall be a fire, And the house of Joseph a flame; But the house of Esau *shall be* stubble; They shall kindle them and devour them, And no survivor shall *remain* of the house of Esau," For the LORD has spoken. (Obad. 1:18, NKJV)

Make no mistake: by his usage of "the house of Esau," Obadiah refers to the ancient Edomites in the Hebrew language, later labeled the Idumeans in the Greek language, who are today known as the Palestinians, which is a derivative from the Hebrew word *Pelesheth*, the Arab term *Filastin*, the Latin word *Palaestina*, and the English word *Palestine*. The Palestinian trail can be traced in part back to the ancient Philistines, and the Edomite descendants of Esau.[219]

Presently the Palestinians have picked up where the Idumean contingency of their ancestors left off. "Nor should you have delivered up those among them who remained In the day of distress." They are still delivering up their Jewish cousins to oppressive conditions. It is as if the Jews who have returned to their motherland, are still living under persecution as in the former times "In the day of distress."

ONWARD WITH OBADIAH'S VISION

> For the day of the LORD upon all the nations *is* near; As you have done, it shall be done to you; Your reprisal shall return upon your own head. (Obad. 1:15, NKJV).

The curse-for-curse-in-kind reprisal against Edom will occur before "the Day of the LORD" occurs; it occurs when "the day of the LORD upon all the nations is near." "The day of the LORD" is defined by most as either the entire seven-year period of the tribulation (i.e., Daniels seventieth-week), or only the second half of that period, spanning 3.5 years.

> For as you drank on My holy mountain, *So* shall all the nations drink continually; Yes, they shall *drink*, and *swallow*, And they shall *be as though they had never been.* (Obad. 1:16, NKJV; emphasis added)

To "drink," "swallow," and "be as though they had never been," finds association with biblical illustrations of judgment. The picture is that of a people being forcibly handed a cup containing a poisonous content. God, insuring that the intended recipients will not possess the antidote, personally conjures up this highly toxic concoction. The affected population group has done something that has greatly disturbed God, and as such has provoked upon them a divine judgment. Pertinent examples to this study can be found in Jeremiah 25:17–26, and Jeremiah 49:12.

The judgment to befall Edom will serve as a precursor to the judgment within "the day of the LORD upon all the nations." Zephaniah

2 also makes clear that this judgment against Edom, which will also extend further into the other confederate member nations, is to serve as an example to the other nations, but more importantly it is a call to the "meek of the Earth" to get right before "the day of the LORD" occurs.

> Gather yourselves together, yes, gather together, O undesirable nation [Israel today in unbelief, gathering in the land], Before the decree is issued, *Or* the day passes like chaff, Before the LORD'S fierce anger comes upon you, Before the day of the LORD'S anger comes upon you! Seek the LORD, all you *meek of the Earth*, Who have upheld His justice. Seek righteousness, seek humility. It may be that you will be hidden In the day of the LORD'S anger. (Zeph. 2:1–3, NKJV, emphasis added)

Zephaniah 2 goes on to describe the conditions subsequent to the Israeli Conquest of the Psalm 83 confederacy. For more information on the details of Zephaniah 2, refer to the *Call to Caution* chapter contained within this book.

ONWARD WITH OBADIAH'S VISION

> But on Mount Zion there shall be deliverance, And there shall be holiness; The house of Jacob shall possess their possessions. (Obad. 1:17, NKJV)

Though we are told in verse 16, that the Psalm 83 confederate nations first, and then the remaining nations at large in the world "shall be as though they had never been," this will not be the case on Mount Zion! "On Mount Zion there shall be deliverance," and holiness.

> "The house of Jacob shall be a fire, And the house of Joseph a flame; But the house of Esau *shall be* stubble; They shall

kindle them and devour them, And no survivor shall *remain* of the house of Esau," For the LORD has spoken. (Obad. 1:18, NKJV)

Obadiah encapsulates the theme scattered throughout his vision; I will bring you Palestinians down (v4), you will be cut off (v5), your treasures searched out (v6), a trap for you (v7), everyone will be cut off by slaughter (v9,) shame shall cover you (v10), the forced drinking from the cup of judgment (v16). Obadiah in v18 determines the defeat of Esau's descendants residing within the modern-day Palestinians will be at the hands of Israel's exceedingly great army. The use of stubble, which when lit burns entirely, evidences the theme earlier presented of the severity of this judgment against Edom.

The South shall possess the mountains of Esau, And the Lowland shall possess Philistia. They shall possess the fields of Ephraim And the fields of Samaria. Benjamin *shall possess* Gilead And the captives of this host of the children of Israel *Shall possess the land* of the Canaanites As far as Zarephath. The captives of Jerusalem who are in Sepharad Shall possess the cities of the South. (Obad. 1:19–20, NKJV; emphasis added)

After reading this chapter, please feel free to read ahead to the *The Future Maps of Isralestine* chapter contained within this book. Greater detail into the profound prophesies of Obadiah 1:19–20 can be found within this chapter. In essence, Obadiah 1:19–20 implies that as a direct result of the Jewish conquest over the Palestinians alluded to in Obadiah 1:18, Israel will be significantly increased in both size and prosperity. The tiny Israel as we recognize it today will soon encompass a major portion of the Middle East, and become one of the wealthiest nations in the world.

Then saviors [*yasha*] shall come to Mount Zion To judge the mountains of Esau, And the kingdom shall be the LORD'S. (Obad. 1:21, NKJV)

The Hebrew word *yasha* can mean deliverers, victors, avengers, or saviors. What Obadiah appears to be stating in verse 21a is that from Mount Zion, Jewish sovereignty will be exercised over the conquered territory of Edom. The phrase "the kingdom shall be the LORD'S" in v21b is a probable reference to the sovereignty over the region by the Jews, as they will be known at that future point once again as "My people Israel." Ezekiel 25:14 addresses this conquest and refers to the Jews again as "My people Israel."

"I will lay My vengeance on Edom [the Palestinians] by the hand of *My people Israel,* that they may do in Edom according to My anger and according to My fury; and they shall know My vengeance," says the LORD GOD. (Ezek. 25:14, NKJV; emphasis added)

PSALM 83
The Arab Confederacy

This chapter takes a close look at Psalm 83 and its prophetic relevancy to the end-times. It was written by Asaph, a Levite musician, and prophet appointed by King David to serve in the tabernacle until the first Jewish temple was completed.[220] Asaph wrote this Psalm when the nation of Israel was experiencing the blessings of the Abrahamic Covenant in an unprecedented manner; they were a people of prominence entering a period of prosperity and residing in their own land under the leadership of their God-ordained king David.

As a people, their focus was on the growth of the nation, and building God, His first house of worship on Earth, i.e., the Jewish Temple, but unexpectedly Asaph introduces a futuristic threat to the Covenant God made with their patriarchs Abraham, Isaac, and Jacob—a warning so severe that the survival of the thriving nation could be in question.

For behold, *Your enemies* make a tumult; And *those who hate You* have lifted up their head. They have taken crafty counsel against Your people, And consulted together against Your sheltered ones. They have said, "Come, and let us cut them off from *being* a nation, That the name of Israel may be remembered no more." For they have consulted together with one consent; They form a confederacy against You: The tents of Edom [Southern Jordan] and the Ishmaelites [Saudi Arabia]; Moab [Central Jordan] and the Hagrites [Egypt]; Gebal [Northern Lebanon], Ammon [Northern Jordan], and Amalek [Sinai]; Philistia [Gaza Strip] with the inhabitants of Tyre [Southern Lebanon]; Assyria [Syria] also has joined with them; They have helped the children of Lot [Moab and Ammon above]. (Psa. 83:2–8, NKJV; emphasis added)

In his Psalm, Asaph identifies two groups: "Your enemies," and "those who hate You." Then in verses 6–8, he specifies the populations that fall into either of these two categories, both of which possess adversarial attitudes against Jehovah, the God of the Jews. Geographically, these peoples throughout time have most closely bordered the nation of Israel. Furthermore, they are the ones who have historically contested the Jewish claims of there being only one God, and they being His chosen people.

Asaph would not necessarily have known the timing destined for the final fulfillment of this prophecy, and to date this event is yet pending, however he should have been well aware of the disposition of hatred that already plagued the region. Long before his time the confederate members listed above, had become infected by the enmity established by Hagar, between herself and Sarah, by Ishmael between himself and Isaac, by Esau between himself and Jacob, and by the children of Lot (Moab and Ammon) between themselves and the children of Israel.

The individuals classified within the group of "those who hate You" are Hagar representing the "Hagarenes," Ishmael father of the "Ishmaelites," Esau who is also called "Edom,"[221] "Moab," and "Ammon" who are the "children of Lot." These five infamous characters are enlisted members of the ten-member confederacy that will ultimately seek to destroy the Jewish nation of Israel. These ancestors all coveted the contents of the Abrahamic Covenant. They felt in some way cheated or in the case of "Moab," and "Ammon" threatened by the covenant, and As such, they outsourced through their descendants that followed a hatred of the Jews.[222]

This adversarial attitude spread rapidly throughout the entire Middle East region and overtook the populations residing in "Gebal, Amalek, Philistia, Tyre, and Assyria." These remaining five confederate members comprise the "Your enemies" group. Unlike Hagar, Ishmael, Esau, Moab, and Ammon of the "those who hate You" group, the "Your enemies" group, has only an indirect association to the contents of the Abrahamic Covenant. Apart from Amalek, who was a distant great-great-grandson[223] of Abraham, they were not the near relatives of Abraham as were the "those who hate You" group, however the contents of the Abrahamic Covenant threatened their own territorial claims as well.

In Genesis 15:18, we are told that all of the land between the river of Egypt, and the river Euphrates, was to be "Grant Deeded" to the Jewish heirs of the Abrahamic Covenant. This prescription put the generally Arab populations within those confines on official notice that they were trespassing on Jewish land, and would need to cooperate with Jewish sovereignty over the region, or else pay the consequences.

As you can imagine, these affected Arab populations considered the ancient hatred attitude, which had been well established within the "those who hate You" group, worthy of adopting for their own territorial purposes. As such, the "Your enemies" group became formed. Throughout history, each individual member within these two groups evidenced their enmity in one way or another toward the Jewish people. Collectively these two groups embraced a common concern over the contents of the Jewish Covenant.

STRIKING SIMILARITIES

Since this prophecy appears destined for fulfillment in the near future, some striking similarities for today should be extrapolated from the historical facts just described. As it was during Asaph's time, the Jewish people are again experiencing a time of blessings. Today they are thriving in their homeland, under the leadership of a king, poised to experience a period of prosperity. Once again, they draft blueprints for the building of a Jewish Temple for Jehovah their God. Lastly, the descendants of the same two groups comprised of "those who hate You" and "Your enemies" are enjoined in an adversarial attitude antagonistic against the restoration of the nation Israel.

As it was in Asaph's time, the prosperity of the nation Israel, should serve to remind the neighboring nations of the contents of the Abrahamic Covenant. These Arab nations are settled on soil promised to Abraham and his descendants, the Jews. Rather than subscribing to the positive side of the Genesis 12:3 clause of the Abrahamic Covenant, whereby all those peoples who would bless the Jews, would in return receive blessings of like kind, they align themselves on the reverse side of the same clause. In contrast, curses are promised to those who oppress and oppose the Jewish people.

Whether the modern-day descendants of these two angered groups consider the consequences of their actions in relationship to the contents of the ancient Abrahamic Covenant or not, their act of confederating against Israel on any level operates under the "threat" of the covenant, rather than the "trust" of the covenant. The lesson to this Jewish generation is the same as it was for Asaph's generation. They are not to forget that Jewish prosperity provokes their neighbors into a precarious position. Either these neighbors can support the process and be accordingly blessed, or they can resist the process and become collectively defiant.

Asaph's prophecy tells us that Israel's Arab neighbors will choose the latter, they will as Asaph declares above in Psalm 83:3–5, consult together with one consent, take crafty counsel against the Jews, formulate into a confederacy and say: "Come, and let us cut them off from being a nation, That the name of Israel may be remembered no more."

What a powerful mandate these two distraught groups formulate "Israel, remembered no more." The ramifications of this war effort are staggering, considering that then and now numerous promises and prophecies rely upon the eternal existence of the nation Israel and the Jewish descendants of Abraham. For these ten confederate members to believe that they can successfully nullify the final fulfillment of the yet unfulfilled promises and prophecies centered upon the Jews and Israel requires a powerful faith.

Interestingly today, all of these ten confederate members are united under one umbrella of faith known as Islam. Apparently, they believe that their god Allah has the ability to void out the contents contained within the Abrahamic Covenant specifically, and the Bible generally. This unity of faith did not exist during the time of Asaph, back then these various populations worshipped their own different deities. Milcom, Chemosh, Asherah, Baal, and many more gods were worshipped, in contrast to the Jewish God Jehovah.

The teachings of their prophet Mohammed cleverly convinced these peoples to abandon their polytheistic practices, in order to embrace his religious package. Islam presents itself as a monotheistic religion, but scholars still debate this premise. Regardless, the fact is that these ten populations prophesied to attempt the future genocide of the Jews are presently all predominately Islamic.

PSALM 83—A PETITION ONLY

Psalm 83 is a prophecy formatted by Asaph into a petition only, it is void of any resolution content, and yet due to the severity of the prophecy it demands a reaction from God. In order to discover the divine response one is required to look elsewhere into the scriptures, as guided by clues contained within Asaph's Psalm 83 petition.

What is of utmost importance to understand is that this prophecy, though it threatens the survival of the Jewish people, is primarily an assault against the character of the covenant making God of Abraham, Isaac, Jacob, and Jesus Christ! This first clue is given in the very beginning passages of the Psalm.

Do not keep silent, O God! Do not hold Your peace, And do not be still, O God!

For behold, Your enemies make a tumult; And those who hate You have lifted up theirhead. (Psa. 83:1–2, NKJV)

We can arrive at the understanding that this is an assault targeted at God, in that if the client nation is exterminated and the name Israel remembered no more, then their covenant-making God, Jehovah, is not a covenant-keeping God, and is therefore nothing more than a liar. The problem therein lies in the fact that if the God of the Jews is a liar, who breaks His promises, then so is the God of the Christians, because Jesus Christ came as the "Seed" of Abraham,[224] in fulfillment of the unconditional covenant God made with Abraham, Isaac, and Jacob. Therefore, Salvation as taught in Christianity, which is by faith in Christ, would likewise be un-assured. [225]

Asaph used the pronouns "Your," and "You," evidencing that he recognized this was an assault against God personally: "Your enemies," "those who hate "You," "counsel against Your people," "against "Your sheltered ones," "they form a covenant against You!" Asaph appears cognizant of the inference; that if the Jews were exterminated, their God Jehovah was a failure, and a liar. Several centuries after Asaph's time, the prophet Jeremiah declared the following:

Thus says the LORD, Who gives the sun for a light by day, The ordinances of the moon and the stars for a light by night, Who disturbs the sea, And its waves roar (The LORD of hosts *is* His name): "If those ordinances depart From before Me, says the LORD, Then the seed of Israel shall also cease From being a nation before Me forever." Thus says the LORD: "If heaven above can be measured, And the foundations of the Earth searched out beneath, I will also cast off all the seed of Israel For all that they have done, says the LORD. (Jer. 31:35–37 NKJV)

Cemented in the Abrahamic Covenant, is the survival of the Jewish people. The other important subsequent covenants, which were created to compliment this Covenant are the Promised Land, (Land Covenant), the Eternal Throne, upon which Jesus Christ will sit as King (Davidic Covenant), and the Eternal Relationship, whereby the Spirit of God indwells the heart of man, both Jew and Gentile, (New Covenant). All of these other facets, the "Land," "Throne," "King," and "Relationship" are based upon the survival of the Jewish people.

Therefore, in conclusion any offensive against God originating upon the Earth is best directed at His promises made through the Abrahamic Covenant. This Covenant was designed to be inclusive of the entirety of God's foreign policy regarding all of humanity. If the Covenant could be voided out on Earth, then the heavens would no longer be able to declare justifiably God's glory[226]. Asaph thus petitions God to uphold His glorified position in the heavens, by protecting his people on Earth.

THE ANGELIC CONFLICT

Hence, when Asaph discovered prophetically the pending confederate attack against the nation Israel, aimed at the genocide of the Jews, he probably realized that this was not an event confined to the reaches of Earth, rather it extended well into the heavens, from which the angelic conflict is outsourced. He therefore acknowledges that it is God's reputation at stake. Any attack against the descendants of Jacob (Israel) is an attack at God's head, as Jacob is the "Apple of God's eye."[227]

Thus concealed within the heart of this pending confederate effort comprised of the Arab states most closely bordering the nation Israel, aimed at the extermination of the Jews, is the scheming of Satan. He intends to pin Arabs against Jews in an attempt to spear God in the "Apple of His eye." Let us not forget a few important powerful characteristics about this enemy of God as pointed out in the scriptures:

1. Satan is extremely cunning in this world, or in other words, powerfully influential over the direction of world affairs. (Gen. 3:1a)

2. The entire world lies under his sway, or persuasiveness. (1 John 5:19)

3. The Devil is a liar and a murderer. (John 8:44)

4. Satan presently possesses the ability to travel between the geographies of heaven and Earth, and upon the Earth is able to travel the entire expanse of it. (Job 1:6)

5. Satan, also known as Lucifer, is a fallen angel who has said in his heart that he seeks to be like the Most High God Jehovah. (Isa. 14:12–14)

So then, can we be clear upon the fact from which we derive our preclusions? Is not the prophecy of Psalm 83, yet pending, an attack outsourced by Satan, who desires to be like the "Most High," aimed at the character of God? Though it will manifest someday as a war in the Middle East between the Arab and Jewish respective kingdoms, it has far greater reaches. Jeremiah prophesied of this pending event that: The Earth shakes at the noise of their fall; At the cry its noise is heard at the Red Sea (Jer. 49:21, NKJV). Yet even further, it reaches into the heavenly realm, whereby the righteous character of God is placed on trial by the angelic conflict. For us Christians we are to fear not because we know the ultimate outcome of the angelic conflict.

War will break out in heaven in the future between Michael the archangel and his good angels against Satan and his fallen angels. Michael's team will prevail, and Satan and his troops will finally be cast out of heaven. Remember that it is Michael the archangel, whose ministry incorporates the preservation of the Jewish people.[228]

Satan will shortly thereafter be imprisoned for the period of 1000 years, which appears to coincide with the timing of the Messianic Kingdom. Ultimately, Satan ends up in the "Lake of Fire," whereby he will be tormented day and night forever and ever.[229]

ADVANCING THE CLOCK

Having prefaced the scope, roots, and motivation of the prophecy, let us advance the clock forward in time, from Asaph to the present. In so doing we skip over centuries of Middle East history, but none of which can be identified as the final fulfillment of the Psalm 83 prophecy.

The stage was set during the worldwide dispersion of the Jewish people out of their homeland Israel, between AD 70 and AD 1948 for Satan to make sinister preparations for their prophesied return. Satan realized that the restoration of the nation Israel would mean the return of the Jews into the region.[230] He also understood that this event would occur in the latter days, meaning that the time of his free passage between heaven and Earth would soon then after be coming to an abrupt end.[231]

What could he possibly contrive to insure that upon the return of the Jew into their Promised Land, they would meet with the most hostile welcoming committee? Indeed, such a hostile committee was in place at the time of their return. It was coincidentally, a committee comprised of several of the members listed in the Psalm 83 confederacy. Immediately upon their return in AD 1948 the nations of Egypt, Jordan, Syria, Lebanon, Iraq, as well as Palestinian guerillas, engaged them in a war conflict.[232] Welcome home bullets and bombs replaced the well-deserved banners and balloons.

More of the same aggression followed in the Six-Day War, an armed conflict in June 1967 between Israel and the Arab states of Egypt, Jordan, and Syria. In six days, Israel conquered the Sinai Peninsula, Gaza Strip, West Bank, and Golan Heights.[233] Then came the War of October 1973 between Israel and the Arab countries of Egypt and Syria. Egypt and Syria initiated the conflict to regain territories that Israel had occupied since the Six-Day War of 1967. Although both sides suffered heavy losses during the 1973 war, Israel retained control of the territories.[234]

How inconsiderate! How inhumane! How could these nations attack a people who had been dispersed out of their homeland for centuries, and ultimately reduced to the lowest of refugee conditions because of the Holocaust? What we see, is that the longstanding hatred of the Jews by the Arabs, did not disintegrate during the centuries of worldwide Jewish dispersion rather it was kept alive and well. It was formatted into a unified force just lying in wait, to be easily provoked by the return of the Jew into the Promised Land.

Satan, who was well aware of God's prophetic program, which strongly referenced the restoration of the nation Israel as the Jewish homeland, took the well-established hatred plaguing the region, and packaged it up into an instrument formed to prevent the successful return of the Jews into their Promised Land.

ISLAM

The religion of Islam originated in the Middle East during that window period of time when the Jews were dispersed out of Israel and into the nations of the world. Muhammad, who lived between 570 and AD 632, founded Islam.[235] His new religion was cleverly designed to convert the worship of the peoples in the region from their various gods, into the worship of one god, his god, whom he labeled as Allah. An excerpt out of Encyclopedia Encarta, helps to give a basic understanding of this point.

> Around the year AD 570 Muhammad, the founding prophet of Islam, was born in Mecca, at the time the central city of the Arabian Peninsula. Some 40 years later Muhammad started preaching a new religion, Islam, which constituted a marked break from existing moral and social codes in Arabia. The new religion of Islam taught that there was one God, and that Muhammad was the last in a series of prophets and messengers. Through his messengers, God had sent various codes, or

systems of laws for living, culminating in the Qur'an (Koran), the holy book of Islam. These messengers were mortal men, and they included among many others Moses, the Hebrew prophet and lawgiver, and Jesus, whom Christians believe to be the son of God rather than a prophet.[236]

"Islam, which constituted a marked break from existing moral and social codes in Arabia." Indeed, Islam presented "a marked break" from the historical worship practices in Arabia, and the entire Middle East for that matter. For centuries, the region worshipped Jehovah, Milcom, Chemosh, Baal, Asherah, Dagon, Molech, and others. Scholars estimate that as many as 360 different gods had been worshipped in the region throughout the time leading up to the arrival of Muhammad.

He declared that he was the last prophet, and his supposed divine message, was to invite all the gods to submit to his god, Allah. This invitation was not restricted to the prevalent polytheistic Arab practices present at that time, but also reached out to the monotheistic religions of Judaism, and Christianity. Of course history informs us that the Jews and Christians did not buy into his propaganda at that time, however the predominant non-Jewish, and non-Christian Arab population in the region did.

"Within two centuries after its rise in the seventh century, Islam spread from its original home in Arabia into Syria, Egypt, North Africa, and Spain to the west, and into Persia, India, and, by the end of the tenth century, beyond to the east. In the following centuries, Islam also spread into Anatolia and the Balkans to the north, and sub-Saharan Africa to the south. The Muslim community comprises about 1 billion followers on all five continents."[237]

What Satan attempted to do through Muhammad, was to incorporate all religions into one. If this plan succeeded it would enable him to dismantle Judaism and Christianity through conversion, or more importantly if Jews and Christians did not convert, it enabled him to ostracize them for their failure to convert. The quote below out of the Koran (Quran) is an example of what Islam truly teaches about Jews and Christians.[238]

> O you who believe [Muslims]! *do not take the Jews* and the Christians for friends; they are friends of each other; and whoever amongst you takes them for a friend, then surely he is one of them; surely Allah does not guide the unjust people.[239] (Surah 5:51, Shakir; emphasis added)

As of May 14, 1948, the predominant Jewish population in the world did not convert into Islam and, as such, they entered back into the Promised Land as non-Muslims. They were simply the Jews, who had been hated in the region by the Arab ancestors from time immemorial.[240] They were that ethnic group that Hitler was unable to exterminate successfully. In the eyes of the Arab-Muslim populations in the region they were coming back to dispossess the Arabs of the real estate they had swallowed up during the centuries of Jewish dispersion into the nations of the world.

To date the Jews still request favor from most of the surrounding Arab nations, for the mere right to exist in the nation Israel as their homeland. This demonstrates that the underlying dominant Arab attitude is, as Asaph prophesied, "Come, and let us cut them off from being a nation, That the name of Israel may be remembered no more."[241]

The world at large is tired of the Middle East entanglement, and continues to forward political solutions aimed at resolving the conflict, however there is very little real estate left in Israel, for the world to pressure the Jews to forfeit into Arab hands.[242] These political attempts also play well into Satan's plan, which is to cut the Jews off from being a nation.

SUMMARY

In summary, Satan schemed up Islam forwarded through the man Muhammad, during the period of the worldwide Jewish dispersion, in an attempt to ignite the longstanding hatred of the Jews, by the Arabs, and unite them in common cause to oppose the return of the Jew back into the Promised Land. The devils ultimate goal is to cut the nation Israel off, that the name Israel will be remembered no more. If this can be done, and every Jew destroyed, then the unconditional covenant that their God made with their patriarch Abraham becomes rendered void and inoperative. If this covenant can be permanently disrupted as such, then God its Maker, is indeed a liar!

Remember that the genocide of the Jews is the campaign of Satan. If he can exterminate every last Jew, he can discredit God, before his angelic piers, and fulfill his desire to exalt his throne above the stars of God, and be like the most high. As quoted earlier in this chapter, Satan is cunning, a murderer, and the whole world presently lies under his sway.

ISLAMIC ARABS

The Psalm 83 confederates have several things in common, they are predominately of Arab descent, they all reign from Muslim dominated countries, they all generally border the modern-day nation of Israel, and they primarily hail from ancestors that were the notorious historical enemies of Israel. Could there be better candidates for Satan to fashion as a first-line offensive against the returning Jews?

I apologize if this material is offensive to some, but scripture tells us, which is also the theme of this book, that the exceedingly great army of Israel will mightily defeat these Islamic Arabs or their Psalm 83 confederate attempt. It is not the intent of this author to upset Islamic Arabs, rather to enlighten them of the pending prophetic events relating to them. Their lives and the lives of their future generation are in jeopardy if they subscribe to the Psalm 83 confederate effort.

By faithfully adhering to the principles of Islam, they appear to have patterned their lives contrary to the true content of the Abrahamic Covenant. It is through this covenant, which God exercises his entire foreign policy toward all humankind. God fully intends at the time of the Psalm 83 confederate effort finally to dispose of the adversarial attitude established in ancient times by their ancestors, Hagar, Ishmael, Esau, Moab, and Ammon. These attitudes infected the region and the other localized enemies of Israel throughout time embraced them.[243]

THE STAGE IS SET FOR THE SHOWDOWN

Psalm 83 required the existence of the nation Israel, in order that the nation could be cut off, and the name Israel be remembered no more. Today this requirement is met. It also required that these Arab nations find common cause in order to unite in a confederate effort to exterminate the Jews. If there is ever a Jew on Earth, there is the potential of a nation Israel to be his or her homeland. Therefore, in order to achieve their goal, "that the name Israel be remembered no more," the Arab confederates must exterminate the Jews. They are presently united in such a common cause, under the umbrella of Islam.

It is interesting that the terrorist organizations confronting the Jewish people today come from the very nations listed in Psalm 83, some examples being the Hezbollah from Lebanon (primarily sponsored by Iran and Syria), and Hamas from the Gaza Strip, the Philistia of old. [244] Al-Qaida, though they hail from Afghanistan, their leader Bin Laden is from Saudi Arabia, the nation predominately formed out of Ishmael. If you study the origin of many of the numerous terrorist groups, they have arisen out of Egypt, Saudi Arabia, Jordan, Syria, Lebanon, the Palestinian territories of the Gaza Strip, and the West Bank. All of these nations are members of the Psalm 83 confederate effort. This evidences their unity of cause, which is to disrupt the further establishment of the nation Israel. Ultimately, this random terrorism will give way to the concerted confederate attack described by Asaph in Psalm 83.

Terrorism as demonstrated in the Middle East is nothing more than the unconventional method of warfare that these above nations adopted and collectively embraced when their conventional methods failed in 1948, 1956, 1967, and 1973. These Arab nations realized that they lacked the military capability at the time to destroy Israel, but they possessed the radical Islamic constituency sufficient to disrupt the final establishment of the nation Israel, i.e., the terrorist population. Each terrorist group grew as they gained sponsorships from these Arab nations. The greater the act of terror, the stronger the support for the sponsoring nation.

Each hell-bent attack composed of wars or acts of state-sponsored terror by these Arab nations against Israel has ultimately served to create an exceedingly great army within the Jewish state. This army was foretold to come in Ezekiel 37:10. There will be a localized face-off between the Jewish Kingdom, represented by Israel, and the Arab Kingdom, represented by the ten-member confederacy, in fulfillment of a Bible prophecy.

> And you will hear of wars and rumors of wars. See that you are not troubled; for all *these things* must come to pass, but the end is not yet. For nation will rise against nation, and *kingdom against kingdom.* And there will be famines, pestilences, and Earthquakes in various places. All these *are* the beginning of sorrows. (Matt. 24:6–7, NKJV; emphasis added)

Nation rose against nation in the World War I and World War II. Subsequent to these wars, the nation of Israel was restored as the Jewish homeland on May 14, 1948. Whereas "nation will rise against nation" referred to war on the broader international scale, "kingdom against kingdom" refers to war on a more localized regional level.[245]

More specifically, what Christ was addressing contextually was prophecy regarding the Jewish people. He continued to prophesy in the next breath:

Then they will deliver you up to tribulation and kill you, and you will be hated by all nations for My name's sake. (Matt. 24:9, NKJV)

What Christ was alluding to was the prophetic future of the Jewish people, first there would be world wars, then a Middle East war, and then the oppressive conditions of the seven-year Tribulation Period. World wars would affect the Jews, in that they were at the time a scattered people residing within those very nations warring against one another. The Middle East war would be more specific in relationship to the Jews, in that they would be restored in their homeland Israel and through time develop an "exceedingly great army," and in that condition would come under assault by the confederacy representing the "Arab kingdom" listed in Psalm 83:6–8. Lastly, the Tribulation Period would be a final attempt at the genocide of the Jewish people by the Antichrist and his armies.[246]

The kingdom-against-kingdom prophecy appears to be broader in scope than just the Arab-Israeli conflict. It has also manifested itself in modern history through numerous other regional disputes, such as North and South Viet Nam, North and South Korea, Bosnia, the Sudan, Russia against Afghanistan, Iran vs. Iraq, the breakaway republics of the former Soviet Union, Georgia and Chechnya, and the list goes on.

THE MOTIVE

In Psalm 83:9–11, Asaph petitions God to format His divine response against the Arab confederacy in the manner of historical precedent.

Deal with them as *with* Midian, As *with* Sisera, As *with* Jabin at the Brook Kishon, Who perished at En Dor, *Who* became *as* refuse on the Earth. Make their nobles like Oreb and like Zeeb, Yes, all their princes like Zebah and Zalmunna. (Psa. 83:9–11, NKJV)

All of these instances above represented historical attempts by various enemies of Israel to take for themselves the pastures of God for a possession. In each instance, God had a hand in putting the effort to an end. By requesting God to respond in a similar fashion, he identifies for us the underlying motive of the Psalm 83 confederacy.

Who said, "*Let us take for ourselves The pastures of God for a possession.*" (Psa. 83:12, NKJV; emphasis added)

These Arab confederates desire to take possession of the Promised Land, i.e., the "pastures of God" for themselves. In essence, they covet the land content contained within the Abrahamic Covenant. They come together and formulate a covenant of their own, which for our purposes we will call The Arabic Covenant.

For they have consulted together with one consent; *Against thee* do they make a [Arabic] *covenant* [*berith*]. (Psa. 83:5, ASV; emphasis added)

Asaph tells of a time to come in his Psalm, whereby the majority of Arabs will make a covenant against God. The Hebrew word is *berith* and we can translate it as "league."[247] These particular Psalm 83:6–8 nations will formulate an Arab League of sorts, which mutually agrees upon the destruction of the nation Israel. In addition, the term *berith* is used in similar covenant context in Genesis Chapter 15:

In that day Jehovah made a covenant [*berith*] with Abram, saying, Unto thy seed have I given this land, from the river of Egypt unto the great river, the river Euphrates. (Gen. 15:18, NKJV)

In an apparent attempt to avoid the ancient and still existing *berith* covenant, the Abrahamic Covenant, these enemies assembled in an Arab League, form a covenant of their own. They do not intend to amend or supplement the land provision within the Abrahamic Covenant, nor do they seek only to supersede the current covenant operating successfully in the region; rather, by destroying the Jews and erasing the name of Israel forever, they seek to eradicate the entire covenant itself.

Interestingly, the nations aligned fall for the most part within the scope of the land of the covenant God made with Abraham. Apparently, deeply and religiously rooted within the minds of these confederating covenant-making Arabs, is the belief that it is in the best interest of their present real estate holdings to extinguish the Jews. In essence, whether they realize it or not, their end intention is the expiration of the Abrahamic Covenant.

Thus, Asaph is correct in suggesting in the beginning of his Psalm, that these conspirators are the enemies of God, formulator of the eternal Abrahamic Covenant. In essence, these nations want to extinguish the Jews, take over their territory, erase the name of Israel forever, and thus re-scramble the letters of the Abrahamic Covenant in their favor to create "The Arabic Covenant."

THE PALESTINIAN CONFEDERACY

> All the men in your confederacy Shall force you to the border;
> The men at peace with you Shall deceive you
> *and* prevail against you. *Those who eat* your bread shall
> lay a trap for you. No one is aware of it.
>
> —OBAD. 1:7, NKJV; EMPHASIS ADDED

The prerequisite reading to this study is Psalm 83, whereby Asaph foretells the formation of an Arab confederacy primarily comprised of Palestinians, Syrians, Saudi Arabians, Egyptians, Lebanese, and Jordanians. There are actually ten population groups listed by their historical names in the Psalm 83:6–8 confederacy, but in the final analysis their modern-day equivalent nations are those listed above. This confederacy, which wishes the final destruction of the modern-day Jewish State of Israel, is the topic of this study. The premise for interpretation is that the Psalm 83 confederacy is the same as the confederacy contained in Obadiah 1:7.

Furthermore, as the *Who-domites?* chapter previously pointed out, the Palestinians of today have a contingency of Edomites amalgamated within their overall composite population. Thus, when this study refers to Esau, his descendants, or the Edomites, it finds its closest association with their modern-day equivalents, the Palestinians.

All the men in your confederacy. The whole (*kol*), or entirety of the ten-member confederacy is of the same conspired mindset.[248] The other nine members agree with Esau, the lead member of the confederacy, *"your confederacy."* They are all of common cause, and this cause drives or forces Esau's descendant Edomites to a border or boundary.

Shall force you to the border. The mutual consensus amongst the confederacy is that the Palestinians must serve in an infantry capacity, and that they are to be stationed at some frontline border lying area. Since this confederacy has mandated the destruction of the nation Israel as per Psalm 83:4, this suggests the strategic area of their deployment to be the borders surrounding the reforming nation of Israel.

The men at peace with you. The men, "all the men," each one, are at peace (*shalom*) with the Palestinians.[249] This is technically Esau's confederacy, and the men who conspire with him pledge their allegiance to his cause. However, the prerequisite for achieving such peace is that Esau, as lead member, holds down the frontline at the borders of Israel. The Palestinians are to entrench themselves in the Isralestine territories that most closely surround Israel.[250]

Shall deceive you and prevail against you. Inherent in the conditional peace and support that the Palestinians receive from "all" of the Arab men in alliance with them is their obligation to occupy these Isralestine territories. In essence, they are not encouraged to assimilate themselves as citizens within the outer lying confederate member territories. This would be unsound strategic deployment of the Palestinians. In fact, most of these member nations make it very restrictive for Palestinians to become naturalized citizens within their respective nations.

They are to maintain their own distinct ethnic identity. Though many of them have ancestral roots from among the surrounding confederate Arab nations, they are discouraged from calling themselves Syrians, Egyptians, Saudi's, etc. We call them the Palestinians, in spite of the fact that up until 1948 no such ethnic label ever existed. Until that time, the world knew them as the Arabs of the grossly undefined territory of Palestine. Though they are currently predominately a population of refugees,[251] mutual confederate consensus leads them to believe that they deserve their own state and citizenry therein. This propaganda promoted by the Arab community has become the successful deception of "all" the men of Esau's confederacy.

The prevalent belief among all the nations listed in Psalm 83:6–8 is that the Palestinians are a distinct people, deserved of their own state. Their belief is that all of Israel, including the Gaza Strip, and the West Bank, is to become earmarked territory for the drafting of another Arab State in the Middle East, a Palestinian State, called Palestine. This goal discourages the successful establishment of an Isralestine scenario, whereby Israel exists cooperatively in the region, with the Palestinians specifically and the Arabs generally. This is the reason for the confederate call to eradicate the nation of Israel as the Jewish State:

> They [all the men in Esau's confederacy] have said, "Come, and let us cut them [the Jewish State] off from *being* a nation, That the name of Israel, [and any Isralestine inklings] may be remembered no more." (Psa. 83:4, NKJV; emphasis added)

The Arab nations who participate alongside the Palestinians in this momentous quest leave the Palestinians little choice but to fight for their own Palestinian statehood. The Palestinian inability as a displaced population group to assimilate adequately into the outer-lying Arab nations leaves them no option but to remain in a refugee status indefinitely. Thus, "all the men" of the Palestinians confederacy have "deceived" them, the Palestinians, and "forced them to the border" of Israel, and in so doing have "prevailed against" them.

Those who eat your bread: All the men of Esau's confederacy are eating Esau's bread in contrast to their own. Again, we see Obadiah use the pronoun "your" in this passage. It is your, Esau's, confederacy, and your, Esau's, bread. Esau is the one who invites all the others to his table to deliberate over his Palestinian plight. They break Esau's bread and agree with him, that Israel must perish as the resolution to the Palestinian problem. Esau does not request these men to open their national borders to his descendant people; rather he beckons their assistance to destroy the descendants of his twin brother Jacob. In essence, the Palestinians request support to destroy the Jewish State, and replace it with a Palestinian State.

The symbolism of these Arab nations eating bread together finds association with a common confederate cause. Deuteronomy 8:3, Matthew 4:4, and Luke 4:4 declare that man does not live by bread alone, but by every word that proceeds out of the mouth of God. It is possible that the prophet Obadiah alludes to the eating of bread in this passage as a spiritual thread that binds these Arabs together religiously. All of the members of Esau's confederacy are predominately Islamic.

They digest Esau's baked bread possibly referring to their ideology that it is the will of their god Allah that they form an allegiance with the Palestinians to destroy the Jews. Islam does not favor the existence of the contrasting religion of Judaism, especially in their Middle East neighborhood. The Jewish State of Israel has its religious roots in Judaism, and this is generally problematic for their Arab Muslim neighbors. The confederacy of Esau is motivated to destroy Judaism, and promote Islam, throughout the entire Middle East.

Shall lay a trap for you: "All the men" who participate in Esau's confederacy entrap his Palestinian descendants. The Hebrew word utilized by Obadiah for trap is *mazor*, and can refer to an ambush, or as defined by *Strong's Hebrew and Greek Dictionary*, to a turning aside from truth, a treachery, a plot, or a wound.

What Obadiah likely alludes to, is that the Palestinian descendants of Esau have allowed themselves to be deceived by "all the men," in their confederacy, and as such have turned aside in a treacherous act from some truth. What truth could they have turned aside from, which ultimately proves to trap or ambush them? This truth must have something to do with the Jewish people and their Jewish State, since this is what the confederacy is attempting to destroy according to Psalm 83.

The truth is that nobody can destroy the Jewish people, according to the covenant their God made to their patriarchs Abraham, Isaac, and Jacob. The LORD promised these patriarchal fathers of the Jewish people an everlasting family tree.[252] In order for the predominately-Islamic confederacy of Esau to accomplish its mission, which is the effectual destruction of the Jewish State, it must attempt to destroy every last Jew in the world. If there were any Jew left, the potential would exist for that Jew to restore a Jewish State in his or her ancient promised land. Furthermore, other scriptures refer to the eternal existence of a Jewish State in the land between the Nile River of Egypt and the Euphrates River of modern-day Iraq.[253]

Therefore, the minor premise is that the confederacy of Esau must believe that they can destroy the Jewish people and their potential for any current or future Jewish state, and the major premise is that the God of the Jews, who promised the eternal existence of a Jewish people and a Jewish state, is in essence a promise-breaking liar. Esau thoroughly knew that the God of his grandfather Abraham and his father Isaac made these promises to the Jewish people in ages past, but his descendants down through the ages have turned aside (*mazor*) from this truth. They have allowed themselves to be successfully deceived into thinking that they can prove the Jewish God to be a liar. They contest the Jewish claims of being heirs of the Abrahamic Covenant and often attempt to substitute their patriarch Ishmael as the rightful heir, rather than Isaac; however, this is all part of the deceit of their religion, Islam. The truth they have turned aside from is that the God of the Jews intends to preserve the Jewish people forever. This is a dangerous miscalculation that will ultimately lead to the destruction of Esau's confederacy.

No one is aware of it. Neither Esau nor all the men in his confederacy realize how severe this miscalculation is. They will leave the God of the Jews no choice but to make an end of their confederate effort aimed at the destruction of the Jewish people and their Jewish State. They will force the enactment of the curse-for-curse-in-kind clause contained in the Abrahamic Covenant (as specified in Genesis 12:3). They will attempt to destroy the Jews, but the Jews will destroy them instead (Ezek. 25:14, Obad. 1:18).

The modern-day Jewish state of Israel will not be eradicated from the formerly recognized territory of Palestine. Isralestine is a phenomenon that is here to stay. The Israel of today, which has become superimposed upon the Palestine maps of yesterday, has providential protection. No adequate tool can be found to exist in the confederate arsenal that can blot out the Jewish survival clause contained in the Abrahamic Covenant. The result of the Israeli conquest over this coming Palestinian confederacy will be the requirement for new Middle East maps to be drawn, which include Isralestine, once and for all.

THE FUTURE MAPS OF
ISRALESTINE

Although approximately 6000 years of recorded history has emanated from the Middle East, today's maps of the area are primarily composed of countries that have relatively recently gained or regained their independence. The Ottoman Empire had ruled over the area from 1517 until 1917, but with its collapse at the conclusion of World War I forfeited its holdings, primarily into British and French hands. Within decades, the Middle East as we presently recognize it formed as follows:[254]

COUNTRY	YEAR OF INDEPENDENCE	TOTAL AREA SQ MILES	POPULATION [255]
Afghanistan	1919	250,000	31,056,997
Egypt	1922	386,662	78,887,007
Saudi Arabia	1932	756,981	27,019,731
Iraq	1932	167,556	26,783,383
Iran	1935 [256]	636,296	68,688,433
Lebanon	1943	4,015	2,874,050
Syria	1946	71,498	18,881,361
Jordan	1946	35,637	5,906,760

One-by-one, these Arab and Persian population groups became autonomous. Territory was generally allotted in alignment with ancestral boundaries. The region was reshaping itself in a relatively orderly fashion, with the exception of the inklings of the international community to appropriate territory for a Jewish state.

In 1917, the Balfour Declaration was introduced to the world. It was designed to partition a portion of the former Ottoman Empire into a Jewish state. In its initial draft, it offered up the territory of Palestine and was to include about 46,000 square miles, extending from the Mediterranean Sea in the west, eastward to the western borders of modern-day Iraq. The Arabs in the region desired sovereignty over this land, and promptly protested this international proposal. Continued Arab agonizing over the matter postponed the issue.

Then, with the conclusion of the Holocaust, the International community arguably forced the Arabs to expect a Jewish State to surface in their neighborhood. The Palestine Partition Plan, UN Resolution GA 181 of 1947, emerged and appropriated 8,000 to 9,000 square miles from the Mediterranean Sea to the Jordan River for the re-creation of Israel. Since Jordan had become a nation in the year prior and consumed most of what the Balfour Declaration intended as territory for the Jewish State, the nation Israel was formed on the little bit of unclaimed land left in the region.

The tiny Israel was added to the long list of Middle East nations:

Country	Year of Independence	Total Area sq miles	Population[257]
Israel	1948	8,019	10,241,366

(Includes the Gaza Strip, and West Bank)

The purpose of this chapter is to redefine the Middle East in accordance with the prophetic content contained within the Bible. In the near future, we can expect another facelift in the Middle East. Publishers will soon be busy reproducing entirely new Isralestine atlases of the area.[258] It is helpful to list the pertinent passages sequentially, and to map them out territorially to better understand how that region will change.

Scripture informed us that when the Jews returned from the nations of the world back into the land of Israel, they would meet with Arab protest. The present resentment toward the reestablishment of Israel by those Arab nations that most closely border it is in direct fulfillment of this predicted attitude. Furthermore, this protest is prophesied to become a confederacy composed of these resistant nations. This coalition has been previously referenced in the chapters: *The Palestinian Confederacy* and *Psalm 83: The Arab Confederacy*. These two chapters do not identify two differing confederacies; rather, they describe the same one.

The Bible tells us that what is now an area conflict will upgrade itself into a war in the Middle East. Arabs will confederate in an attempt to extinguish the nation Israel. Israel will defeat them, resulting in the expansion of their national borders well into these Arab territories. This expansion will bear some resemblance to the former borders of the ancient territories allotted to the Twelve Tribes of Israel. Additionally, Arab exiles are destined for detention camps within the described areas.

THE CONFEDERACY

The first map below depicts a border around the confederate nations. These are the nations most closely bordering Israel today. They are listed in Psalm 83:5–8.

> For they have consulted together with one consent; They form a confederacy [league] against You: The tents of Edom and the Ishmaelites; Moab and the Hagrites; Gebal, Ammon, and Amalek; Philistia with the inhabitants of Tyre; Assyria also has joined with them; They have helped the children of Lot.[259] Selah (Psa. 83:5–8, NKJV, emphasis added)

Edom: Southern Jordan and Palestinian refugees
Ishmaelites: Saudi Arabia
                       (Ishmael was one of the fathers of the Arabs)
Moab: Central Jordan and Palestinian refugees
Hagrites:[260] Egypt
Gebal: Northern Lebanon
Ammon: Northern Jordan and Palestinian refugees
Amalek: The Negev and Sinai Peninsula areas
Philistia: The Gaza Strip and Hamas
Tyre: Southern Lebanon and Hezbollah
Assyria: Syria and Northern Iraq

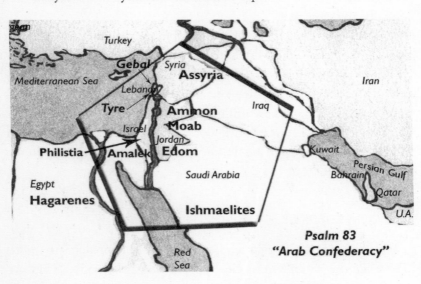

Fig. 6. Map by Lani Harmony, www.gallery3nine.com.

For the purposes of this book, the territories identified by their historical titles have been labeled as the "Inner Circle" of nations. They consist of those core nations that most closely border the tiny nation of Israel. These nations present the first confederate attempt at destroying the reforming nation of Israel. Foretold are three confederacies that will conspire for the same cause, which is the extinguishing of the Jewish race.

The second such confederacy is prophesied in Ezekiel Chapters 38 and 39. For this book, we will call those nations the "Outer Circle," and they are on the following map. At the time of the formation of their coalition, the Inner Circle of nations will have met their end at the hands of the "exceedingly great army" of Israel.[261] In victory, Israel will extend its territorial embrace into the width and breadth of those Inner Circle nations mapped above. As such, the expanding nation of Israel will become neighbor to the Outer Circle grouping of nations mapped below.

The Outer Circle of nations will not welcome Israel into their neighborhood; rather, they will formulate an attempt to seize the wealth acquired by Israel resulting from their conquest over the Inner Circle of nations. As the map below displays, the second confederacy enlists those nations that border the primary bodies of water surrounding Israel. This appears to be done in an attempt to challenge Israel's ability to distribute its increased commerce capacity into the International community. Ezekiel details for us the motive of the Outer Circle of nations:

> Thus says the LORD GOD: "On that day it shall come to pass *that* thoughts will arise in your mind, and *you will make an evil plan: You will say, 'I will go up against a land of unwalled villages;* I will go to a peaceful people, who dwell safely, all of them dwelling without walls, and having neither bars nor gates'" (Ezek. 38:10–11, NKJV; emphasis added)

The Outer Circle of nations, led by Russia "will make an evil plan" designed to invade Israel," who at the time of this Russian-led advance, will be residing peacefully. Israel will be victorious over the Inner Circle of nations, and thus generally freed from the further torment of Arab terror and hatred.

*To take plunder and to take booty, to stretch out your hand against
the waste places that are again inhabited,* and against a people
gathered from the nations, who have acquired livestock and
goods, who dwell in the midst of the land. Sheba, Dedan, the
merchants of Tarshish, and all their young lions will say to you,
"Have you come to take plunder? Have you gathered your
army to take booty, to carry away *silver and gold,* to take away
livestock and goods, to take *great plunder?*" (Ezek. 38:12–13,
NKJV; emphasis added)

These passages aptly describe the motive of the Outer Circle of
nations. They seek "to take plunder and to take booty" from Israel.
They intend "to stretch out your hand against the waste places that
are again inhabited." This confederacy stretches out its hand in an apparent attempt to blockade Israel from competing in the open market.
The "merchants of Tarshish" also emphasizes the commerce theme,
as do terms like "silver and gold," "livestock and goods," and "great
plunder!"

The map on the next page displays the nine confederate members
and their approximate historical locations, of the Outer Circle of nations. These nations are identified by their ancient names in Ezekiel
38:1-6 in the New King James Version as; Magog, Rosh, Meshech,
Tubal, Persia, Ethiopia, Lybia, Gomer, and Togarmah.

Unlike the Inner Circle, which experiences defeat at the hands
of the "exceedingly great army" of Israel, the Outer Circle of nations
meet their defeat via divine intervention.[262] Israel becomes a powerful
entity because of these two victories over the Inner Circle and Outer
Circle.

As such, the third confederacy, spearheaded by the world leader
at the time, will act promptly to neutralize Israel's enormously grown
international esteem. This world leader, more commonly referred to
as the Antichrist, will accomplish this by confirming a seven-year covenant with the nation of Israel.

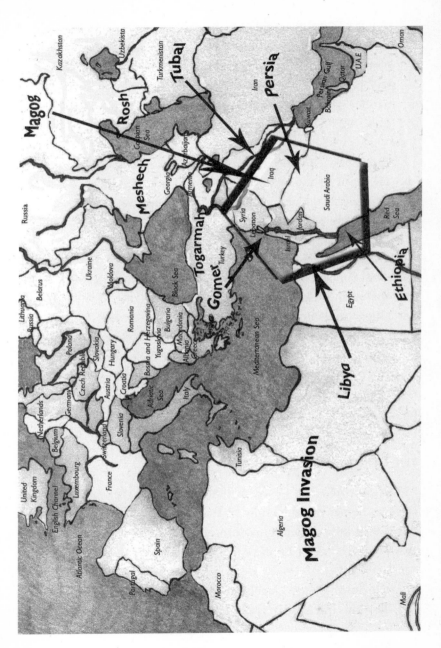

Fig. 7. Map by Lani Harmony, www.gallery3nine.com.

Then he [Antichrist] shall confirm a covenant with many for
one week; But in the middle of the week He shall bring an end
to sacrifice and offering.[263] And on the wing of abominations
shall be one who makes desolate, Even until the consum-
mation, which is determined, Is poured out on the desolate.
(Dan. 9:27, NKJV; emphasis added)

As this passage states, the Antichrist breaches this covenant at the
midway point of the seven-year covenant and commences his campaign to destroy the nation Israel and extinguish the Jewish race once
and for all. He enlists the remaining nations of the world, which at
that time will be conspicuously void of the Inner Circle and Outer
Circle of nations. Not all inhabitants of the world will join his effort;
some will support the Jewish race; however, his effort concludes all
attempts to annihilate the Jews.

This chapter does not attempt to detail the events or results of
the final campaign of the Antichrist; rather, I've chosen to display the
re-mapping of the Middle East as a result of the conquest by the Jews
over the Inner Circle of Arab nations. You will find some of the best
text from which to glean further information in the Old Testament
book of Obadiah.

THE CONQUEST

"The house of Jacob [Jews] shall be a fire, And the house of Joseph
[Jews] a flame; But the house of Esau [Palestinians] *shall* be stubble;
They shall kindle them and devour them, And no survivor shall *re-
main* of the house of Esau," For the LORD has spoken.[264]

The South [Negev] shall possess the mountains of Esau, And
the Lowland shall possess Philistia. They shall possess the
fields of Ephraim And the fields of Samaria. Benjamin *shall
possess* Gilead. (Obad. 1:18–19, NKJV)

Simply stated, the declarations made in these passages are that the Jews are going to "devour" "the house of Esau," and "possess" more territory after their conquest. By referring to "the house of Esau," Obadiah identifies the descendants "of Esau," the Edomites. In modern times, the prophecy plays out primarily against the Palestinians, who have Edomite contingencies scattered throughout the Gaza Strip, the West Bank, and surrounding Palestinian refugee communities in the Middle East. You will find a more detailed explanation below.

"The South shall possess the mountains of Esau." This statement refers to the border expansion of Israel to the south, on into Southern Jordan. Modern-day Southern Jordan was recognized in ancient times as Edom. Edom was the territory established by Esau and his descendants. The Hebrew word Obadiah uses for south is *Negeb* or *Negev*, which is located in the southern portion of Modern-day Israel.

"The Lowland shall possess Philistia. They shall possess the fields of Ephraim And the fields of Samaria." The Lowland, *shephelah* in the Hebrew, references the territory just above Negev. Obadiah progresses upward, describing the jurisdictional changes that result in correlation with the Israeli victory over the Palestinians of the Gaza Strip and portions of the West Bank.

"Benjamin shall possess Gilead." By possessing Gilead, the Jewish army repossesses the northern-most part of the modern-day West Bank. This brings to a bitter conclusion the final attempt of the Palestinians to homestead the Holy Land.

THE PRISONERS

And the *captives of this host of the children of Israel* Shall possess the land of the Canaanites As far as Zarephath. The captives of Jerusalem who are in Sepharad Shall possess the cities of the South. (Obad. 1:20 NKJV; emphasis added)

It is unclear whether this passage includes the return of more Jews back into the land of Israel after the Israeli Conquest over the Arabs, or if it suggests that Palestinian Prisoners of War will be captured and detained by the exceedingly great army of Israel. Some teach that the "captives of Jerusalem who are in Sepharad" refers to the return of Jewish people back into Israel from Spain and other associated areas.[265] However, for arguments sake, I present the Palestinian prisoner of war possibility below.

The Hebrew word Obadiah uses for "this host," is *cheyl*, which is defined as "a collateral form of; an army; also (by analogy) an entrenchment, or bulwark."[266] "This host," the ones referenced in verse 18 as the "houses of Jacob and Joseph," and known in verse 19 as "the possessors" of the expanded tribal territories; "This host" in verse 20 also relocates Palestinian exiles. The Hebrew word used here by Obadiah for "possess," is *yaresh*, and in this instance we can translate it as "supplanted."

The inference is that the Israeli army will take prisoners of war and detain them in designated areas. Israel will establish two camps for these POW's: one to the north "As far as Zarephath," which is modern-day Lebanon, and one to "the South," referring to the Negev also identified in verse 19.

SUMMARY

This chapter points out that the Modern-day nation of Israel is but a mere fragment of its appointed size. Soon, Israel will likely grow territorially to approximately 125 times its present size. It could grow from 8,019 total square miles at present, which includes the Gaza Strip and West Bank, to about 1,000,000 total square miles sometime after the Israeli conquest over the Inner Circle of surrounding Arab nations.

This territorial expansion likely engulfs much of Lebanon, Syria, Jordan, Egypt, and parts of Saudi Arabia. The Jews will feel justified in stretching out their hand in sovereignty over all of these lands for two primary reasons. First, they will have conquered these nations militarily and, secondly, they will remember their patriarchal father Abraham owns this land.

> On the same day the LORD made a covenant with Abram, saying: "To your descendants I have given this land, from the river of Egypt to the great river, the River Euphrates." (Gen. 15:18, NKJV)

This is not to suggest it is certain that the final fulfillment of Genesis 15:18 will manifest completely due to the collapse of the Inner Circle; however, significant strides in that direction will result. Furthermore, although this chapter tends to summarize Israel's coming expansion, other sections of this book exposit in detail what scripture predicts will happen to these Inner Circle nations and how Israel is able to possess their lands.

Try to imagine the United States of America enlarged territorially to the extent that she possesses 75 percent of all the landmass on Earth. For instance, the continents of North America, South America, Europe and Asia, all placed under the umbrella of America.[267] Relatively speaking, this is what will proportionately occur to the tiny nation of modern-day Israel; she will expand extensively in the Middle East.

In essence, it is preposterous for the international community to preclude that the propensity of what was promised to the Jews territorially is adequately appropriated presently. The inhabitants of this world are in store for a shocking revelation when they witness the transformation of Israel today into the Isralestine of tomorrow.

THE SECOND TIME

A Jewish Sequel

I n his Chapter 11, Isaiah presents glimpses of several important prophetic episodes. He predicts the first coming of the Messiah, which is now past tense, the present whereabouts of the Messiah, and lastly the future return of the Messiah. In addition to these Messianic prophecies, Isaiah foretells of the second and final mass migration of the Jews from among the nations of the world, back into the land of Israel.

> Then it will happen on that day that the LORD Will again recover the *second time* with His hand The remnant of His [Jewish] people, who will remain, From Assyria, Egypt, Pathros, Cush, Elam, Shinar, Hamath, And from the islands of the sea. He will set up a banner for the nations, And will assemble *the outcasts of Israel*, And gather together the *dispersed of Judah* From the *four corners of the Earth*. (Isa. 11:11–12, NKJV; emphasis added)

In essence, he declares that the Jews will again perform in the Middle East Theater. They will be cast for a second and final time in their infamous role of "My people Israel." The powerful episodes, previously scripted in the scriptures, performing in modern times, will culminate in a final act, whereby the Messianic Hero returns to rescue His people from their final doom!

The Bible nowhere refers to a third, fourth, or fifth such time of recovery, therefore Isaiah's second time, must be the final time. Is this restoration of the Jewish people back into the Promised Land the second and final time? This chapter suggests it is, and the opening scenes of The Second Time: A Jewish Sequel are now playing upon the world stage.

Many of the Hebrew prophets foretold of this present return of the Jews, and they warned it would provoke a hostile protest from the surrounding Arab kingdom. They went on to declare that because of this hostility, the Jews would be compelled to establish a powerful army in self-defense. Though this chapter briefly comments upon Isaiah's Messianic prophecies, it concludes with an emphasis upon the conquest of this Israeli army over the surrounding Arab nations.

Isaiah addresses the Arab populations comprised of Palestinians, Jordanians, Egyptians, and Syrians by their ancestral equivalents, Philistia, Edom, Moab, Ammon, Egypt and Assyria. These nations make up six of the ten-member nation confederacy listed in Psalm 83 destined to formulate an end-times attempt at the annihilation of Israel as a nation.[268]

In his Chapter 11, Isaiah helps to give understanding into the victory of the nation Israel over these Arab groups. He declares that the Jews will fly down in battle upon the Palestinians of the Gaza territory. They will conquer and plunder all of Syria. Jordan will be captured and annexed into Israeli territory. Furthermore, the waterways of Egypt become disturbed, enabling the Jews to easily cross over and capture territory there as well.

These conquest events occur in concert with the second and final recovery of the Jews. As such, we have just cause to consider the plausibility of this present worldwide recovery of the Jews back into the nation Israel, as the beginning of final feature presentation of the divine plan of God. This movie can now be seen worldwide through modern technologies. You will not want to miss any part of this motion picture, so sit down and pay close attention to every detail.

Before the analysis of the final feature, it is important to preview the prophecies contained in Isaiah's Chapter 11. These prophecies provide the necessary introductory material to understand better the stage upon which the final story takes place.

THE FIRST COMING

> Then a shoot will spring from the stem of Jesse, And a branch from his roots will bear fruit. The Spirit of the LORD will rest on Him, The spirit of wisdom and understanding, The spirit of counsel and strength, The spirit of knowledge and the fear of the LORD. (Isa. 11:1–2, NKJV)

Without going into a lengthy Bible study, the meaning of these two verses is generally understood to be as follows: First, the Messiah will be a Jew, and at the time of His arrival on the world scene, the Jewish people will find themselves in a condition of depravity. When the Messiah first comes, the Jews will not be likened to a fully-grown, fruitful tree; rather, they will look more like the stump of a tree that has been chopped down. Isaiah makes the analogy that the Messiah will be to Israel like the shoot of a new branch beginning to grow out from a tree stump. Secondly, in verse two when he comes He will be filled with the Holy Spirit of God.

Just as Isaiah predicted, such was the case at the first advent of the Messiah, Jesus Christ! The Jews were under Roman occupation, and they were likened to that tree, which had been chopped down with only its trunk remaining. Furthermore, the Sanhedrin had reduced the all-important religion of Judaism into a condition of hypocrisy, by altering it into a system of self-righteousness.[269] From that apostate Jewish condition, out of Israel the true righteousness would sprout forth. A Messiah would come who would be filled with the Spirit of the LORD, wisdom, understanding, counsel, might, knowledge, and the fear of the LORD. These Seven Spirits represent the fact that the Messiah will be entirely filled with the Holy Spirit.[270]

THE SECOND COMING

> And He will delight in the fear of the LORD, And He will not judge by what His eyes see, Nor make a decision by what His ears hear; But with righteousness He will judge the poor, And decide with fairness for the afflicted of the Earth; And He will strike the Earth with the rod of His mouth, And with the breath of His lips He will slay the wicked. Also righteousness will be the belt about His loins, And faithfulness the belt about His waist. (Isa. 11:3–5, NKJV)

These above passages portray Messianic judgment. The wicked will be slain, but the meek of the Earth will receive fair and equitable treatment for their faith. Judgment results at the time of the Second Coming of Christ, not at the point of His First Coming. Matthew 25:31–46, details some of the events destined to occur within the judgment process scheduled to take place at the point of the Second Coming of Christ, "When the Son of Man comes in His glory, and all the holy angels with Him, then He will sit on the throne of His glory."[271]

At that point, He will bear in actuality the title "Branch of David." The distinction between these two Messianic titles is that the "root of Jesse" identifies with the first coming of Christ, and the "Branch of David" His second coming.[272]

THE MESSIANIC KINGDOM

And the wolf will dwell with the lamb, And the leopard will lie down with the young goat, And the calf and the young lion and the fatling together; And a little boy will lead them. Also the cow and the bear will graze, Their young will lie down together, And the lion will eat straw like the ox. The nursing child will play by the hole of the cobra, And the weaned child will put his hand on the viper's den. They will not hurt or destroy in all My holy mountain, *For the Earth will be full of the knowledge of the LORD* As the waters cover the sea. (Isa. 11:6–9, NKJV; emphasis added)

These above conditions much emulate the original Garden of Eden environment, prior to the fall of Adam and Eve. Creation resided in cooperation with man, rather than in its present state of chaotic confusion. This cooperative complimentary condition will be restored in the one thousand year Messianic Kingdom period.[273] The "Earth will be full of the knowledge of the LORD" at that time, which presently is not the case. Currently the world is generally ignorant of the knowledge of the LORD, and as such is cleverly swayed by Satan into a condition of continual sin.[274]

This condition of sin suffers the world, and finds direct connection with humanities less than full knowledge of the LORD. The crucifixion of Christ on the cross, served as the ultimate priestly act of substitution for the sin induced suffering of the world. Christ declared while hanging from the cross; "Then Jesus said, 'Father, forgive them, for *they do not know* what they do.'" (Luke 23:34, NKJV; emphasis added)

This acknowledgment of Christ, Who as the Messiah was filled with the "Seven Spirits," i.e., the Holy Spirit, among which includes the "Spirit of knowledge and of the fear of the LORD," evidences the fact, that though He died for suffering humanity, this humanity generally lacked the necessary knowledge of the LORD, to even grasp the significance of the event.

The Bible teaches that sin leads to suffering, furthermore that its ultimate wages are death.[275] Hosea 4:6 declares the lack or rejection of the knowledge of the LORD ultimately results in the suffering and or destruction of people.[276] The more cunning personage of Satan, toward their demise, easily manipulates people left to their own ignorant devices. During the one thousand year Messianic Kingdom, Satan will be bound and separated from any ability to interact with humanity.[277] Furthermore, the Earth will be filled with the knowledge of the LORD. Therefore, as Isaiah states above, suffering and destruction will be non-existent in Israel, and at the most minimal throughout the rest of the world, during the Messianic Kingdom period.

THE GLORIOUS RESTING PLACE (THE MESSIAH'S PRESENT WHEREABOUTS)

> Then *in that day* The nations will resort to *the root of Jesse,* [the Messiah] Who will stand as *a banner* [standard of salvation] *for the peoples* [all of humanity]; And His resting place will be glorious. (Isa. 11:10, NKJV; emphasis added)

This passage is pivotal in understanding the rest of Isaiah's Chapter 11, in that the fulfillment of the events described therein apparently occurs "in that day." In essence, in that same day that "The nations will resort to "the root of Jesse," Who will be erected or, more specifically, resurrected, as "a banner for the peoples," the events Isaiah further describes will occur.

When the Messiah becomes the "standard" of salvation for all of humanity, in contrast to the former means of salvation through proselytizing into Judaism, "in that day," the rest of the events of Isaiah Chapter 11 occur. "His resting place will be glorious." Alludes to His present position whereby He; "the root of Jesse," sits down at the right hand of God, waiting for the time of His enemies to be likened to His footstool.

> But this Man, after He had offered one sacrifice for sins forever, *sat* [*kathizo*] *down* [*kathizo*] at the right hand of God, [glorious resting place] from that time *waiting till* His enemies are made His footstool.[278] For by one offering He has perfected forever those who are being sanctified. (Heb. 10:12–14, NKJV, emphasis added)

THE SECOND RETURN OF THE JEWISH REMNANT

> Then it will happen on *that day* [same day there shall be a Root of Jesse, v10] that the LORD Will again recover the second time with His hand The remnant of His people, who will remain, From Assyria, Egypt, Pathros, Cush, Elam, Shinar, Hamath, And from the islands of the sea. (Isa. 11:11, NKJV; emphasis added)

> He will set up a banner [standard of salvation] for the nations [Gentiles], And will assemble the *outcasts of Israel*, And gather together the *dispersed of Judah* From the four corners of the Earth. (Isa. 11:12, NKJV; emphasis added)

This phrase "that day," used in both verses 10 and 11 by Isaiah represents a space of defined time. The Hebrew word *yom*, which can be interpreted literally as "a day, or an age, or figuratively as a space of defined time," is used.[279] In this instance, Isaiah refers to some space of defined time between the First and Second Comings of Christ, whereby Christ, bannered as the standard of salvation, resembles the Messianic title "the Root of Jesse." Contained within this space of defined time the Jews labeled by Isaiah, as the "outcasts of Israel" and "the dispersed of Judah," will be re-gathered back into the holy promised land of Israel. They will be returning from the remotest locations reaching as far out as "From the four corners of the Earth."

The Hebrew word for banner, which is used in both Isaiah 11:10 and Isaiah 11:12, is *nes*. This word can be interpreted as "banner, ensign, signal, or standard."[280] Isaiah 11:10 is quoted by the apostle Paul in the New Testament in Romans 15:12. Paul interprets this Isaiah passage for us, in the context of the Messiah, Jesus Christ as the "root of Jesse," being bannered as the standard for salvation, the hope for the Gentile nations.

> And again, Isaiah says, "The Root of Jesse will spring up [1st coming of the Messiah], one who will arise [from His present glorious resting place] to rule over the nations [in the Messianic Kingdom]; the Gentiles [now and in the future] will hope in him [bannered as the standard of salvation]." (Rom. 15:12, NKJV)

Isaiah calls this a "second time" that a Jewish gathering takes place. There are three primary views as to the timing of this second recovery. Some say this was fulfilled after the seventy years of Babylonian captivity. Others believe this is occurring presently, and lastly some believe that this is fulfilled at the end of the seventieth week of Daniel. (i.e., the Seven-Year Tribulation Period).

There are four decent arguments against this referring to the Jewish return out from the Babylonian captivity, which occurred around the time of 539 BC. First Christ, as "the root of Jesse," had not yet come, and this second gathering occurs in that same *yom* period that Christ, "the root of Jesse" rests in "His glorious place."

Second, this gathering is from the "four corners of the Earth," whereas the return out of Babylon was far more limited. Third, if this second gathering has already seen its final fulfillment, this would make this present gathering a third time, and the Bible nowhere refers to any such "third time." Lastly, Israel remained a divided kingdom upon the return out of Babylon, whereas Isaiah prophesies in his next verse, that they will become a united kingdom this second time.[281]

The arguments against the second time occurring at the end of the Seventieth Week of Daniel, also known as the Great Tribulation, are that the title of Christ at that time will be more likened to the "Branch of righteousness" rose up to King David, rather than "the root of Jesse."[282] It also presupposes that Israel today united, at some future point before the Great Tribulation becomes a divided country once again. This is highly doubtful. Presently, Northern Kingdom (Ephraim) is no longer in opposition to the Southern Kingdom (Judah); they are united in their fight for their right to exist as one nation, the nation Israel.

Furthermore, this argument imagines that the extent of the dispersion in the three and one half years of the Great Tribulation extends worldwide.[283] Granted, the antics of the Antichrist during the Tribulation will cause many Jews to disperse once again from Israel. However, Christ, as the "root of Jesse," has instructed them at the time of His first advent to flee only to the mountains (of Bozrah) and not into the countries of the world at large.[284] Therefore, upon his return as the "Branch of righteousness" rose up to "King David," the gathering of the Jews into Israel will be notably from, but not limited to, the mountains (of Bozrah).

Subsequently, Gentiles escort remaining Jews found outside the land after the second coming of Christ back to Israel.

> Thus says the LORD of hosts: "In those days ten men from every language of the nations shall grasp the sleeve of a Jewish man, saying, 'Let us go with you, for we have heard *that* God *is* with you.'" (Zech. 8:23, NKJV)

Lastly, and most importantly, the events that occur in Isaiah 11:14 because of this gathering are not likely Messianic Kingdom events. In the Messianic Kingdom, swords will give way to plowshares, but in verse 14 Isaiah goes on to describe events of a military nature.[285] He foretells the conquering of Gaza, Syria, and Jordan, by the "exceedingly great army" of Israel.[286]

Therefore, the possibility remains high that this current gathering (*Aliyah*) of the Jewish people into Israel in unbelief could be "the second time" referenced here in Isaiah 11:11. [287,288] Isaiah says; "It shall come to pass in that day." In what day is he referencing? The day that Christ, identified as the "root of Jesse," "rests in His glorious place" and represents the "standard to the people." Presently the Jewish peoples have been gathering from the above Syria, Northern Iraq (Assyria), Egypt (Pathros), Ethiopia (Cush), Iran (Elam), Southern Iraq (Shinar), Upper Syria (Hamath), and the islands of the sea (Mediterranean?).

> He will set up a banner [the Messiah] for the nations [humanity], *And* will assemble the outcasts of Israel [Northern Jews], And gather together the dispersed of Judah [Southern Jews] From the four corners of the Earth [Jews dispersed worldwide]. Also the envy of Ephraim shall depart, And the adversaries of Judah shall be cut off; Ephraim shall not envy Judah, And Judah shall not harass Ephraim. (Isa. 11:12–13, NKJV; emphasis added)

All Jews from the Northern and Southern kingdoms, who were dispersed out of Israel into the nations of the Earth are returning to the Land of Israel. They are no longer prophesied to be a divided kingdom, but God is reuniting them as one nation, the nation Israel. Prior to the worldwide dispersion of the Jewish people out of Israel, which commenced in AD 70 the country was a divided kingdom; the Northern Kingdom was referred to as Israel, Ephraim, or sometimes Samaria. The Southern Kingdom was predominately referred to as Judah.

THE ISRAELI CONQUEST

> But *they* shall fly down upon the shoulder of the Philistines toward the west; Together *they* shall plunder the people of the East [Haran, N. Syria Gen 29:1–5]; *They* shall lay their hand on Edom and Moab; And the people of Ammon shall obey *them*. (Isa. 11:14, NKJV; emphasis added)

This is the telling passage "they shall fly down," "they shall plunder," "They shall lay their hand on," "And the people of Ammon shall obey them." Isaiah declares that "they, they, They, and them," are the Jewish people re-gathered out of the countries of the world. He announces that "they, they, They, and them" are no longer a divided kingdom fighting amongst each other; rather, "they, they, They, and them," become engaged in a serious regional conflict against Gaza, Syria, and Jordan.

Gaza, Syria, and Jordan are three of the more prominent members in the Psalm 83:6–8 confederacies. This confederacy forms to destroy the nation Israel. Since this Psalm 83 prophecy is not yet fulfilled, and requires a non-divided kingdom of Israel in order to be fulfilled, we can surmise that the nation Israel united today, meets this requirement.

Isaiah 11:14 alludes to Syria as "the people of the East." This can be determined by referring back to the first biblical usage of "the people of the East," which is found in Genesis 29:1–5. It alludes to people Jacob met who were from Haran. The same Hebrew words are used in both scriptural instances "the people" (*ben*) "of the East" (*qedem*).[289]

> So Jacob went on his journey and came to the land of the people [*ben*] of the East [*qedem*]. And he looked, and saw a well in the field; and behold, there *were* three flocks of sheep

lying by it; for out of that well they watered the flocks. A large stone *was* on the well's mouth. Now all the flocks would be gathered there; and they would roll the stone from the well's mouth, water the sheep, and put the stone back in its place on the well's mouth. And Jacob said to them, "My brethren, where *are* you from?" And they said, "*We are from Haran.*" Then he said to them, "Do you know Laban the son of Nahor?" And they said, "We know him." (Gen. 29:1–5, NKJV; emphasis added)

Jacob sojourns out of the land of Canaan, which best represents Israel proper today, in an attempt to locate his future wife. He goes to Haran, which would today be located in modern-day northern Syria. Therefore, by association Isaiah is informing his readers that Northern Syria is scheduled for plundering.

A comparative study between Isaiah 11:14 and Isaiah 17:1 suggests that the extent of the Israeli assault against Syria, reaches from the southern most to the northern most boundaries of the nation.

But they shall fly down upon the shoulder of the Philistines toward the west; *Together they shall plunder the people of the East* [Haran, Northern Syria]; They shall lay their hand on Edom and Moab; And the people of Ammon shall obey them. (Isa. 11:14, NKJV; emphasis added)

The burden against Damascus [Southern Syria]. "*Behold, Damascus will cease from being a city*, And it will be a ruinous heap." (Isa. 17:1, NKJV; emphasis added)

Isaiah's implied usage of Haran, which is located at the northernmost tip of Syria, depicts the massive reach of the plundering of the people (*ben*) of the East (*qedem*). Not only will Damascus in the

South of Syria cease to be a city, but it also appears as though the entirety of Syria will be struck.[290]

We were informed by Isaiah 11:13 NKJV: "Also the envy of Ephraim shall depart, And the adversaries of Judah shall be cut off; Ephraim shall not envy Judah, And Judah shall not harass Ephraim."

We see today in the midst of the Middle East conflict that no such enmity between Judah and Ephraim exists. The "envy" of old, which caused the kingdom to divide into two, has departed as foretold by Isaiah. Israel is a united kingdom today, attempting to survive the clear and present danger of the "perpetual enmity" described in Ezekiel 35:5, of the surrounding Arab nations.[291]

THEY SHALL LAY THEIR HAND ON EDOM

Another clue of discernment that argues against this second Jewish gathering occurring after the return of Christ at His Second Coming is that Isaiah states that the Jews "shall lay their hand on Edom." This is highly unlikely to occur subsequent to the second coming of Christ, i.e., in the Messianic Kingdom, for the following two reasons:

1. The Messianic Kingdom period is a time of peace on Earth.
2. Edom will already be desolated.

As stated earlier in this study, the Messianic Kingdom is a time whereby swords give way to plowshares, creation operates in cooperation with humanity, the Messiah reigns on Earth, and the world is filled with the Knowledge of the LORD. Thus it is highly unlikely that the Jews "shall lay their hand on Edom," at that time. To "lay their hand on Edom" would imply a military conquest, captivation of sovereignty over the territory, and the subsequent customary exploitation of the spoils of war.

Edom experiences two end-time judgment sequences, first by the

Jews and secondly by the Messiah at His Second Coming, which render it desolate.[292] As such Edom, much like Babylon will be a desolated geography throughout the entirety of the Messianic Kingdom
period. In this desolated condition, the territory of Edom, which is
modern-day Southern Jordan, will offer the Jews nothing of desire
upon which to lay their hands. Furthermore, the hand of the Jews,
i.e., their military, will be disbanded on or about the commencement
point of the kingdom period. They will not be laying their hands
upon anything at that time, but the ministerial instructions to them
from the Messiah.

Whereas the Jews will not exploit Edom in the Kingdom, "They
shall lay their hand on Edom," prior to the commencement of the
Kingdom period. It is prophesied in Ezekiel 25:12–17, and Obadiah
1:18, and various other scriptures, that the Israeli military will successfully execute the vengeance of the LORD against the Palestinians and
their cohorts listed in Psalm 83:6–8, the fulfillment of which places
Jewish sovereignty over Edom. This would account for the availability
of Edom to become the final place of refuge for the faithful Jewish
remnant.

The faithful Jewish remnant is the end-times generation of Jews,
who survive the devastating antics of the Antichrist during the heavily
prophesied Tribulation Period. This period, also referred to in scripture as the "time of Jacobs trouble," "the Day of the LORD," and
"Daniel's Seventieth Week," just to name a few, is characterized by
the most severe Holocaust attempt against the Jews in their history.
It will vastly overshadow the Holocaust of the Jews by Hitler and the
Germans.

"And it shall come to pass in all the land," Says the LORD,
"*That* two-thirds [of the Jews] in it shall be cut off *and* die, But
one-third shall be left in it: I will bring the *one*-third [faithful
Jewish remnant] through the fire, Will refine them as silver
is refined, And test them as gold is tested. They will call on

My [Jesus Christ the Messiah] name, And I will answer them [by returning to the Earth to rescue them]. I will say, 'This *is* My people' [My people Israel]; And each one [each one will believe in Christ] will say, 'The LORD *is* my God.'" (Zech. 13:8–9, NKJV)

As a result of the horrific events of the Tribulation, a Jewish remnant will recognize that Jesus Christ was the Messiah that their fathers before them had failed to identify as such. Hosea informs us that because of their persecution during the Tribulation Period, this end time's remnant of Jews will call out for the return of Christ. This invokes the return of Christ for His Second Coming.

I [Jesus Christ, the Messiah] will return again to My [glorious resting] place
Till they [the Jewish remnant] acknowledge their offense [generational rejection of Christ as Messiah].[293] Then they [the Jewish remnant] will seek My face; In their affliction [Tribulation] they will earnestly seek Me. [Jesus Christ] (Hos. 5:15, NKJV)

What can be discerned from all of this is that the Jewish people will face entire extermination at the hands of the Antichrist and his armies. Their survival as a race depends on outside divine deliverance. The once infamous "exceedingly great army" of Israel will be obliterated and void of any further ability to defend against the onslaught of the Antichrist. As a result, the Jews flee out of Israel, and many of them move immediately East into the territory of Edom.

The territory of Edom will be the preferred choice for three primary reasons: First, Edom will have already been conquered prior by the exceedingly great army of Israel, thus placing it under Israeli sovereignty. Second, the Messiah at the time of His First Coming gave prophetic instructions for this end-times Jewish generation to flee into the mountain range of Edom, to a place called Bozrah, modern-day Petra. Third, the cliffs and caverns of Petra present this remnant of Jews a fortress of protection from the Antichrist in His campaign of Armageddon.

Many books line the Christian bookshelves that adequately describe the Tribulation Period, the Campaign of Armageddon, the final hiding place of the faithful Jewish remnant, and the Second Coming of Christ the Messiah; as such this author will defer to those sources for details rather than further specifications in this book.[294] However, since the exploits of the exceedingly great army of Israel line the pages of this book, the reader is encouraged to read and understand this book thoroughly, before the time of the dismantling of the exceedingly great army of Israel during the Tribulation Period.

This faithful Jewish remnant finds itself held up in hiding in Petra/Southern Jordan, surrounded by the assembled armies of the world spearheaded by the Antichrist. They are utterly helpless to defend against the assault about to annihilate them as an ethnicity. They cry out to Jesus Christ as their Messiah, and ask Him to come and deliver them out of their predicament. He responds, and henceforth the numerous prophecies regarding the Second Coming of the Messiah find their final fulfillment.

THE DECLARATION OF DANIEL

At this point, it is germane to understand what the prophet Daniel declared regarding Edom and the end-times faithful Jewish remnant. He states that the Antichrist enters into the "Glorious Land" of Isralestine, likely referring to territories under Jewish sovereignty, which at that future time should encompass parts of what are modern, day Lebanon, Syria, Jordan, and Egypt.[295] The Jews will come into possession of these countries because of their successful defeat of the Psalm 83:1–8 confederacy via the means of their "exceedingly great army."

> He [the Antichrist] shall also enter the Glorious Land, and many *countries* shall be overthrown; but these shall escape from his hand: *Edom, Moab*, and *the prominent people of Ammon*. (Dan. 11:41, NKJV; emphasis added)

The Antichrist comes in heavy-handedly conquering many countries, but does not overthrow Edom, Moab, and Ammon. These three territories comprise what is today referred to as the nation of Jordan. Jordan became a nation in 1946, but prior this land was referred to down through the generations as Edom, Moab, and Ammon. By way of reminder Isaiah declared of these three places In Isaiah 11:14 that, "They (the Jews) shall lay their hand on Edom and Moab; And the people of Ammon shall obey them."

Daniel declares that Jordan escapes the escapades of the Antichrist, yet Isaiah informs us that Jordanians do not escape the grasp of the "exceedingly great army" of Israel.[296] The next paragraph orchestrates the chronological order of events prophesied over Edom, Moab, and Ammon.

First, the Jordanians align themselves as a member nation in the Psalm 83:6–8 confederacy. Second, this confederacy engages in a major war against Israel. Third, Israel exacts victory via the hands of its "exceedingly great army." Fourth, Israel establishes sovereignty over Jordan. Fifth, the Antichrist initiates a military campaign to overthrow the glorious land of Isralestine, which is so called because it is comprised of countries predominately under Israeli sovereignty, including Jordan. Sixth, the Antichrist avoids Jordan, and marches through Israel proper instead.

The reason this crazed individual comes into future Isralestine is to overthrow it. Since this land, will at that time be generally sovereign to the government of Israel; we can surmise that the Antichrist has come to kill Jews. This reminds us of what Zechariah said pointed out earlier in this chapter:

"And it shall come to pass in all the land [the Glorious Land of future Isralestine]," Says the LORD, "*That* two-thirds [of the Jewish population] in it shall be cut off *and* die, But *one-*third shall be left in it." (Zech. 13:8, NKJV)

There are a couple possible reasons why the Antichrist does not initially overthrow "Edom, Moab, and the prominent people of Ammon." First all of these areas by then will be generally desolated by the war between the Arabs and Jews. By territories, the setting at the time of the genocidal campaign of the Antichrist should be as follows:

1. *Southern Jordan (Edom).* This territory presently is desert and is minimally populated. In addition, the Mountain range of Seir traverses through Edom, making it generally undesirable for day-to-day living. Much of these mountains are impassable, making it an obstacle to the Antichrist in his campaign to overthrow this element of the Jewish kingdom. Lastly, it will have been hard hit by the Arab-Israeli war, meaning that very few Jews will find it desirable to migrate there. As such, Jews for the Antichrist to kill will be sparsely found there.[297]

2. *Central Jordan (Moab).* This terrain today is primarily desert, not extremely desirable for habitation. This territory may at that time also be the location of the valley of "Hamon Gog." The valley of "Hamon Gog" becomes the designated area of the mass burial grounds for millions of dead soldiers killed in association with the Russian-Iranian confederacy described in Ezekiel Chapters 38 and 39.[298] This prophetic episode, whereby Russia and its coalition form against Israel, occurs after the Israeli Conquest of the "Glorious Land," but before the Antichrist marches into the "Glorious Land." Due to the desolated desert environment, coupled with the possibility that Moab becomes

burdened by the largest cemetery since the flood of Noah, the Antichrist will find few Jews there for the killing as well.

3. Northern Jordan (Ammon). Daniel stated "but these shall escape from his hand: "Edom, Moab, and the prominent people of Ammon." Who are these prominent people? In Isaiah 11:14 we were informed that They shall lay their hand on Edom and Moab; And the people of Ammon shall obey them. Both Isaiah and Daniel have listed these same three locations and in the same order.

By connecting the dots, we can determine that the people whom Isaiah says, "Ammon shall obey," are those reigning over them. Since the events Daniel describes occur subsequent to the events Isaiah describes, we can surmise "the prominent people of Ammon" referred to by Daniel are those governing Jordan at the time that the Antichrist marches into "Glorious Isralestine." According to Isaiah, those sovereign over Jordan at that time are the Jews.

Therefore, "the prominent people of Ammon" whom Daniel declares will escape the march of the Antichrist would be either Jewish governors or some form of a vassal Jordanian government subservient to Israeli sovereignty. Because the Antichrist is on a campaign to overthrow the "Glorious Land" and kill all the Jews, his focus is on the supreme leadership headquartered in Israel, rather than their ambassadors stationed in Ammon. This could be the reason that "the prominent people of Ammon" escape.

He [the Antichrist] shall stretch out his hand against the countries, and the land of Egypt shall not escape. He shall have power over *the treasures of gold and silver, and over all the precious things of Egypt*; also the Libyans and Ethiopians *shall follow* at his heels. (Dan. 11:42–43, NKJV; emphasis added)

Following the trail of the Antichrist further, we see that he avoids Jordan, moves through Israel proper, and heads down into Egypt. Why does he set Egypt within his sights? Daniel says he gains power over the great wealth of Egypt "the treasures of gold and silver, and over all the precious things of Egypt." History instructs us that in war campaigns the victor gains notoriety on the world scene with every conquest. It also teaches that many armies have sustained themselves through the spoils of war. However, more than this, the Antichrist appears to attack Egypt because at that time there will likely be a significant population of Jews residing there.

Skipping ahead to Isaiah Chapter 19, we find interactive prophecy regarding Egypt and Israel encouraging this possibility.

> In that day, Egypt will be like women, and *will be afraid and fear* because of the waving of the hand of the LORD of hosts, which He waves over it. And the land of Judah [Southern Israel] *will be a terror to Egypt*; everyone who makes mention of it will be afraid in himself, because of the counsel of the LORD of hosts which He has determined against it. In that day *five cities in the land of Egypt will speak the language of Canaan* [Hebrew] *and swear by the LORD of hosts; one will be called the City of Destruction.*
>
> In that day there will be *an altar to the LORD* in the midst of the land of Egypt, *and a pillar to the LORD* at its border. (Isa. 19:16–19, NKJV; emphasis added)

Isaiah says that there will come a day when Egypt will be terrified of Israel. The reason for this is probably that the exceedingly great army of Israel will be successfully combating the Arab nations of Psalm 83:6–8 that come against them in a confederate effort. Egypt is one of the enlisted member nations within this ten-member confederacy.[299] Israel will prevail over this confederate effort and Egypt, along with many of the other nations involved, will become captured by Israel.

Israel will then establish "five cities in the land of Egypt." These cities will experience a migration of Jews into those cities. As a result, these Jews will establish their language, culture, and religion therein. Isaiah states that they "will speak the language of Canaan (Hebrew) and swear by the LORD of hosts."

One of these five Jewish Cities "will be called the City of Destruction." Jewish tradition evidences the common historical practice of renaming a city or location in an attempt to identify a powerful epic event that occurred there. One of the reasons for this practice was so that future Jewish generations would be caused to learn and reflect upon the lessons of the significant episode.[300] This city will likely meet its destruction at the hands of the "exceedingly great army" of Israel, at which point the city will be aptly renamed "the City of Destruction."

But *news from the east and the north shall trouble him*; therefore he shall go out with great fury to destroy and annihilate many [Jews]. And he shall *plant the tents of his palace between the seas and the glorious holy mountain*; yet he shall come to his end, and no one will help him. (Dan. 11:44–45, NKJV; emphasis added)

The Antichrist intercepts troubling news while he is basking in the glory of his victory over Egypt. The newsworthy information comes from the east and the north. In the Old Testament of the Bible, there are no translations using the word "Northeast" or "Eastnorth," but we can surmise that is where Daniel is directionally describing. Breaking news comes out of the territory directly "Northeast" of Egypt. This identifies the location of modern-day Southern Jordan, which is ancient Edom. This is the territory directionally "Northeast" of Egypt.

How could any news disturb the Antichrist, who at that time will be exalted in his recent victory over Egypt? Perhaps this will be the headline from the Jerusalem Post or its equivalent during that period:

Jews Escape to Edom

A multitude of Jews has fled Israel in an emergency mass exodus into Southern Jordan. The Jews are taking refuge in the protective cliff fortresses of ancient Bozrah, Edom. Known today as Petra, its rugged mountain terrain offers the Jews a form of temporary protection from the ongoing slaughter taking place in the Glorious Land of Isralestine.

Apparently, the troubling news is that a massive exodus of Jews is occurring directly northeast of his location in Egypt. This would be the faithful Jewish remnant referenced earlier in this chapter. The Antichrist then moves to "plant the tents of his palace between the seas and the glorious holy mountain." This move by the Antichrist sets the stage for the heavily prophesied campaign of Armageddon. The targets of this campaign are the Jewish faithful who have fled into Edom, or modern Southern Jordan. They will hide in the cliff fortresses of the mountain ranges of ancient Seir.

As stated earlier in this study, the faithful remnant recognizes its offense and realizes Jesus Christ is the Messiah.[301] They repent as a nation and beckon the return of Christ. This motivates Christ to come to the Earth again. During this visit, He rescues the faithful Jewish remnant and defeats the Antichrist. Daniel foretells the destruction of the Antichrist in Daniel 11:45 quoted earlier: "he [the Antichrist] shall come to his end, and no one will help him." The Antichrist meets his end through the crushing might of Jesus Christ, in fulfillment of Genesis 3:15.

And I will put enmity Between you [Satan] and the woman, And between your [Satan] seed [the Antichrist] and her Seed [the Messiah]; He [Jesus Christ the Messiah] shall bruise your head [destroy the Antichrist], And you shall bruise His heel. (Gen. 3:15, NKJV)

Isaiah on Egypt:

> The LORD will utterly destroy the tongue of the Sea of Egypt [Red Sea]; With His mighty wind He will shake His fist over the River [The Nile River], And strike it in the seven streams, *And make men cross over dryshod.* (Isa. 11:15, NKJV; emphasis added)

In keeping with the establishment of a Jewish presence in Egypt, Isaiah declares the geography of Egypt will be re-shaped through a series of what appear to be natural disasters. The result better facilitates Jewish migration into Egypt. The tip of the Red Sea will experience a devastation of sorts that serves to dry it up.[302] Furthermore, the Nile River will undergo tornado-like conditions, which will establish dry land over "the seven streams," referring to tributaries of the Nile River. All of the above will enable Jews to "cross over" into Egypt on "dryshod."

Could similarities exist between this future crossover into Egypt on dryshod and the historical Hebrew exodus out of Egypt, which fit the same description?

> Then Moses stretched out his hand over the sea [Red Sea]; and the LORD caused the sea to go *back* by a strong east wind all that night, and made the sea into *dry land,* and the waters were divided. So the children of Israel went into the midst of the sea on the *dry ground,* and the waters *were* a wall to them on their right hand and on their left. (Exod. 14:21–22, NKJV; emphasis added)

A possible point of comparison would be that "the tongue of the Sea of Egypt" referred to in Isaiah 11:15 might be close in proximity to the location of the historical miracle whereby the waters parted, facilitating the ancient Hebrew exodus out of Egypt. Remember that

according to the covenant made between God and the Jewish patriarch Abraham, the Jews believe they are entitled to a landmass that
extends to the Nile River.

> On the same day the LORD made a covenant with Abram,
> saying: "To your descendants I have given this land, from the
> river of Egypt [Nile River]) to the great river, the River Eu-
> phrates." (Gen. 15:8, NKJV)

Therefore, as a result of the Israeli Conquest over Egypt, and in
light of the Promised Land given to Abram, later renamed Abraham,
the Jews will feel justified in their mass migration campaign into
Egypt.[303] As they populate Egypt, the potential for the final fulfillment
of Isaiah's prophecy could occur:

> In that day five cities in the land of Egypt will speak the lan-
> guage of Canaan [Hebrew] and swear by the LORD of hosts;
> one will be called the City of Destruction. In that day there
> will be an altar to the LORD in the midst of the land of
> Egypt, and a pillar to the LORD at its border. (Isa. 19:18–19,
> NKJV)

Isaiah concludes his Chapter 11 by referencing "a highway for the
remnant of His people who will be left from Assyria." This highway is
opened for unrestricted travel between Syria and Israel sometime after
Israel's conquest over its Arab enemies. This highway further facilitates the return of Jews who have remained outside the land of Israel
until after the coming Middle East war.

> There will be a highway for the remnant of His people Who
> will be left from Assyria, As it was for Israel In the day that he
> came up from the land of Egypt. (Isa. 11:16, NKJV)

This scripture referencing a "remnant of His people who will be left from Assyria," is coincidentally quoted in Isaiah 11:11, just a few passages earlier.

It shall come to pass in that day *That* the LORD shall set His hand again the second time To recover the remnant of His people who are left, From Assyria and Egypt, From Pathros and Cush, From Elam and Shinar, From Hamath and the islands of the sea. (Isa. 11:11, NKJV)

In Isaiah 11:11 "the remnant of His people who are left, From Assyria" refers to Jews coming into Israel prior to the Israeli Conquest over the Arabs. These Jews are the ones migrating from 1948 through the present. This second reference of "the remnant of His people who are left, From Assyria," described in Isaiah 11:16, appears to identify those Jews who kept residency among the nations of the world and did not join the first wave of Jewish migration into Israel.

The opening of this highway is only made possible by the fact that Israel will gain supremacy of the region. This highway will offer safe passage to the Jews who would like to emigrate from the north into what will then be referred to as the Glorious Land. Since the first group of re-gathered Jews will still maintain a contingency residing within Israel at the time, the second wave of Jewish migration coming in on this highway does not constitute a third worldwide gathering of the Jews. Furthermore, Isaiah Chapter 19 also describes this highway.

In that day there will be *a highway* from Egypt to Assyria, and the Assyrian will come into Egypt and the Egyptian into Assyria, and the Egyptians will serve with the Assyrians. In that day Israel will be one of three with Egypt and Assyria—a blessing in the midst of the land, whom the LORD of hosts shall bless, saying, "Blessed *is* Egypt My people, and Assyria

the work of My hands, and Israel My inheritance." (Isa.
19:23–25, NKJV; emphasis added)

If the highway described in Isaiah 19:23 is the same as that described in Isaiah 11:16, it appears to remain accessible from the time
of its opening after the Israeli Conquest into the Messianic Kingdom
period. This can be deduced from the fact that the final fulfillment
of these Isaiah 19 passages, whereby "Israel will be one of three with
Egypt and Assyria—a blessing in the midst of the land" occurs in
the Messianic Kingdom period. Some scholars teach that the ancient
"Kings Highway" becomes extended into Syria and becomes the highway described here.

19

ZEPHANIAH'S CALL TO CAUTION

> Seek the LORD, all you meek of the Earth,
> Who have upheld His justice.
> Seek righteousness, seek humility.
> It may be that you will be hidden
> In the day of the LORD'S anger.
>
> —ZEPH. 2:3 NKJV

The Hebrew prophet Zephaniah delivers a powerful message to the "meek of the Earth."[304] This message has application for those residing on the planet now and from this point forward. In his second chapter, he commands the world population to be cognizant of, and to direct their lives in accordance with, three specific powerful prophetic events.

1. The return of the Jewish people into Israel
2. The restoration of their fortunes as the Client Nation
3. The Day of the LORD

In addition to this important message to the meek of the Earth, Zephaniah dedicates a major portion of his chapter toward activities that will occur at the time of the Israeli Conquest over the Psalm

83 confederated Arab armies. He alludes to Jewish victories over the Palestinians and Jordanians. These two contemporary groups are generally, but not exclusively, comprised of the descendant peoples from Philistia, Moab, Ammon, and Edom.[305]

These four historical ethnicities are enlisted in the Psalm 83:5–8 Arab confederacy, destined to attack Israel. Zephaniah foretells a time when the peoples of Philistia, Moab, and Ammon, i.e., the modern-day Palestinians and the Jordanians will be found guilty of homesteading the Holy Land. Their borders presently penetrate the Gaza Strip, the West Bank, and border the Golan Heights, which scripture tells us will ultimately be territories deeded to the Jewish people. Since the restoration of Jewish fortunes includes enlarged real estate holdings, this border encroachment presents a major obstacle to the conversion of the Holy Land into Jewish sovereignty.

Zephaniah sets the stage as follows: The Jews return into the land of Israel and conquer the Arab alliance represented in part by the Palestinians and Jordanians. As a result, Israeli fortunes are greatly enhanced as they come into possession of the plunder and spoils of war. In the process, Allah is greatly reduced as a god figure, and Islam is severely affected.[306] Then Zephaniah appears to allude to the advance against the then regionally superior Israel by the Russian confederacy spoken of in Chapters 38 and 39 of Ezekiel, which is commonly referred to as the Magog Alliance. [307]

Lastly, he declares that these events occur before the day of the LORD arrives, which is the period most associated with the expiration date of the Earth in its present condition of existence, i.e., the Tribulation Period. He prophesies all of the above for the primary purpose of invoking the "meek of the Earth" into the worship of God.

1. THE RETURN OF THE JEWISH PEOPLE INTO ISRAEL

"Gather yourselves together, yes, gather together, O undesirable nation!" (Zeph. 2:1 NKJV)

Zephaniah introduces the second chapter of his book by pointing the world's attention toward the return of the Jewish people into their ancient homeland of Israel. The verse quoted above could be considered his headline as it sets the stage for the all-important call to caution message he is about to deliver.

In essence, he describes the heavily prophesied repopulation of the Jewish people back into the land of Israel. Furthermore foretold in his headline is their national spiritual condition at the time of their return. He uses the Hebrew words *lo kasaph* for "undesirable" or "shameless." These words might also be translated as "without longing." It portrays the Jewish people returning to their ancient homeland void of the appropriate spiritual attitude that should accompany their return.

The first biblical use of the word *kasaph* is found in the following passage:

"And now you have surely gone because you greatly long [*kasaph*] for your father's house" (Gen. 31:30a, NKJV). In this first usage of *kasaph*, Jacob, the father of Israel greatly longs to return to the house of his father Isaac.[308] This house was in the land of Canaan.[309] Conversely, though the world witnesses the return of the Jewish people back into Israel, which was the place of their patriarchal father Jacob's house, they are *lo*, or without the same great longing.

Certainly, by the time of the rebirth of the nation Israel in 1948, the Jewish people found themselves in desperate need of their ancient homeland, but their disposition differed greatly from that of Jacob's. Jacob was in fellowship with the God of his grandfather Abraham and his father Isaac. He believed in the promises covenanted through them. Whereas Jacob was in a condition of belief at the time of his return to the Promised Land, the Jewish people today are generally gathering in unbelief.

Not only are the Jewish people returning without belief in Him, whom the Christians believe to be the Messiah, Jesus Christ, they are also void of the same effective faith as was characterized by their patriarchal father Jacob upon his return into the land of Canaan. The reason they lack the similar *kasaph* of Jacob is that they are returning without the similar "faith" of Jacob.

Zephaniah banners this newsworthy information for all of the generations of men and women that find themselves present upon the Earth during that period when God orchestrates the return of the unbelieving Jew back into the land of ancient Israel. Undeniably, the rebirth of the nation Israel should be the number-one attention getter of the world since its inception in 1948. Zephaniah speaks to you and me who reside in that time, as well as our descendant generations to follow until the return of Christ at His Second Coming!

> For the LORD their God will be mindful of them and *restore their fortunes.* (Zeph. 2:7c RSV; emphasis added)

Not only will the world witness their return, but also the restoration of their status as the client nation of God, the infamous "My people Israel." Zephaniah 2:4–12 gives some detail into the means through which their fortunes are restored and they become empowered once again as the holy people.

> Before the decree is issued, *Or* the day passes like chaff, Before the LORD'S fierce anger comes upon you, Before the day of the LORD'S anger comes upon you! (Zeph. 2:2 NKJV)

Furthermore, these three Zephaniah passages quoted at the onset of this study pronounce the return of the Jew into the land of Israel and the subsequent restoration of fortunes all to occur before "the day of the LORD." "The day of the LORD" is considered by most scholars to eventuate either throughout the seven-year Tribulation Period, or during the span of the second 3.5 years of that same period (often referred to as the "Great Tribulation"). This seven-year tribulation is scheduled to be the last seven years on our present Earth's timeline, then followed by the thousand-year Messianic Kingdom period.[310] As

Zephaniah declares, "the day of the LORD" is characterized by the outpouring of God's fierce anger and wrath upon the planet, targeted at its unsaved population.

The stage is now set for this study, which will serve to outline the details that Zephaniah chapter two determines to be important for the "meek of the Earth" to discern. His message cautions them to seek the LORD as they witness the events described in this all-important chapter. Due to the catastrophic circumstances that occur during the day of the LORD, Zephaniah pleads with them that they might do what it takes to be hidden from the events of the day of the LORD.

2. THE RESTORATION OF THEIR FORTUNES

Therefore thus says the LORD GOD: "Now *I will restore the fortunes of Jacob,* and have mercy on the whole house of Israel; and I will be jealous for my holy name." (Ezek. 39:25 RSV; emphasis added)

I will multiply upon you [Israel] man and beast; and they shall increase and bear young; *I will make you inhabited* as in former times, *and do better for you* than at your beginnings. (Ezek. 36:11 NKJV; emphasis added)

Included with the return of the Jewish people to their homeland is the restoration of their fortunes. This is an important area of Bible prophecy not to be overlooked. Zephaniah, in his call to caution, causes the meek of the Earth to consider carefully this important episode. When they witness Israel empowered, they are to recognize that the time to take action and be hidden from the day of the LORD is running out.

At some point Israel will indeed enter into a period of prosperity, which far exceeds their present holdings of national wealth. As a nation, they will become the benefactor of vast amounts of booty and plunder, the spoils of war, which come to them as conquerors over the surrounding Arab nations enlisted in the Psalm 83:1–8 confederacy. They will expand their borders, meaning their real estate portfolio will be greatly enhanced, and they will acquire livestock, silver, gold, and other forms of booty in large quantities.

We are informed in Ezekiel Chapters 38 and 39 that when Israel finds itself as a nation residing in such a prosperous condition that a large confederate effort spearheaded by Russia and Iran will form against them. In Ezekiel 38:10–13 Israel is identified as "the quiet people who live in safety, all of them living without walls, and having no bars or gates." They are a "people who were gathered from the nations, who are acquiring cattle and goods." They are in possession of "plunder," "silver and gold," "cattle and goods," and "a great amount of booty." All of these are Old Testament terms for identifying a condition of peace and prosperity. The use of the terms plunder and a great amount of booty emphasizes wealth obtained through the spoils of war.

Therefore when Zephaniah tells us in verse 2:7c that "the LORD their God will be mindful of them (The Jewish People) and restore their fortunes," we are to find further association with the events described in Ezekiel Chapters 38 and 39.[311]

I will display my glory among the nations; and all the nations shall see my judgment that I have executed [on the Russian-Iranian confederacy], and my hand that I have laid on them. The house of *Israel shall know that I am the LORD their God, from that day forward.* And the nations shall know that the house of Israel went into captivity [worldwide dispersion which began in AD 70 and concluded in 1948] for their iniquity, because they dealt treacherously with me. So I hid my face from them and gave them into the hand of their adversaries, and they all fell by the sword. I dealt with them according to their uncleanness and their transgressions, and hid my face from them. Therefore thus says the LORD GOD: Now *I will restore the fortunes of Jacob, and have mercy* on the whole house of Israel; and *I will be jealous for my holy name.* (Ezek. 39:21–25 NRSV; emphasis added)

The Russian confederate advance is defeated, and Israel's fortunes are further restored. In the process the "glory" of God is displayed among the nations, and Israel comes into a greater reverence of the God of Moses. Ultimately, that "glory" which was long ago shown to Moses in Exodus 33:18–23 is again put on display.

In both instances, Jewish history and Jewish future, the glory of God finds association with the proclamation of the name of the LORD, and the bestowal of mercy to him, whom the LORD chooses. This indeed occurred at the time of Moses, the glory of God was accompanied by the proclamation of the name of the LORD, and the declaration that God would shower mercy on whom He chooses, which in the case of Moses primarily referred to the client nation of Israel.

At the future display of the glory of God as described by Ezekiel to occur at the judgment of the Russian confederacy, the same results occur to the benefit of the Jewish people. Mercy is granted to the whole house of Israel as their fortunes are further restored, and the upholding of the holy name of the LORD is also accomplished. God has chosen the defeat of the Russian confederacy as the specific episode through which to uphold His Holy Name.

The point of importance is that alongside the upholding by God of His Holy Name is the extension of His mercy upon the whole house of Israel. The whole house of Israel most likely refers to the entirety of the Jewish ethnicity present on Earth at that time, whether they be in a condition of belief (*kasaph kasaph*), or unbelief (*lo kasaph*). As a nation, they will again be thoroughly recognized as the client nation "My people Israel," and they will experience the restoration of their fortunes. For the Jewish people it will be as Ezekiel declares:

The house of *Israel shall know that I am the LORD their God, from that day forward.* (Ezek. 39:22 NRSV; emphasis added)

As a people, they will then enjoy mercy, prosperity and world recognition. Unfortunately, this episode will not cause the nation as a whole to believe in Jesus Christ as their Messiah; rather, they will think to respond to this display of the glory of God by reinstating the Mosaic Law.[312]

3. THE DAY OF THE LORD

Sometime shortly thereafter, the Jewish leadership will abuse this merciful condition and confirm the false seven-year covenant with the Antichrist, which will issue in the day of the LORD, whereby the LORD exhibits His fierce anger.[313] By recollection, this is what Zephaniah calls to caution to the meek of the Earth. He pleads with them to worship God before the day of His fierce anger arrives.

As mentioned previously, Israel greatly enhances its prosperity via the spoils of war, which result from their conquest over the confederacy of the surrounding Arab nations. Furthermore discussed is that the timing of this conquest over the Arabs occurs prior to the Advance of the Russian confederacy. Both events significantly lend themselves to the restoration of Israel's fortunes.

"GAZA SHALL BE DESERTED, AND ARAB HOMES EVACUATED"

After Zephaniah's introductory call to caution to the "meek of the Earth," he continues on to introduce the devastating effects that fall upon the Arab confederate members, Philistia, Moab, and Ammon. In so doing, he carries on with his theme that the Jewish people are gathering into the land of Israel, and that in the process their fortunes are being restored. The modern-day equivalent of these Arab groups, are the Palestinians of the Gaza, the Palestinians of the West Bank, and the Jordanians of Northern and Central Jordan.

These specific Arab populations currently present themselves as formidable obstacles to the stretching out territorially of the returning Jews. As we read the words of Zephaniah, it becomes clear that these Arabs are considered trespassers and as such, they will be forcibly evicted before the Day of the LORD arrives. He outlines a series of conditions that will occur because of the Israeli victory over the Palestinians and Jordanians. The reason for this prophetic material is to serve as a "call to caution" to the "meek of the Earth."

> Seek the LORD, all you humble of the land, who do his commands; seek righteousness, seek humility; perhaps you may be hidden on the day of the LORD'S wrath. For *Gaza* shall be *deserted*, and *Ashkelon* shall become *a desolation*; *Ashdod's people* shall be *driven out* at noon, and *Ekron* shall be *uprooted*. Ah, inhabitants of the seacoast, you nation of the Cherethites! The word of *the LORD is against you, O Canaan, land of the Philistines*; and I will destroy you until no inhabitant is left. (Zeph. 2:3–5 NRSV; emphasis added)

Zephaniah describes a destruction to come that devastates several cities of ancient Philistia. Philistia is an enlisted member of the Psalm 83 Arab confederacy, which will advance against Israel, but will be destroyed by Israel. Gaza, Ashkelon, Ashdod, and Ekron were four of the five prominent historical cities, known as the Pentapolis.[314] Zephaniah prophesies of a future time when Gaza will be deserted, Ashkelon desolated, the people of Ashdod driven out, and Ekron uprooted.

The lesson will be for that generation which experiences these four cities residing in those specific conditions that the day of the LORD is to shortly follow. This should cause the "meek of the Earth" to redeem the time and seek righteousness, and humility and to continue to uphold the justice of the LORD. The aim is that they may increase in number and many more might be hidden from the day of the LORD.

Many are the commentaries that suggest prophesies regarding Philistia have already found their final fulfillment, and that the Philistines have become an ethnicity gone extinct. Though it may be difficult today to trace any residue of the ancient Philistines, the territory of Philistia is clearly identified in end-times prophecy through Psalm 83. Therefore, if what Zephaniah declares about these four cities should occur in the present or near future, it would likely find its closest association with the Palestinians of the Gaza area.

By Zephaniah's ordering of events, we are also caused to conclude that this prophecy regarding the desertion of Gaza, desolating of Ashkelon, driving out of Ashdod, and the uprooting of Ekron, is destined to occur sometime after the commencement of this present Jewish return back into the land of Israel, and yet before the day of the LORD. As such, it seems that this prophecy has yet to find its final fulfillment.

The Gaza of today is a coastal strip of land that the Palestinian Refugees occupy and believe to be part of their heritage. However, long before there were Palestinians or even Philistines, this land was allotted to the tribe of Judah. Historically it was Jewish territory. Presently, it serves in part as a launch site for various types of short-range rockets aimed at Jewish civilian targets in Israel. By no stretch of the imagination is Gaza deserted at the time of the writing of this chapter. Gaza is extending outwardly in an attempt to enlarge its borders.

And you, O seacoast, shall be *pastures, meadows for shepherds and folds for flocks.* The seacoast shall become the possession of the remnant of the house of Judah, on which they shall pasture, and in the houses of Ashkelon they shall lie down at evening. *For the LORD their God will be mindful of them and restore their fortunes.* (Zeph. 2:6–7 NRSV; emphasis added)

We are further told that after Gaza is deserted, Ashkelon desolated, Ashdod driven out Ekron uprooted, and no Palestinian inhabitants reside along the Southwestern seacoast of Israel, that the seacoast
will become the possession of the Jewish people. It will be for "pastures, meadows for shepherds, folds for flocks." The vacated houses of
Ashkelon will provide shelter for the shepherds and their flocks.

Presently, Gaza is not deserted; rather, Palestinians occupy it. Ashkelon and Ashdod are modern-day cities under Jewish jurisdiction.
Ekron today is most likely known as Tel Miqne, located approximately
23 miles southwest of Jerusalem. It has been the site of numerous
noteworthy excavations in recent times, but is not today a city in its
scope that is comparable to Gaza, Ashkelon, or Ashdod. Therefore,
it will be up to the "meek of the Earth" to constantly observe the
events that unfold in these Mediterranean seacoast areas, to see how
this prophecy sets up and plays out.

Presently, this area is undergoing a serious "Land for Peace" struggle between the Palestinians and the Israelis. The final frontier as to
which group dominates over which territories is likely not yet determined. At some point, however, the prophecy of Zephaniah will take
place, Gaza will be deserted, and the houses of Ashkelon will be where
the remnant of the house of Judah will lie down at evening time.

It is interesting that a scenario has already occurred in modern history relative to Ashkelon, which might prove insightful. It is known as
the Israeli National Master Plan of June 1949.

The Israeli national master plan of June 1949 designed Al
Majdal as the site for a regional urban center of 20,000
people. Mass repopulation of the vacated Arab houses by
Jewish immigrants or demobilised soldiers began in July
1949 and by December the Jewish population had increased
to 2,500. During 1949, the town was renamed Migdal Gaza,
and then Migdal Gad. Soon afterwards it became Migdal
Ashkelon. In 1953 the nearby neighborhood of Afridar was

incorporated and the current name Ashkelon was adopted. By 1961, Ashkelon ranked 18th amongst Israeli urban centers with a population of 24,000.[315]

It is doubtful the Israeli National Master Plan of June 1949 represents the final fulfillment of Zephaniah's prophecy that "Ashkelon shall become a desolation (to the Arabs)," "and in the houses of Ashkelon they (Jews) shall lie down at evening;" however, at the very least it suggests a Jewish mindset willing to occupy homes that are evacuated by Arabs.

REPOSSESSING JORDAN, THE GOLAN HEIGHTS, AND THE WEST BANK

Now Zephaniah shifts his attention to the modern-day nation of Jordan. He refers to this territory through the usage of the ancient names of Moab and Ammon. Moab encompassed the land, which was primarily located in Central Jordan, and Ammon was what is now Northern Jordan. Upon the return of the Jew into the Promised Land, the people of Jordan are guilty of two things: they commit anti-Semitic acts against the Jewish people, and they trespass in on the eastern and northeastern borders of the traditional tribal territories of Israel.

> I have heard *the taunts of Moab and the revilings of the Ammonites,* how they have *taunted my people* [Israel] *and made boasts against their territory.* Therefore, as I live, says the LORD of hosts, the God of Israel, Moab shall become like Sodom and the Ammonites like Gomorrah, a land possessed by nettles and salt pits, and a waste forever. *The remnant of my people* [Israel] *shall plunder them, and the survivors of my nation shall possess them.* (Zeph. 2:8–9 NRSV; emphasis added)

Jeremiah the prophet, whose ministry briefly overlapped with Zephaniah's, also expounds upon this trespassing of the Ammonites into the Jewish tribal territory of Gad. He foretells, as does Zephaniah, of the forcible eviction of the Arabs by the Jews, and the subsequent Israeli repossession of the land in question.

> Against *the Ammonites*. Thus says the LORD: "Has Israel no sons? Has he no heir? Why *then* does Milcom *inherit Gad*, And *his people dwell in its cities?* Therefore behold, the days are coming," says the LORD, "That I will cause to be heard an alarm of war In Rabbah of the Ammonites; It shall be a desolate mound, And her villages shall be burned with fire.[316] *Then Israel shall take possession of his inheritance*," says the LORD. (Jer. 49:1–2 NKJV; emphasis added)

Jeremiah asks the Jordanians; "Has Israel no sons? Has he no heir?" The answer is obvious: of course Israel has descendants—they are repopulating the Holy Land in our day! He goes on to ask, then why are Jordanians trespassing in the Holy Land, which long ago was deeded to the Twelve Tribes of Israel, i.e., the twelve sons of Jacob? Gad was one of the twelve sons of Israel.

Therefore, Jeremiah emphasizes the similar point of Zephaniah, that for the Jordanian thievery of the Holy Land, at the time of the return of the Jew back into the land of Israel the Jordanians will come under military conflict. Because of military defeat over the Arab populations that occupy the land in question, Israel will inherit more Promised Land. This fits in fulfillment with the prophecy to restore the fortunes of the Jewish people prior to the "Day of the LORD."

Once upon a time, Ammon and Moab were legitimately appropriated the territories to the East of the allotted territories of the Twelve Tribes.[317] The Hebrews were taught to respect the territorial divides. However, at present the descendants of Ammon and Moab do not respect the boundaries established of old, and the prophets afore mentioned suggest that the Jordanians and the Palestinians will suffer the curse-for-curse-in-kind consequence contained in the Genesis 12:3 clause of the Abrahamic Covenant for their homesteading of the Holy Land.

Technically speaking, it may be that Golan Heights, West Bank, and the Gaza Strip are under the spotlight of the prophetic theater. These territories reside well within the borders of the land formerly possessed by the Twelve Tribes of Israel. Terms like *Palestinians*, and *Jordanians* were not available to Zephaniah at the time of his prophetic writings; thus, the "meek of the Earth" must extrapolate the times of their signs as they traverse through these periods of Middle Eastern territorial mayhem.

The point is clear that unintended Arab parties are presently consuming prime property. Real estate in Israel comes at no small price tag, and yet today it is given away hastily to the Arabs in exchange for an illusive peace. There is a seesaw, back-and-forth battle for possession of the Promised Land that has plagued the region and burdened the international community since May 14, 1948, when Israel was restored as the Jewish nation. The Jews generally want to maintain the borders established after the Six-Day War of June 1967, and the Arabs would like to re-establish pre-1948 borders.

Scriptures already included in this study, once again listed below, do not allow for assimilation of the Holy Land into Arab control. A point soon forthcoming will find the Arabs displaced from the territories once allotted to the Twelve Tribes of Israel.

For the LORD their God will be mindful of them and restore their fortunes. (Zeph. 2:7)

"Then Israel shall take possession of his inheritance," says the LORD. (Jer. 49:2)

The remnant of my people [Israel] shall plunder them, and the survivors of my nation shall possess them. (Zeph. 2:9)

These scriptures and many more like them line the prophetic pages of the Bible. The point is clear that God's plan for the Jewish people will move forward on schedule, and He will restore unto them their fortunes. Part of this portfolio is the precious real estate of the Twelve Tribes of Israel. God deeded this land ages ago to Abraham and his descendants.

And the LORD said to Abram, after Lot had separated from him: "Lift your eyes now and look from the place where you are—northward, southward, eastward, and westward; for *all the land which you see I give to you and your descendants forever.* And I will make your descendants as the dust of the Earth; so that if a man could number the dust of the Earth, *then* your descendants also could be numbered. Arise, walk in the land through its length and its width, *for I give it to you.*" (Gen. 13:14–17, NKJV; emphasis added)

The Jews came into realization of much of this land after they had been delivered out of the four-hundred years of captivity in Egypt. Joshua led them in numerous battles as they marched as a people back into the Promised Land, and from a condition of victory, he distributed the land to the Twelve Tribes of Israel.

So Joshua took the whole land, according to all that the LORD had said to Moses; and Joshua gave it as an inheritance to Israel according to their divisions by their tribes. Then the land rested from war. (Josh. 11:23, NKJV)

Similarly, today the Jews return from hundreds of years of worldwide captivity, and they will retake the same territories and in the process their fortunes will be restored. As it was at the time of Abraham, so it remains today: real estate is a possession deemed to be of great value. A quick query on the Internet regarding the price tag of real estate for sale in Israel today finds many properties priced well over one-million dollars per parcel. However, more than an expensive price tag, real estate provides shelter, productivity, defensibility and more to its possessor. When God says He will be "mindful of them and restore their fortunes," one must indeed consider real estate as an important part of this national wealth.

The fact remains intact that the land in question is God's to deed to whom He so chooses, and He has not chosen to bequeath it to the Arabs, who presently seek to seize it from the Jews. After the Jews are finished with the political attempts to resolve the issue, they will ultimately conclude that the land does not belong to the Arabs, but that it is theirs for the taking and that it can only be regained via the means of military conflict. When the "meek of the Earth" experience this magnificent episode, they need to "seek the LORD" with all fervor and redeem the time for the salvation and protection of their loved ones.

THE SHRIVELING OF ISLAM

> This shall be their lot in return for their pride, because they scoffed and boasted against the people of the LORD of hosts [My people Israel]. The LORD will be terrible against them; he will *shrivel all the gods of the Earth,* and to him shall bow down, each in its place, all the coasts and islands of the nations. (Zeph. 2:10–11 NRSV; emphasis added)

In keeping with the Israeli Conquest over the Palestinians and the Jordanians, two member groups of the Psalm 83:6–8 Arab confederacy, Zephaniah alludes to the shriveling up of their respective gods. In Zephaniah's day, a defeated people evidenced that their god was unable to deliver them victorious. If a nation, tribe or ethnic group was defeated or destroyed, their god or gods would lose credibility by association. Therefore, the prophet causes the reader to remember that the two go hand-in-hand; a plundered people equaled a shriveled god.

At the time of the writing of this prophecy, the Moabites worshipped the god called Chemosh.[318] The Ammonites worshipped Milcom.[319] When Mohammed, born around AD 570 and the primary founder of the religion of Islam, came onto the scene, the Arabs of the Middle East worshipped many gods. Mohammed cleverly packaged the polytheism that plagued the region and presented the Arabs and the world with the religion of Islam. Though it had the appearance of a monotheistic religion, it incorporated many of the common polytheistic worship practices of the time.

Today, the subject god of Zephaniah's prophecy is Allah, the god of Islam. All of the other ancient Arab gods of the region were made to give way to the rise of Allah. Therefore, when we are informed that the god of the Palestinians and Jordanians will shrivel up, we are being foretold of the beginning stages of the demise of Islam. Islam is a religion bent on cursing the Jews, and scripture tells us that anyone seeking to curse the Jews will be cursed in retaliation.[320]

More on this is found in the appendix of this book entitled *The Xenocide of the Gods of the Earth*, but for now we should make the association that Islam is dealt a major blow at the time of the fulfillment of Zephaniah's prophecy. Islam has grown into a major religion with handcuffing arms well into the international community; therefore, Islam will not likely be eliminated at the time. However, the meek of the Earth will see the shriveling up process of Allah begin as a result of the Israeli conquest over the Psalm 83 Arab confederacy. They should be called to further caution as they begin to see Allah wither.

The Magog confederacy, led by Russia and Iran, which this author suggests sequentially follows the Psalm 83 confederacy, is likewise primarily operative under Islamic influence. The nations enlisted in this grouping are predominately Muslims. This Russian-Iranian confederacy will also experience defeat as hooks are put in its jaws to move against the expanding nation of Israel.[321] Because of the divine defeat of this confederacy, Islam will dramatically diminish in scale. This acknowledgement segues into the next chronologically prophetic passage of Zephaniah regarding Ethiopia.

> You Ethiopians also, You shall be slain by My sword. (Zeph. 2:12, NKJV)

In this brief passage, Zephaniah reminds the "meek of the Earth," not to forget the epic prophetic episode that follows, whereby the Magog (Russian-Iranian) alliance advances against Israel. Ethiopia is enlisted in this confederate group and therefore through association we must consider the possibility that Zephaniah is alluding to this specific prophetic event. This event is thoroughly described by Ezekiel, in the 38th and 39th Chapters of his prophetic book.

Since this episode in Israel's future is not the subject of this book, the Magog event is only referenced here in passing. However, the point Zephaniah makes is that God will slay Ethiopia with the weapon of His choice, "My sword." As one studies the divine defeat of the Russian Confederacy described in Ezekiel 39:1–6, they recognize that it is God Who personally delivers Israel from this major assault.

SUMMARY

In conclusion, the time is at hand to consider Zephaniah's call to caution. At the time of this writing, the reformation of the nation Israel is underway. A strong, wealthy Jewish nation is on the horizon. Don't be surprised to see the Israeli Defense Force evict the Hamas from ancient Philistia, and the other terrorist entities out of Isralestine proper. Gaza will soon be deserted, serving as an end-time sign that the day of the LORD'S anger is shortly to follow.

Wherever the place and whenever the time, it is wise to keep a watchful eye on the events revolving around Isralestine. The LORD desires that the meek of the Earth be duly informed, so that they may get right with Him, in order to be hidden from the disturbing events destined to befall the inhabitants of the Earth during the day of the LORD.

At the request of the LORD, Zephaniah inscribed centuries ago this invaluable prophetic information in Chapter 2 of his book, for you, the "meek of the Earth." He said that the Jewish people would re-gather in their ancient homeland and that they would do so in a condition of unbelief. Then he describes the Jews overcoming the Palestinians and their Arab cohorts, thereby taking back territory once belonging to their twelve tribal ancestors. This event brings with it a severe blow to the religion of Islam, the religion of the defeated Arabs.

Jewish fortunes are enormously increased and Russia is lured into coming after the great booty of the Israeli-Arab war. Russia forms its own coalition, which includes Iran and Ethiopia, among others, and comes down against Israel from the north to take the spoils. God divinely destroys this Russian-led confederacy. This defeat displays the glory of God and further dismantles the religion of Islam.

All of the above has been foretold by Zephaniah, as well as among other Old Testament Jewish prophets, in order that the "meek of the Earth" would be called to caution as they witnessed the unfolding of these specific events. This select population group, upon witnessing all of the above, can then be certain that the day of the LORD is the next significant prophetic event on the calendar. They are to seek the righteousness of Christ, in order that they may "be hidden, In the day of the LORD'S anger."

TO THE MEEK OF THE EARTH...

To you, the "meek of the Earth," *anav erets* in the Hebrew, to whom Zephaniah's message is intended, there are a few more comforting words inscribed elsewhere in scripture for you to hear.

Thou, *even* thou [the LORD], *art* to be feared: and who may
stand in thy sight when once thou art angry? Thou didst
cause judgment [in the day of the LORD] to be heard from
heaven; the Earth feared, and was still, When God arose to
judgment, to save all the meek of the Earth [anav erets].Selah
(Psa. 76:7–9, KJV; emphasis added)

The word judgment is used two times in the above passage. In
verse 8 it is judgment (*diyn* in the Hebrew), referring to the wrath of
God poured out upon the unsaved population of the Earth during the
"day of the LORD." In verse nine, the word in Hebrew used for judgment is *mishpat*, alluding to the favorable pronouncement or reward
presented concurrently to the meek of the Earth *anav erets*.

For evildoers shall be cut off; But those who wait on the
LORD, They shall inherit the Earth. For yet a little while and
the wicked *shall be* no *more;* Indeed, you will look carefully for
his place, But it *shall be* no *more.* But the meek shall inherit
the Earth, And shall delight themselves in the abundance of
peace. (Psa. 37:9–11, NKJV)

This information is relatively self-explanatory; those who wait on
the LORD in verse nine are the meek of the Earth in verse 11. For
their faith, they will be rewarded with an inheritance. The wicked evildoers as they are referred to will be no more; they will be cut off. God
will judge this unsaved portion of Earth's population, and the meek
will inherit the Earth *anav erets*. The word for inherit used in both
verse nine and 11 is the Hebrew word *yarash*, and it often refers to an
occupation that results from the seizure of property. The departure of
the unsaved population is preparatory for the inheritance of the meek
of the Earth. For their faith and patience, they will peacefully reside
in the restored Earth, during the thousand-year millennial kingdom
reign of Jesus Christ, the Messiah.

His [The Messiah Jesus Christ's] delight *is* in the fear of the
LORD, And He shall not judge by the sight of His eyes, Nor
decide by the hearing of His ears; But with righteousness He
shall judge the poor, And decide with equity for the meek of
the Earth [*anav erets*]. He shall strike the Earth with the rod
of His mouth, And with the breath of His lips He shall slay
the wicked. (Isa. 11:3–4, NKJV; emphasis added)

The same theme is taught by Isaiah the prophet, that the meek of
the Earth will be treated equitably for their faith. Though the Messiah
will slay the wicked unsaved population during the day of the LORD,
the meek of the earth will be granted entrance into the one thousand
year Messianic era. They will experience a restored Earth much like
that which existed in the Garden of Eden.[322]

The wolf also shall dwell with the lamb, The leopard shall lie
down with the young goat, The calf and the young lion and
the fatling together; And a little child shall lead them. The
cow and the bear shall graze; Their young ones shall lie down
together;
    And the lion shall eat straw like the ox. The nursing child
shall play by the cobra's hole,
    And the weaned child shall put his hand in the viper's
den. They shall not hurt nor destroy in all My holy mountain,
For the Earth shall be full of the knowledge of the LORD As
the waters cover the sea. (Isa. 11:6–9, NKJV)

These passages provide a glimpse into kingdom life. Creation
again interfaces cooperatively with man, as it was in the beginning
stages in the Garden of Eden. So then how can one be hidden from
the events of the day of the LORD and inherit salvation? One must
be classified among the meek of the Earth as appropriately defined by
the scriptures. Observe that it is the Messiah, Jesus Christ, Who will

equitably reward this group. Therefore, they must be members of His elect group, i.e., those who believe in Him. They must be saved in the fashion outlined in the scriptures. Listed below are a few of the more notable passages describing the process of one's salvation.

That if you confess with your mouth the Lord Jesus and believe in your heart that God has raised Him from the dead, you will be saved. For with the heart one believes unto righteousness, and with the mouth confession is made unto salvation. For the Scripture says, "Whoever believes on Him will not be put to shame." For there is no distinction between Jew and Greek, for the same LORD over all is rich to all who call upon Him. For "whoever calls on the name of the LORD shall be saved." (Rom. 10:9–13, NKJV)

But God, who is rich in mercy, because of His great love with which He loved us, even when we were dead in trespasses, made us alive together with Christ (by grace you have been saved), and raised *us* up together, and made *us* sit together in the heavenly *places* in Christ Jesus, that in the ages to come He might show the exceeding riches of His grace in *His* kindness toward us in Christ Jesus. For *by grace* you have been saved through faith, and that not of yourselves; *it is* the gift of God, not of works, lest anyone should boast. (Eph. 2:4–9, NKJV; emphasis added)

That whoever believes in Him [Messiah] should not perish but have eternal life. For God so loved the world that He gave His only begotten Son [Jesus Christ], that whoever believes in Him should not perish but have everlasting life. For God did not send His Son into the world to condemn the world, but that the world through Him might be saved. (John 3:15–17, NKJV)

Jesus answered and said to him, "Most assuredly, I say to you, unless one is born again, he cannot see the kingdom of God." (John 3:3, NKJV)

First, note from the previous scriptures that salvation is a gift from God. It is outsourced from His great love for us. It is His wish that no man, woman, or child would perish, but that all would inherit eternal life. In order to receive the love of God, one must believe in its most obvious expression, which is the sending of His only begotten Son, Jesus Christ, to die sacrificially for our sins.

Scripture says that God, the heavenly father, gave His son to us for our salvation; Jesus Christ is the gift. We are requested to believe this. This belief leads us to confess with our mouths that He is LORD, and to believe in our hearts that God raised Him from the dead. In so doing, one becomes "born again," through their faith in Jesus Christ as their Messiah. Christ Himself tells us through the passage below that this is the only way.

Jesus said to him, "I am the way, the truth, and the life. No one comes to the Father except through Me." (John 14:6, NKJV)

Therefore, as one receives Christ into their hearts, one is classified among the meek upon the Earth. This is the natural transformation of the believer, who upon receiving Jesus Christ as their Messiah, seeks to turn from wicked ones and wicked ways. As Zephaniah described at the beginning:

Seek the LORD, all you meek of the Earth, Who have upheld His justice.
Seek righteousness, seek humility. It may be that you will be hidden In the day of the LORD'S anger. (Zeph. 2:3, NKJV)

The believer becomes engaged in a quest to humbly search out a lifestyle of righteousness crafted in the ways of the LORD. The meek of the Earth attempt just living in an unjust and wicked world environment. They pray, read the word of God, meet regularly, and love one another, and in so doing they make their earnest attempt to be pleasing to the LORD. The individuals who have put their faith in Christ are the ones who have found the way of escape from the day of the LORD'S anger.

Appendix 1

THE ORACLE OF THE RHETORICAL
Contesting the Content of the Covenant

Jeremiah Chapter 49 asks a series of serious rhetorical questions intended for the Jordanians, Palestinians, and Syrians of today to answer. Though he wrote these questions over 2,500 years ago, they were intelligently and intentionally woven into prophecies that are to find their final fulfillments in modern times. As such, these questions must be, and furthermore, can only be, answered by these present Middle Eastern populations.

AGAINST THE JORDANIANS

Jeremiah asks the Jordanians, who are in part the descendants of the Ammonites, why they are homesteading the Holy Land promised to the Jewish descendants of Abraham.

> Against the Ammonites. Thus says the LORD: *"Has Israel no sons? Has he no heir? Why then does Milcom inherit Gad, And his people dwell in its cities?* (Jer. 49:1, NKJV; emphasis added)

Notice the passage begins with "Against the Ammonites," which puts this specific population group on alert that the information to follow has judgmental implications. God will find these people guilty of something contrary to the will of God! Psalm 83:1–8 describes a coalition of Arab forces that forms in the end-times to destroy the nation Israel. Among them are the Jordanians, Palestinians, and the Syrians. The Psalm refers to them by their ancient equivalents, the Ammonites, Edomites, and Assyrians. It is for this reason that this line of rhetorical questioning is aimed against them.

Jeremiah asks the Jordanians if Israel has "no sons" left to inherit the Promised Land presented to Abraham by his God. This Promised Land was to span from the Nile River in Egypt, eastward toward the Euphrates River, which courses through the middle of modern-day Iraq.[323] God promised Abraham about 4,000 years ago that he would have heirs through the lineage of his son Isaac and grandson Jacob that would someday possess all this prime property.[324]

When Jeremiah asks: "Has Israel no sons? Has he no heir?" he is referring to Jacob, grandson of Abraham, who was later renamed Israel by the God of Abraham.[325] "Has Jacob no descendants?" Considering the foreknowledge of Jeremiah's God, Who took into consideration that the Jewish people would be confronted by attempted genocide via the Germans, this is an astoundingly apropos question! Today we could appropriately format the question to read:

> Against the Jordanians, did Hitler successfully annihilate the Jewish people, thus leaving Jacob no descendants? If not, why then does Allah inherit one of the tribal territories appropriated to the descendants of Israel, and you Jordanians trespass therein?

"Milcom" was the god of the Ammonites during Jeremiah's day. On or around the time of the advent of Islam in AD 622, the Ammonite descendants, in connection with many other Middle Eastern Arabs, forfeited their many gods in favor of the one god called Allah. As such, any unfulfilled prophecies regarding the ancient Middle Eastern gods will now find their fulfillment by association through Allah, god of Islam. Remember that the Jewish prophets had no Allah to refer to at the time of their writings, so when they referenced an Arab god, they did so by their customary names at the time.

The Jordanians are today accountable for their present occupation of land promised to the nation Israel. The nation of Jordan, as it was so recognized by the international community in 1946, sits squarely in the middle of the Promised Land of Israel. More specifically, the Ammonites most closely represent the Northern portion of modern-day Jordan, which Jeremiah says belongs to the Jewish tribe of Gad. "Why then does Milcom inherit Gad, And his people dwell in its cities?" (Jer.49:1c).

The Jordanians are to deduce from the major premise that if their god overtakes Gad, then the people of that god would feel authorized to possess the same subject territory. During the time of Jeremiah, the common belief was that the god of a people would be the entity that would lead them to victory over peoples and possession over places.

In modern application, the shoe fits as follows: The Jordanians worship their god Allah in lands promised to the Jewish tribe of Gad. This infers that Allah has given to the Jordanians the ancient land appropriated to the tribe of Gad and, as such, they are free to "dwell in its cities." Jeremiah asks them "Why?" Is it because there are no Jewish descendants to claim this real estate as their inheritance?

Indeed, if there were no more Jews, the Jordanians would certainly be free to possess the territory appropriated to the ancient tribe of Gad. Who or what God could prevent them from doing so? Certainly, the God of the Jews and Christians could not stop them, since that God would be a promise-breaking liar. Jeremiah formats the question in such a way that if there are still Jews, how dare the Jordanians trespass upon their inherited Promised Land? He holds them accountable for giving any other justifiable reason for such unacceptable behavior.

The Jews were dispersed into the nations of the world for 1,878 years. They were confronted with genocide but were protected from their final destruction by their promise-keeping God Jehovah. They have been severely disciplined, more so than any other ethnic group in the history of the world. Today the world witnesses their divinely orchestrated return back into a small notch of the Promised Land. What, then, can be the justifiable Jordanian argument for stealing land from those to whom God promised it? Jeremiah's God would like to hear their answer!

AGAINST THE PALESTINIANS

I hope that by the time you read this appendix you have read the chapter in this book entitled *Who-domites?: Who Are The Edomites Today?* If not, I encourage you to do so at this point. It is paramount that that the reader possesses an understanding of who the Edomites were in order to understand in part who the Palestinians are presently.

The Edomites originally occupied the territory we recognize today as Southern Jordan. Throughout their history, many of them migrated into Israel proper, whereby they eventually became known as Idumeans, which is the Greek term for Edomites. A small contingency within the Palestinian population of today has ancestry traceable back to the Edomites. As Jeremiah moves from his advance against the Ammonites, he next fires his rhetorical questions in succession against the Edomites, best represented today by the Palestinians.

> Against Edom. Thus says the LORD of hosts: "*Is wisdom no more in Teman? Has counsel perished from the prudent? Has their wisdom vanished?*" (Jer. 49:7, NKJV; emphasis added)

The Palestinians enjoin themselves alongside their Arab partners in the confederate effort prophesied in Psalm 83. The Bible describes them in that prophecy as the "tents of Edom," most likely referring to their refugee condition. When the "tents of" phrase appears in the

Bible to describe a people, it either refers to a military encampment on the march to battle or a displaced population of refugees.

The other members Psalm 83:6–8 foretells to unite with the Palestinians in their plight are the Lebanese, Syrians, Jordanians, Saudi Arabians, and Egyptians. It is a confederacy composed of all the territories that most closely border Israel. It is important to recognize what their confederate mandate is, according to the Psalmist:

> They have taken crafty counsel against Your people [The Jews], And consulted together against Your sheltered ones. They have said, "Come, and let us cut them off from being a nation, That the name of Israel may be remembered no more." For they have consulted together with one consent; They form a confederacy [league] against You: The tents of Edom [Palestinians] and the Ishmaelites [Saudi Arabians]; Moab [Jordanians] and the Hagrites [Egyptians]; Gebal, Ammon [Jordanians], and Amalek; Philistia [Palestinians] with the inhabitants of Tyre [Lebanese]; Assyria [Syrians] also has joined with them;
>
> They have helped the children of Lot [Ammon and Moab/Jordanians]. (Psa. 83:3–8, NKJV)

It is against this backdrop that Jeremiah's rhetorical questions find their legitimacy. This confederacy, including the Palestinians, "consults together with one consent." They take "crafty counsel against" the Jews, from which they formulate a plan mandating the destruction of the modern-day Jewish state. Their goal is to eradicate the nation from the face of the Earth, "That the name of Israel may be remembered no more." Jeremiah asks them where the wisdom is in their futile plan. Not only is this campaign ignorant, it will prove to be a fatal mistake for these confederate populations.

These three rhetorical questions are directed at Edom, who is listed first in the grouping of the ten confederate members of Psalm 83.

Esau, twin brother of Jacob (also referred to as Israel), founded Edom. The Edomites and Israelis shared a common kinship through these twin brothers. These twins were both acutely aware of the promises made to their grandfather Abraham by his God. As such, they passed on their common knowledge of the Abrahamic Covenant through their future generations.

This covenant assured Abraham he would have descendents forever. These heirs are the Jewish people. Furthermore, the covenant promised a land to Abraham and his Jewish descendants. When Jeremiah asks of Edom: "Is wisdom no more in Teman? Has counsel perished from the prudent? Has their wisdom vanished?" we are to recognize that it is the wisdom of the Abrahamic Covenant to which Jeremiah refers. The Palestinians are accountable for recalling the former wisdom the Edomites once possessed.

Teman was the grandson of Esau, making Abraham his great-great-grandfather. Teman was one of the chiefs of Edom during his generation, and was renown in the region for his wisdom.[326] This wisdom included an acutely detailed understanding of the contents of the Abrahamic Covenant. What was common knowledge to Teman and accredited to him as "wisdom," has vanished from his Edomite-then-Idumeans descendants who are now in part Palestinians.

This line of questioning causes the Palestinians to consider the futility of their mischievous confederate plan with their neighboring Arab cohorts. Their plan is to destroy the Jewish people and to take over their promised land. Jeremiah points out through his rhetorical questions "wisdom has vanished" from the Palestinians, and as such, they have not presented their Arab partners with the "prudent counsel" once possessed by their patriarch Teman!

Yes, wisdom is no more in Teman.
Yes, counsel has perished from the prudent.
Yes, their wisdom has vanished.

They did not remember the contents of the Abrahamic Covenant, which guaranteed the survival of the Jewish people and their possession of the promised land of Israel. These important facts are the "counsel that has perished," and the "wisdom that has vanished!"

Unfortunately, in the absence of this invaluable information the Psalm 83 confederates set themselves up for a no-win situation. How can they in Psalm 83:4 "cut them off from being a nation, That the name of Israel may be remembered no more?" How also do they plan to in Psalm 83:12 "take the pastures of God for a possession?" In order to fulfill their confederate mandate they will need first to render the Abrahamic Covenant void and inoperative, which in essence will require their god Allah to overcome Jehovah, God of Abraham.

Therefore, the Palestinians must deduce from the minor premise, that in order to destroy the Jewish nation, the name Israel must be remembered no more, this major premise: that they have abandoned the wisdom of their patriarchs and now believe their god Allah is more powerful than the God Jehovah of Abraham. The Jeremiah who asks these rhetorical questions has admittedly also stated that there is one and only one way for a god to accomplish the destruction of the nation Israel!

> Thus says the LORD, Who gives the sun for a light by day, The ordinances of the moon and the stars for a light by night, Who disturbs the sea, And its waves roar (The LORD of hosts *is* His name): "If those *ordinances* depart From before Me," says the LORD, "*Then the seed of Israel shall also cease* From being a nation before Me forever." (Jer. 31:35–36, NKJV; emphasis added)

These passages beg the question: Does Allah, god of the Palestinians and their Arab cohorts, have the power to cause the ordinances outlined by Jeremiah to depart from the control of the LORD of hosts? Jeremiah's God Jehovah would like to hear their answer!

AGAINST THE SYRIANS

Moving northward into Syria, Damascus becomes the target of the next rhetorical question. Jeremiah 49:23 opens with "Against Damascus" and four judgment passages later ends with "I will kindle a fire in the wall of Damascus." The question in the midst of these passages reads:

> Why is the city of praise not deserted, the city of My joy? (Jer. 49:25, NKJV)

Simply put, why is Jerusalem, the city of God's joy, not deserted?[327] The Bible poses this question to the city of Damascus, the capital of Syria. It is taught by many to be the oldest continuously inhabited city on Earth, dating back to the time of Abraham around 2000 BC. Furthermore, Damascus presently allows many notable terrorist groups to freely conduct organizational activities within its city limits. Ironically, it turns out Jerusalem will not be deserted, but Damascus will be destroyed for taking part in an attempt to destroy Jerusalem, "the city of praise." Isaiah informs us that:

> The burden against Damascus. "Behold, Damascus will cease from *being* a city, And it will be a ruinous heap." (Isa.17:1, NKJV; emphasis added)

Jeremiah similarly declares:

> Damascus has grown feeble; She turns to flee, And fear has seized *her*. Anguish and sorrows have taken her like a woman in labor. Why is the city of praise not deserted, the city [Jerusalem] of My joy? Therefore her young men shall fall in her streets, And all the men of war shall be cut off in that day," says the LORD of hosts. "I will kindle a fire in the wall of

Damascus, And it shall consume the palaces of Ben-Hadad [the palaces of the would-be King of Syria at that time]." (Jer. 49:24–27, NKJV)

In a remarkable turn of events, God enacts the curse-for-curse-in-kind clause of Genesis 12:3 and contained in the Abrahamic Covenant against Damascus, Syria. Syria, as a member of the Psalm 83 confederacy, attempts to destroy the nation Israel; however, in the process it becomes destroyed in retaliation from Israel.

Unfortunately for Islam, this future episode will not bid well for its god Allah. As such, the Syrians, along with the entirety of the Muslim community scattered throughout the world, are to deduce from the minor premise that since the Jerusalem of God's joy cannot be destroyed, the major premise is the God Jehovah of the Jews and Christians is indeed the true God.

This becomes the obvious and only logical explanation as to "Why is the city of praise not deserted, the city of My joy?" It is not deserted because the coming Psalm 83 war effort against the Jews will be unsuccessful! The nation Israel will be victorious over the Arab confederacy, and Damascus will at that time "cease from being a city," and "it will be a ruinous heap."

Damascus will be destroyed for attempting the expulsion of the Jews from Jerusalem, "the city of praise, the city of Jehovah's joy." But since Jerusalem will remain inhabited by Abraham's descendants, the Jews, is there any other explanation for why Jerusalem is not deserted, apart from the fact that the God Jehovah is the true God? Jeremiah's God Jehovah would like to hear their answer.

Appendix 2

THE XENOCIDE OF THE GODS OF THE EARTH!

The Jewish prophet Zephaniah declares the God of the Jews will reduce to nothing all the false gods of the Earth. Presently, the population on Earth has a multiplicity of gods competing for their worship. Estimates suggest there are more gods masquerading about than there are days in a calendar year.[328] The Muslims have Allah, the Hindu's have Shiva, Krishna, Brahma, Vishnu, and many more. Zephaniah informs us that his God, Jehovah, will execute the xenocide of these and every other god imposter parading himself or herself about the Earth![329]

> The LORD will be awesome to them, *For He will reduce to nothing all the gods of the Earth*; People shall worship Him, Each one from his place, Indeed all the shores of the nations. (Zeph. 2:11, NKJV; emphasis added)

If the major premise reduces to nothing the entire menu of gods, apart from the God of the Jews and Christians, then the minor premise must be that the miscellaneous false religions of the world will likewise be reduced to nothing, since their gods will soon be abandoning their posts. This means that approximately one-billion Muslims scattered amongst the nations of the world will find themselves at some point in time without their god Allah.

If the major premise for the Muslims of today is that God reduces Allah to nothing, the minor premise must be that Islam as a major world religion has an expiration date. Contrary to teachings from some mosques, synagogues and pulpits, Allah the god of Islam is not the same as Jehovah, God of the Jews and Christians. Ask an Islamic terrorist on his way to blow himself up if he thinks Allah and Jehovah are one in the same. His final words are not *Jehovah Jireh*, which means, "the LORD Jehovah will provide;" rather, he utters the words *Allah Akkbar*, translated as "Allah is the greatest," defining Allah as the greater god.

Zephaniah inserts this powerful one-passage prophecy in the midst of prophecies associated with judgments outsourced from the God of the Jews against several modern-day Middle Eastern, Islamic nations. I outline this judgment sequence further in the chapter *A Call to Caution*. It is in the context of this judgment against the nations oppressing the Jews that the God of the Jews states He will assault the gods (lowercase *g*) of the Earth, and in so doing, reduce them to nothing.

He goes on to say people will then turn their worship toward Him, rather than the famished gods of the Earth. This worldwide worship will exist in the Messianic Kingdom. Therefore, the god-reduction process must occur in advance of the kingdom age.

Zephaniah inserts this declaration at the conclusion of three-passage description of judgments destined against Moab and Ammon. At the time of Zephaniah's prophetic ministry, approximately 630 to 620 BC, both Moab and Ammon worshipped two notable "gods of the Earth." Moab worshipped Chemosh, and Ammon Milcom. To the Jews of Zephaniah's time, these gods, along with Astheroth, goddess of the Sidonians, were two of the more prominent god figures on the scene. Their reductions in prominence are described as follows:

For because you have trusted in your works and your treasures, You also shall be taken. And *Chemosh* shall go forth into *captivity*, His priests and his princes together. (Jer. 48:7, NKJV; emphasis added)

Woe to you, O Moab! *The people of Chemosh perish*, For your sons have been taken captive, And your daughters captive. (Jer. 48:46, NKJV; emphasis added)

Wail, O Heshbon, for Ai is plundered! Cry, you daughters of Rabbah, Gird yourselves with sackcloth! Lament and run to and fro by the walls; *For Milcom* shall go into *captivity* With his priests and his princes together. (Jer. 49:3, NKJV; emphasis added)

These passages allude to the defeat and captivity of the peoples, priests, princes, and their gods Chemosh and Milcom. The theme of defeat, plunder, captivity, and god reduction all worked hand-in-hand, and was well understood in historic times. Ancient armies commonly prayed to their deity for victory before entering into battle. In defeat, the conclusion was that the god of the victor was greater than the god of the loser.

Scriptural references to the concept of gods protecting the peoples and the lands:

Do you not know what I and my fathers have done to all the peoples of other lands? Were the gods of the nations of those lands in any way able to deliver their lands out of my hand? (2 Chr. 32:13, NKJV)

He also wrote letters to revile the LORD God of Israel and to speak against Him, saying, "As the gods of the nations of other lands have not delivered their people from my hand, so the God of Hezekiah will not deliver His people from my hand." (2 Chr. 32:17, NKJV)

"Who among all the gods of these lands have delivered their countries from my hand, that the LORD should deliver Jerusalem from my hand?'" (Isa. 36:20, NKJV)

Has any of the gods of the nations at all delivered its land from the hand of the king of Assyria? (2 Kings 18:33, NKJV)

Who among all the gods of the lands have delivered their countries from my hand, that the LORD should deliver Jerusalem from my hand? (2 Kings 18:35, NKJV)

And they [the Jews] were unfaithful to the God of their fathers, and played the harlot after the gods of the peoples of the land, whom God had destroyed before them. (1 Chr. 5:25, NKJV)

The famishing and resulting captivity of a god finds its end and greatest example in the book of Revelation:

Then I saw an angel coming down from heaven, having the key to the bottomless pit and a great chain in his hand. He laid hold of the dragon, that serpent of old, who is *the Devil and Satan, and bound him* for a thousand years. (Rev. 20:1–2, NKJV; emphasis added)

The point is that God, through a series of defeats accomplished through varying means, accomplishes His purpose of the Zephaniah passage. These gods will be subdued and will submit to the greater God. He will shrivel all the gods of the Earth and, in the case of Moab and Ammon, they will experience defeat at the hands of the Israeli Conquest; their gods will be reduced in stature.

> "I have heard the reproach of Moab [Central Jordan], And the insults of the people of Ammon [Northern Jordan], With which they have reproached My people, And made arrogant threats against their borders. Therefore, as I live," Says the LORD of hosts, the God of Israel, "Surely Moab shall be like Sodom, And the people of Ammon like Gomorrah; Overrun with weeds and saltpits, And a perpetual desolation. The *residue of My people* [Israel] *shall plunder them, And the remnant of My people shall possess them*." (Zeph. 2:8–9, NKJV; emphasis added)

> "Therefore, behold the days are coming," says the LORD, "That I will cause to be heard *an alarm of war* In Rabbah of the Ammonites; It shall be a desolate mound, And her villages shall be burned with fire. *Then Israel shall take possession* of his inheritance," says the LORD. (Jer. 49:2, NKJV; emphasis added)

Check the historical records and it appears this defeat at the hands of the Jewish military over Moab and Ammon has not occurred. If this is the case, then should this conquest occur in the not so distant future, the god reduced would be Allah, presently the god of worship in Moab and Ammon, which is geographically located in modern-day central and northern Jordan.

Islam became the monotheistic package of the polytheistic religions of the region. The former gods of the Middle East have generally submitted their worshippers into the care of the one capricious god now known as Allah. At the time of Zephaniah and Jeremiah's prophetic ministries, there was no Jordan; rather, it was Ammon, Moab, and Edom. Similarly, there was no Allah, only Chemosh and Milcom.

Yet it is clear that if we are told Satan himself will be reduced (already mentioned as the major premise), then certainly the minor premise holds true; Allah, since he is not one in the same with Jehovah, will be likewise famished.

God will not necessarily complete the famishing of Allah at the conclusion of the Israeli Conquest, as this segment of Israel's prophetic future appears to be limited to the surrounding nations of the region listed in Psalm 83:6–8. Islam as a religion has expanded into the borders of Iran, Russia, Turkey, Libya, and many other countries. However, by the conclusion of the Magog Invasion He will have devastated most of Islam.

The Magog invasion involves a confederacy headed by Russia and Iran, destined to rise against the nation Israel in the end-times. Ezekiel outlines the events surrounding this prophetic episode in his Chapters 38 and 39. The God Jehovah of the Jews divinely defeats this Russian-led coalition. This amazing victory will likely expire the longstanding reign of Allah over his remaining deluded constituents, as it will officially identify him as an imposter.

Notes

1. Gen. 17:8 refers to the land promised by God to Abraham, and Gen. 15:18 determines the landmass in question to stretch from the river of Egypt to the Euphrates River.
2. 1 Cor. 15:51–55, 1 Thess. 4:15–18.
3. Ezek. 38–39.
4. Rev. 20 ascribes the Messianic Kingdom period, the high point of Old Testament prophecy, to span the duration of 1,000 years. We find events fulfilled within that period in the writings of Isaiah, Jeremiah, Ezekiel, Daniel, Hosea, Joel, Amos, Obadiah, Micah, Nahum, Zephaniah, Haggai, and Zechariah.
5. *Inner Circle* and *Outer Circle* are terms utilized in this book to associate two confederate advances foretold to come against Israel in the end-times. They are further explained in the chapter *The Future Maps of Isralestine*. Visit www.isralestine.net for more information.
6. More on the restoration of Jewish fortunes is found in the *Call to Caution* chapter of this book.
7. The use of *peace* rather than *piece* is a play on words. The piece of the puzzle identifies the location of the peace we presently long for in the Middle East.
8. The prophet Ezekiel had a vision, described in Ezek. 37:1–13, which presented the Jewish people outside the Holy Land in a worldwide dispersion scenario. Furthermore, it foretells the horrifically grave circumstances that occur to the whole house of Israel that climactically concludes their dispersion sequence. In essence, the prophet envisioned the Holocaust centuries ago.
9. The Roman Army served as the instrument, utilized for the desolation of the land and dispersion of the Jewish people out of the Holy Land, which was prescribed in the Mosaic Law (Lev. 26:30–33).

10. Ezek. 35:5. For more detail, read the chapter *Ancient Hatred* within this book.

11. I detail the restoration of Jewish fortunes in the chapter *Call to Caution.*

12. Examples of typological usages in the Bible of mountain or mountains: Dan. 2:45, Ezek. 37:22, Ezek. 19:9.

13. *New American Standard* Hebrew and Greek dictionaries. *Yashab*: to dwell. *Betach*: securely.

14 Deut. 12:10, Ezek. 28:26.

15. *Holman Bible Dictionary.* Solomon became the third king of Israel and reigned forty years about 1000 BC.

16. *The Magog Invasion* by Chuck Missler of Koinonia House Ministries is a good source for referencing the member nations of this coalition. Also, *Epicenter* by Joel Rosenberg, in Chapter 9 identifies the nations he believes to be involved in the Russian-Iran coalition of Ezek. 38 and 39.

17. Determining modern-day equivalents is a task undertaken within various portions of this book. The main chapters presenting investigation into these current identities are *Who-domites? Who Are the Edomites Today?*, *Olam Ebah: The Ancient Arab Hatred of the Jews*, *The Psa. 83 Report*, *Obadiah's Mysterious vision*, *Psa. 83*, and *The Arab Confederacy.*

18. Ezek. 25:13–14, Obad. 1:18, Jer. 49:1–2,10.

19. Gen. 12:3. I will bless those who bless you, And I will curse him who curses you; And in you all the families of the Earth shall be blessed. (NKJV)

20. "Curse-for-curse-in-kind" is a phrase I first heard from Dr. Arnold Fruchtenbaum of Ariel Ministries. He may have coined the phrase, which aptly describes the curse component of Gen. 12:3.

21. Rev. 20:6 references the duration of the Messianic Kingdom era.

22. Ezek. 36:4 NKJV, emphasis added.

23. Ezek. 36:12, NKJV.

24. Some teach that Psa. 102:1–14 was a prophecy relative to the

Holocaust and subsequent reformation of the Jewish State of Israel. Refer to David Dolan's book: *Israel in Crisis* Chapter 2: The Last Generation, Psa. 102 section.

25. Gen. 22:17.

26. Read the *My People Israel* section in the *Exceedingly Great Army* chapter of this book.

27. http://www.ariel.org/ or http://www.khouse.org/ accessed as of 2/24/08.

28. Ezek. 37:10, Psa. 83:1–8. Read the entire chapter in this book called *Exceedingly Great Army.*

29. For more information visit www.isralestine.net

30. Gen. 12:3 promises to bless those who bless Abraham and his Jewish descendants, or curse those who curse them.

31. Hagar was Jealous of Sarah, wife of Abraham. Ishmael was jealous of Isaac, son of Abraham. Esau was jealous of Jacob, son of Isaac and grandson of Abraham. Moab and Ammon were generally covetous of the promises of God passed Abraham, Isaac, Jacob, and their descendants. We examine this enmity further in the chapter *Ancient Hatred.*

32. Aliyah (Hebrew: "ascent" or "going up") is a term widely used to mean "Jewish immigration to the Land of Israel." *Wikipedia Encyclopedia.*

33. To understand who Edom represents today, read the chapter in this book called *Who-domites?*

34. Ezek. 35:5. Also read the chapter *Olam Ebah The Ancient Hatred* contained in this book.

35. We make the connection between Edom and the Palestinian Refugees in the chapter of this book entitled *Who-domites?* Palestinian-inspired terror is developed in the chapter *The End of Terror.*

36. Gen. 4:1–13, 1 John 3:12.

37. Jer. 31:31–34 foretells a New Covenant that God would make with the Jews.

38. Matt. 25:40.
39. Gen. 4:13–14, NKJV.
40. Hos. 1:9–10 foretells of a time that the Jewish people would be reclassified as "not My people."
41. Ezek. chapters 38 and 39 describe a time when a group of nations spearheaded by Russia and Iran attempt to war against Israel.
42. *Yisrael Yashab Betach*, Israel Dwelling Securely.
43. Egypt is included through the listing in Psa. 83:6 of the Hagarenes, also referred to as the Hagrites in some Bible translations. Hagar was an Egyptian according to Gen. 16:1. *Holman's Bible Dictionary*, and *The International Standard Bible Encyclopedia* connect the Hagarenes to Hagar.
44. Dan. 9:27 describes this seven-year period, and divides it in half. It speaks of one week, but scholars understand this to represent one week of years; in essence, seven years.
45. Zech. 13:8.
46. The exceedingly great army of Israel delivers this slaughter. Ezek. 24:15, 37:10 Obad. 1:18.
47. Gen. 36:1. Now this *is* the genealogy of Esau, who is Edom.
48. Jer. 49:2 says modern-day Northern Jordan will be a desolate mound. (NKJV)
49. You can find greater detail in the chapter *The Future Maps of Isralestine* at www.isralestine.net.
50. Esau fathered the Edomites in Edom, which is modern-day Southern Jordan. Gen. 36:1,9,43.
51. Greater detail is found in the chapter *The Future Maps of Isralestine*.
52. Primary supporting passages are Ezek. 28:24–26, and Ezek. 38:8,11,14.
53. Hos. 5:15.
54. NKJV, abbreviated passage.
55. Exod. 1:22.
56. Gen. 12:3.
57. Several passages to reference would be 1 Kings 16:13,16; 1 Kings 21:26, and Ezek. 8:10,12.

58. Hos. 1:9.
59. Rom. 9:3–5.
60. Isa. 42:6, 49:6, 60:3.
61. Isa. 42:6, 49:6, 60:3.
62. Gen. 13:14–16,17:3–8.
63. Wiersbe's expository outlines on the New Testament quotation "the fullness of the Gentiles" refers to the number of Gentiles that will be saved during this church age. When the body of Christ is completed, He will catch it away in the air; then will begin the seven-year Tribulation here on earth, "the time of Jacob's trouble."
64. Dan. 9:27, Isa. 28:15.
65. This event has not yet occurred, almost 2000 years after. That centuries have passed since the destruction of the Jewish genealogical records further evidences the supernatural orchestration of the emergence of these pure-bred Jewish witnesses. Only a God, who knows the beginning from the end, would be able to trace their tribal origins.
66. John 1:29,36 refer to Jesus Christ as the sacrificial Lamb of God.
67. Rev. 7:9–17.
68. *Holman Bible Dictionary.*
69. http://www.state.gov/r/pa/prs/ps/2003/20062.htm. Accessed 3/1/08.
70. Baal: Lord of Canaanite religion and seen in the thunderstorms, Baal was worshiped as the god who provided fertility. He proved a great temptation for Israel. (*Holman's Bible Dictionary*) Baal or some derivative of the word is referenced 76 times in the Old Testament of the NKJV. Examples: Exod. 14:2,9 ; Josh. 12:7, 13:5,17.
71. http://www.un.org/unrwa/overview/index.html. Accessed 3/1/08.
72. The Turkish Ottoman Empire maintained sovereignty over these territories from 1517 to 1917.
73 http://domino.un.org/UNISPAL.NSF/fd807e46661e3689852570d00069e918/e210ca73e38d9e1d052565fa00705c61!OpenDocument. Accessed 3/4/08.

74 You can add the sum of these numbers from the *The Future Maps of Isralestine* chapter of this book.

75. Deut. 32:10, Zech. 2:8.

76. Ezek. 37:10.

77. Psa. 83:6–8. Egypt, Saudi Arabia, Jordan, Syria, Lebanon and more. Ezek. 25:14, Obad. 1:18.

78. Scripture points to ancient Bozrah, now called Petra, located in Southern Jordan, as the place whereby Christ returns to save the faithful Jewish remnant from the destruction of the Antichrist and his armies. Isa. 34:5–13, 63:1–8.

79. Psa. 83:1–8.

80. Esau is the founder of the territory of Edom. Gen. 36:1, 19; Gen. 25:25–26 regarding the brothers.

81. Gen. 32:28 regarding Jacob to Israelites, and Gen. 36:9,43 regarding Esau to Edomites.

82. http://www.peacefaq.com/palestinians.html. Accessed 2/28/2008. Partially quoted from this web link.

83. http://en.wikipedia.org/wiki/West_Bank. Accessed 2/28/2008. This site includes a map of the West Bank.

84. Some Bible translations refer to the Hagarenes as the Hagrites.

85. Zech. 13:8, Rev. 12:1–6. A recommended reading about the campaign of Armageddon can be obtained through Ariel Ministries, sponsored by Dr. Arnold Fruchtenbaum. As of 2/28/08 their website address is www.ariel.org.

86. 134–104 BCE John Hyrcanus, Ethnarch & High Priest of Jerusalem, "Age of Expansion", annexed Trans-Jordan, Samaria, Galilee, Idumea. Forced Idumeans to convert to Judaism, hired non-Jewish mercenaries, etc. http://en.wikipedia.org/wiki/History_of_ancient_Israel_and_Judah. Accessed 2/28/08.

87. *The Works of Josephus: Book of the Wars 6*, Chapter 8.

88. Refer to The Bar Kokhba Revolt map at http://en.wikipedia.org/wiki/Bar_Kokhba_revolt. Accessed 2/28/08.

89. Hos. 1:9–10. Regarding "My people Israel," Ezek. 25:14, 36:12, 38:14,16, 39:7.

90. Jer. 49:15, Obad. 1:2.

91. "Previous to the arrival of the British, the Arabs in Palestine had thought of themselves as Arabs rather than as Palestinians." Quotation from http://www.fsmitha.com/h2/ch17jeru.html. Accessed 2/28/08.

92. Read the chapter *The Ancient Hatred* for more on the relationship between Esau and Jacob.

93. http://www.kinghussein.gov.jo/his_nabateans.html . Online office of King Hussein I. Accessed 2/28/08.

94. *International Standard Bible Encyclopedia,* "Asmonians."

95. *The Wars of the Jews,* Book 4, Chapter 4.

96. *The Wars of the Jews,* Book 4, Chapter 4:1.

97. *The Wars of the Jews,* Book 4, Chapter 4:2 and Chapter 5:1–4.

98. *The Wars of the Jews,* Book 4, Chapter 5:5.

99. *The Wars of the Jews,* Book 5, Chapter 9:2.

100. *The Wars of the Jews,* Book 6, Chapter 8:1.

101. From *Time Immemorial* by Joan Peters. Chapter 8, 2nd page.

102. http://masada2000.org/ in the *Palestine?* section.

103. From *Time Immemorial* by Joan Peters. Chapter 8, 5th page.

104. From *Time Immemorial* by Joan Peters. Chapter 8, 11th page (600,000 Jews estimated).

105. From *Time Immemorial* by Joan Peters. Chapter 8, 5th page.

106. http://en.wikipedia.org/wiki/Palestine_%28region%29. Accessed 2/28/08.

107. http://en.wikipedia.org/wiki/Palestine_%28region%29. Accessed 2/28/08.

108. Matt. 24:7, Mark 13:8, Luke 21:10.

109. Jordan gained its statehood in 1946. http://en.wikipedia.org/wiki/Jordan. Accessed 2/28/08.

110. *New American Standard* Hebrew and Greek dictionaries.

111. Ezek. 37:10.

112. http://lexicorient.com/e.o/abraham.htm regarding the age of Abraham.

113. *New American Standard* Hebrew and Greek dictionaries. *Olam* meaning "long duration," ancient, ancient times, days of old, everlasting, long ago, long time, without end, permanent, perpetual, and ebah enmity, hostility, hatred.

114. Gen. 36:1.

115. Psa. 83:1–8.

116. Gen. 12:2–3.

117. Quotation from the Bible Knowledge Commentary, Old Testament.

118. Gen. 17:17, 18:12.

119. Gen. 17:17.

120. Gen. 21:17–20.

121. Gen. 21:21.

122. Surah's 2.125, 2.127, 2.133, 2.136, 2.140, 3.84, 4.163, 6.86, 14.39, 19.54, 21.85, 38.48.

123. Gen. Chapter 14 records a historical conflict during the time of Abraham's life. He joins the conflict in an attempt to rescue his relative, Lot. Abraham successfully accomplishes his mission, and in the process gains broader notoriety in the region. The presumption is that the numerous kings referenced in Gen. 14 must have known of Abraham due to his victory in the conflict.

124. Psa. 83:6.

125. *Strong's Exhaustive Concordance of the Bible* (King James Version).

126. Heb. 12:16–17.

127. Gen. 25:23.

128. Gen. 36:1.

129. Gen. 19:37.

130. Psa. 83:8. Assyria also has joined with them; They have helped the children of Lot. *Selah*.

131. Amos 1:13, Jer. 49:1.

132. Gen. 12:4–5.

133. Gen. 15:18.

134. Gen. 11:27.

135. Gen. 19:37.
136. Num. 22:2–4.
137. Num. 22:2–6.
138. Gen. 13:5–16.
139. Judges 3:12–14.
140. Judges 3:28–30.
141. Gen. 25:24–26.
142. Gen. 36:1. Also read the *Who-domites? Who Are The Edomites Today?* chapter contained in this book.
143. Deut. 1:8, Deut. 29:13.
144. Find further commentary on the crimes against Israel listed by Obadiah in the *Obadiah's Mysterious Vision* chapter within this book.
145. http://en.wikipedia.org/wiki/1948_Arab-Israeli_War. Accessed 3/2/08.
146. Obad. 1:7. All the men in your (Esau's) confederacy Shall force you to the border; The men at peace with you Shall deceive you and prevail against you. Those who eat your bread shall lay a trap for you. No one is aware of it.
147. Ezek. 37:10. Also read the chapter contained in this book called *Exceedingly Great Army*.
148. Obad. 1:15.
149. *Holman Bible Dictionary* suggests the ministry of Malachi to be sometime after 450 BC, whereas Easton's Bible Dictionary sets the timing around 420 BC.
150. Read the chapter called *Who-domites?* contained within this book.
151. Obad. 1:2 and Jer. 49:15 both predicted the diminishment in scale of the Edomite kingdom.
152. We made this connection in the *Who-domites?* chapter.
153. *New American Standard* Hebrew and Greek dictionaries, H8606.
154. *New American Standard* Hebrew and Greek dictionaries, H5378. *Strong's Hebrew and Greek Dictionary*, H5377.
155. *Strong's Hebrew and Greek Dictionary*, H4204.

156. http://www.camera.org/index.asp?x_context=7&x_issue=11&x_article=795. *Yassir Arafat's Timeline of Terror,* dated 11/13/2004 by CAMERA: Committee for Accuracy in Middle East Reporting in America. Accessed 3/2/08.

157. Gen. 12:3.

158. Ezek. 37:10. Also read the *Exceedingly Great Army* and *Who-domites?* chapters contained in this book.

159. Gen. 36:1. Also read the *Who-domites?* chapter within this book.

160. Gen. 32:28.

161. This concept is further developed in the chapter of this book labeled the *Who-domites?*

162. *New Revised Standard Bible Translation,* also translated similarly in the New International Version.

163. *New American Standard* Hebrew and Greek dictionaries.

164. Exod. 33:22 exemplifies typologically the cleft of a rock as a place of spiritual protection or covering.

165. Isa. 40:31. But those who wait on the LORD Shall renew their strength; They shall mount up with wings like eagles, They shall run and not be weary, They shall walk and not faint.

166. Stars in biblical typology are often used to represent the angels. Rev. 1:20, Rev. 12:4, Job 38:7, Dan. 8:10, Jude 1:12. Isa. 14:3.

167. He probably lived between 2166 BC and 1991 BC. http://en.wikipedia.org/wiki/Abraham. Accessed 3/1/08.

168. Gen. 12:3. I will bless those who bless you, And I will curse him who curses you.

169. Edomites later became known by their Greek name, Idumeans, and now are best identified as a contingency within the Palestinians. Edo-Palestinians is used here as a bridge term to identify the Edomite remnant within the Palestinian ethnicity. More can be found on this in the chapter called *Who-domites?*

170. Obad. 1:4.

171. *Parson Bible Atlas.*

172. *Holman Bible Dictionary.*

173. Isa. 40:31, Exod. 19:4, Deut. 28:49, 32:11, 2 Sam. 1:23, Jer. 48:40, 49:22, Job 39:27, Lam. 4:19, Ezek. 1:10, Hos. 8:1, Matt. 24:28, Luke 17:37, Rev. 4:7, 12:14.

174. A quote from the Koran, a primary source of Islamic scripture. Author is uncertain of the accuracy, origin, and translation this specific Surah and encourages readers own research into its authenticity.

175. http://www.foxnews.com/story/0,2933,48822,00.html. Saddam pays 25K for suicide bombers, FOX news 3/26/2002. Article by Ken Layne. Accessed 3/1/08.

176. Palestinianism. http://www.ynet.co.il/english/articles/0,7340,L-3159505,00.html. Accessed 3/1/08. http://www.ynetnews.com/Ext/Comp/ArticleLayout/CdaArticlePrintPreview/1,2506,L-3159505,00.html. Accessed 3/1/08.

177. This scripture is quoted in Heb. 2:7–9 as a reference to Jesus Christ, but the point is that Jesus Christ became a man and, in that condition and for that short time, like all men was made lower than the angels.

178. Jude 1:9. Yet Michael the archangel, in contending with the devil, when he disputed about the body of Moses, dared not bring against him a reviling accusation, but said, "The Lord rebuke you!"

179. Read the appendix in this book entitled *The Xenocide of the Gods of the Earth.*

180. *Strong's Hebrew and Greek Dictionary,* H4204.

181. *Strong's Hebrew and Greek Dictionary,* H2114.

182. Psa. 83:6.

183. Psa. 83:6–8.

184. For further information, read the chapter called *The Palestinian Confederacy.*

185. Psa. 83:4.

186. "The Saudi government has been the principal financial backer of Afghanistan' s odious Taliban movement since at least 1996. It has also channeled funds to Hamas and other groups that have

committed terrorist acts in Israel and other portions of the Middle East." Quote from Ted Galen Carpenter. Accessed 3/2/08 at http://www.cato.org/pub_display.php?pub_id=3841. Furthermore, the Hezbollah terrorist group has a presence in Lebanon, and the Hamas of the Gaza Strip smuggle weapons through Egypt. http://www.iht.com/articles/2006/07/18/news/iran.php. Accessed 3/1/08. http://www.jpost.com/servlet/Satellite?cid=118122856975 2&pagename=JPost/JPArticle/ShowFull. Accessed 3/1/08. http://www.weaponsurvey.com/kbase/egyptandsmuggling.htm. Accessed 3/1/08.

187. Gen. 13:15. For all the land which you see I give to you and your descendants forever. [16]And I will make your descendants as the dust of the Earth; so that if a man could number the dust of the Earth, then your descendants also could be numbered.

188. Jihad is translated as "struggle," and Intifada means "shaking off." These terms find association with the modern-day Middle East conflict and its associated Islamic tactics of terror. In essence, the Arabs struggle to shake off the establishment of the nation Israel.

189. Psa. 83:6.

190. Among the Palestinian refugees is a contingency of the descendants of Esau, who were known as Edomites. Further explanation of this connection is delivered in the *Who-domites?* chapter.

191. Bat Yeor. http://en.wikipedia.org/wiki/Bat_Yeor.

192. Zionism. http://www.channel4.com/history/microsites/H/history/browse/glossary.html.

193. Psa. 83:6 refers introduces the term the "tents of Edom." Psa. 83 foretells a confederacy that will come against Israel, and the "tents of Edom" are listed as one of the members.

194. Further details about these two judgments can be found in the chapter *The Final Palestinian Farewell* contained within this book.

195. Psa. 83:6.

196. To understand the Edomites and their history, read the *Who-*

domites? chapter within this book.

197. Teman was a grandson of Esau, one of the "dukes of Edom." Gen. 36:11, 15, 42.

   Easton's Bible Dictionary. The Temanites were renowned for their wisdom Job 2:11; compare Jer. 49:7. *Holman's Bible Dictionary.*

198. Gen. 36:1.

199. Gen. 32:28.

200. Edom and the Edomites are connected with the Palestinians in the chapter *Who-domites?*

201. Greater detail on these three questions is found in the appendix *Oracle of the Rhetorical*

202. The details of this reprisal are further explained in the *Reprisal of Edom* chapter of this book.

203. Obad. 1:18, Ezek. 25:14, Psa. 83:1–8.

204. Many Psalms depict Israel as "her." Psa. 48:12–13, 87:5. Also see Jer. 3:8, 3:20, Ezek. 36:17, and Rev. 12:1–6.

205. Ezek. 37:10.

206 Further detail on this report is found in the connecting *Obadiah's Mysterious Vision* chapter.

207. The King James, New King James, American Standard, New American Standard, Revised Standard, and New International Versions translate the word "least" as "small." The New Living Translation says "cut you down to size."

208. Read the chapter called the *Who-domites?* contained within this book.

209. This passage is commented upon in more detail in the chapter call *The Palestinian Confederacy.*

210. Obad. 1:18, Ezek. 25:14.

211. The *Who-domites?* chapter in this book describes the Edomite descent and locates a remnant of the Edomites within the modern-day Palestinians.

212. Dan. 11:45, Zech. 12:7

213. The *Ryrie Study Bible NASB Expanded Addition* suggests Obadiah

existed in either 841 or 586 BC. Also, an excerpt from the New
Commentary on the Whole Bible: Old Testament Volume. In
the book, it is clear that Jerusalem has already been overthrown
(1:11–16, 20), and the prophet refers to the cruelty of the
Edomites toward the Jews on that occasion (cf. also Lam. 4:21, 22;
Ezek. 25:12–14; Psa. 137:7). This would seem to indicate the book
was written sometime soon after Jerusalem's fall to the Babylonians
in 587/86 BC.

214. Ezek. 35:5. Also read the chapter *Olam Ebah: The Ancient Arab Hatred of the Jews.*

215. Surah 5:51 in the Koran discourage Muslims from befriending Jews and Christians because it considers them unjust people.

216. Greater detail is given about this confederacy in the chapter called "The Palestinian Confederacy."

217. Dates and notes regarding the three sieges were obtained from *Easton's Bible Dictionary.*

218. Jer. 25:1–12 and Jer. 29:10.

219. Read the chapter in this book called *Who-domites?*

220. 1 Chron. 6:39,48–2 Chron. 29:30.

221. Gen. 36:1

222. Read the chapter in this book called *Olam Ebah: The Ancient Arab Hatred of the Jews.*

223. Amalek was Esau's Grandson, who was Abraham's grandson Gen. 36:12, 1 Chron. 1:36.

224. Gen. 22:18, 26:4, 28:14, Gal. 3:16.

225. Eph. 2:8–10, John 3:16.

226. Psa. 19:1.

227. Deut. 32:8–10.

228. Rev. 12:7–10 and Dan. 12:1.

229. Rev. 20:1–3, 7–10.

230. Ezek. 38:8,16.

231. Rev. 12:7–10, Job 1:6.

232. http://encarta.msn.com/encyclopedia_761588322/Arab-Israeli_ Conflict.html. Accessed 3/5/08.

233. http://encarta.msn.com/encyclopedia_761570433/Six-Day_War. html. Accessed 3/5/08.

234. http://encarta.msn.com/encyclopedia_761564886/Arab-Israeli_ War_of_1973.html. Accessed 3/5/08.

235. http://encarta.msn.com/encyclopedia_761553918/Muhammad_ (prophet).html. Accessed 3/5/08.

236. http://encarta.msn.com/encyclopedia_761579171/Islam.html (emphasis added above). Accessed 3/5/08.

237. http://encarta.msn.com/encyclopedia_761579171/Islam.html. Accessed 3/5/08.

238. http://etext.virginia.edu/etcbin/toccer-new2?id=HolKora. sgm&images=images/modeng&data=/texts/english/modeng/parsed &tag=public&part=5&division=div1. Accessed 3/5/08.

239. http://islamawakened.com/Quran/5/51/. Accessed 3/5/08.

240. Book written about the Middle East in modern times by Joan Peters *From Time Immemorial.*

241. Psa. 83:4.

242. Read the *Isralestine—God's Roadmap Plan To Peace* chapter of this book.

243. Read the chapter called *The Ancient Hatred.*

244. "Iran and Syria are linked by more than an alliance. They are linked by their patronage of a terrorist organization: Hezbollah, which is sponsored by Iran, supported by Syria and operates out of Lebanon." Quote from Tom Fenton. http://www.cbsnews.com/ stories/2005/02/22/opinion/fenton/main675330.shtml. Accessed 3/5/08.

245. Christ appears to be drawing his disciples attention to events surrounding Isa. 19:2.

246. Zech. 13:8.

247. *Strong's Exhaustive Concordance of the Bible,* and the *New American Standard* Hebrew and Greek dictionaries. This Hebrew term is also found in Obad. 1:7, and likely refers to the same Psa. 83:5–8 Arab League.

248. *Kol* is the Hebrew word utilized, and it refers to the whole or entirety of this confederacy.

249. *Shalom* is the Hebrew word for peace used by Obad. in this passage.

250. Isalestine in this instance refers to the modern-day Jewish state of Israel and the territorially disputed areas that border Israel, like the Gaza Strip, the West Bank, and the numerous other locations where Palestinian refugee camps still exist in the Middle East Region. Also refer to http://www.hayozma.org/App_Themes/eng/Files/IsraeliInitiative-Refugees.pdf pages 7–10. Accessed 3/4/08.

251. Edom is referenced in first position within this confederacy, as the tents of Edom, according to Psa. 83:6. This is a likely reference to the Edomites being refugees at the time of the formation of their confederacy.

252. Gen. 22:15–19, 26:1–5, 28:10–16, Gen. 12:1–3, Gen. 13:14–17.

253. Gen. 15:18.

254. Associated dates were located from the World Fact Book–Central Intelligence Agency at https://www.cia.gov/cia/publications/factbook/geos/ir.html. Accessed 3/4/08. Refer to country drop-down list.

255. Total Area Size and Population are as of the year 2006 and were referenced at www.infoplease.com/atlas/middleeast.html. Accessed 3/4/08. Specific details can be found by clicking on the country links.

256. Iran was known as Persia until 1935.

257. Total Area Size and Population are as of the year 2006 and were referenced at www.infoplease.com/atlas/middleeast.html. http://www.infoplease.com/ipa/A0107652.html. Accessed 3/4/08. Some other sources suggest the total area in sq miles of Israel to be 9,000–10,000.

258. Isralestine refers to the foretold expansion of the modern-day Jewish State of Israel over the formerly recognized territory of

Palestine, and is not suggesting that the name Isralestine is destined to become the literal name for the future area.

259. The Hebrew term for confederacy used in this passage is *Berith*, and can be defined also as "a league" according to *The New American Standard* Hebrew and Greek dictionaries.

260. Hagrites are called the Hagarenes in the New King James Version, making a better argument for these people having descended down from the Egyptian matriarch Hagar (Gen. 16:1), the mother of Ishmael (Gen. 16:15).

261. Ezek. 37:10 foretells the emergence of a superior army subsequent to the restoration of the Jews into the nation Israel. This army is developing into a superior force with advanced weaponry at the time of the authoring of this book. Further detail about its purpose is found in the chapter *The Exceedingly Great Army*, contained in this book.

262. Ezek. 39:1–6.

263. The Hebrew word for "week" is *Shebuya*, and emphasizes "a period of seven," not necessarily days. Most scholars teach this usage by Dan. to represent "a period of seven" years.

264. A parallel passage is found in Ezek. 25:14.

265. Sepharad: After the Peshitta (second century), it was identified with the Iberian Peninsula. The descendants of the Iberian Jews are still called Sephardim, and Sepharad is the modern Hebrew for Spain. http://en.wikipedia.org/wiki/Sepharad. Accessed 3/5/08. Refer also to the teachings of Ariel Ministries *Obadiah Commentary* obtainable through http://www.ariel.org.

266. *Strong's Exhaustive Concordance*, H2426.

267. The land area of the world is estimated at 148.94 million sq km per http://www.answerbag.com/q_view/2497. Accessed 3/5/08. The land area of the United States of America is 9,166,601 sq km as per http://www.infoplease.com/ipa/A0108121.html. Accessed 3/5/08.

268. Psa. 83:1–8.

269. The Sanhedrin was the highest Jewish council in the first century. The council had 71 members and was presided over by the high priest. The Sanhedrin included both of the main Jewish parties among its membership. *Holman Bible Dictionary.*

270. John 3:34–36, Rev. 5:6 portrays Jesus as the Lamb of God filled with the Holy Spirit in a heavenly ceremony. The term Seven Spirits is used to refer to the Holy Spirit.

271. Matt. 25:31, NKJV.

272. A careful Hebrew word study illustrates that the title of Messiah as "The Branch" is not used here in Isa. 11:1. That word for "The Branch" in Hebrew is tsemach. The word used here in Isa. 11:1 is netser and is better defined as a sprout rather a branch. The Hebrew word tsemach is used in Isa. 4:2, Jer. 23:5, 33:15, Zech. 3:8,6:12, relative to the Messiah as a "righteous Branch" raised up to King David.

273. Rev. 20:2–7.

274. 1 John 5:19–20.

275. Rom. 6:23, James 1:15.

276. Hos. 4:6a "My people are destroyed for lack of knowledge."

277. Rev. 20:1–3, Rev. 20:7.

278. The Greek term kathizô means "to sit down in an appointed place in order to rest." It is used twice, back to back, in this Heb. 10:12 passage to evidence the fact that Messiah seated at the right hand side of God is fulfilling the prophecy of Isa. 11:10 whereby "His resting place will be glorious."

279. *Strong's Hebrew and Greek Dictionary,* H3117

280. *Strong's Hebrew and Greek Dictionary,* 5251 and *New American Standard* Greek and Hebrew dictionaries, 5251.

281. Isa. 11:13.

282. Jer. 23:5 and Jer. 33:15.

283. The Great Tribulation is commonly referred to as the second half of the seven-year Tribulation Period.

284. *Bozrah* means "inaccessible" in the Hebrew. It is closely associated

geographically with *Petra*, which means "rock" in the Greek. They were both located in what is today Southern Jordan. Scriptures like Isa. 34:6, 63:1 refer to Bozrah as the place where the Messiah returns to earth and battles his enemies. Many commentaries suggest it is a place where a remnant of Jews will seek refuge during the Tribulation Period. Furthermore, it is likely the area Christ instructed the Jewish remnant to flee to for protection in Matt. 24:16, and Mark 13:14.

285. Isa. 2:4, Joel 3:10, Mic. 4:3.

286. Ezek. 37:10.

287. Zephaniah 2:1 references a Jewish re-gathering in the land of Israel, in a condition of unbelief.

288. Aliyah is a Jewish term associated with the return of Jews into the nation Israel.

289. *Strong's Hebrew and Greek Dictionary.*

290. Jer. 49:23 refers to the northern Syrian places of Hamath and Arpad in a likewise scenario.

291. Ezek. 35:5. "Because thou hast had a perpetual enmity, and hast given over the children of Israel to the power of the sword in the time of their calamity, in the time of the iniquity of the end." This passage speaks contextually about historical hatred of Israel throughout the Middle East region. It suggests that this hatred was never abandoned, but resurfaced in 1948 at the rebirth of the Jewish State of Israel.

292. More information on these Edom judgments is contained in *The Final Palestinian Farewell* chapter.

293. The offense spoken of by Hos. is the Jewish generational rejection of Christ as the prophesied Messiah. The inception of the offense occurred at the time of the First Coming of Christ, when the Jewish leadership denied Him as Messiah on the grounds of demon possession (Matt. 12:24).

294. One of the best ministerial sources for these commentaries is Ariel Ministries founded by Dr. Arnold Fruchtenbaum. He has written

numerous books and study materials, such as *Israeology*, and *The Footsteps of the Messiah*. Presently Ariel can be accessed at: http://www.ariel.org.

295. This usage of the term identifies Israel expanded well beyond its modern-day borders, in fulfillment of prophecy.

296. Ezek. 37:10 foretells the army we see developing in Israel in modern times.

297. More detail about the devastated condition of Edom is found in *The Final Palestinian Farewell* chapter.

298. Ezek. 39:11. "It will come to pass in that day *that* I will give Gog a burial place there in Israel, the valley of those who pass by east of the sea; and it will obstruct travelers, because there they will bury Gog and all his multitude. Therefore, they will call *it* the Valley of Hamon Gog."

299. Psa. 83:6 refers to the Hagarenes in the ASV translation. This connects Egypt to the confederacy of nations in the Psalm, through the Egyptian matriarch Hagar, the mother of Ishmael.

300. Exod. 17:7, Num. 11:3, Josh. 5:9.

301. Hos. 5:15.

302. Isa. 11:15a Following Masoretic Text and Vulgate; Septuagint, Syriac, and Targum read dry up.

303. Gen. 17:5.

304. Zephaniah's ministry occurred during the reign of Josiah (640–609 BC). Most scholars date the book in 630 or between 630 and 621. (*Holman Bible Dictionary*)

305. Edomite descendants exist within the Palestinian ethnicity, as do descendants from Moab, Ammon, and Philistia, among many others. Though Zephaniah doesn't specifically reference Edom in chapter two of his book, their current existence within the Palestinian ethnicity of today should not be discounted as his theme describes events relative to the peoples and territories inclusive of both Jordanians and Palestinians.

306. Zeph. 2:11.

307. Zeph. 2:12 speaks of the defeat of Ethiopia, which is one of the member nations of the Magog alliance, as identified in Ezek. 38:5.

308. Gen.32:28, Gen. 49:2.

309. Gen. 31:18. Canaan of old later became part of Israel proper.

310. Rev. 20:4.

311. Translated from the Revised Standard Version of the Bible.

312. Ezek. 39:12,14,16 describe the land being cleansed in the aftermath of the destruction of the Magog Alliance. This was a prescription of Levitical Law found in Num. 19:16, Deut. 21:23.

313. Dan. 9:27 and Isa. 28:15,18 speak of a false covenant confirmed between the Jews and the Antichrist.

314. *Holman Bible Dictionary* states PENTAPOLIS a league of five Philistine city-states which banded together to oppose the Israelite occupation of Canaan. See Philistines.

315. http://en.wikipedia.org/wiki/Ashkelon.

316. Rabbah is the ancient title of the modern-day capitol city of Jordan, which is Amman.

317. Deut. 2:8 "And when we passed beyond our brethren, the descendants of Esau who dwell in Seir, away from the road of the plain, away from Elath and Ezion Geber, we turned and passed by way of the Wilderness of Moab. ⁹ Then the LORD said to me, 'Do not harass Moab, nor contend with them in battle, for I will not give you any of their land as a possession, because I have given Ar to the descendants of Lot as a possession.'"

Deut. 2:16 "So it was, when all the men of war had finally perished from among the people, ¹⁷that the LORD spoke to me, saying: ¹⁸"This day you are to cross over at Ar, the boundary of Moab. 19And when you come near the people of Ammon, do not harass them or meddle with them, for I will not give you any of the land of the people of Ammon as a possession, because I have given it to the descendants of Lot as a possession.'"

318. Jer. 48:46.

319. Jer. 49:1,3.

320. The Gen. 12:3 clause contained in the Abrahamic covenant calls for a curse for curse in kind.

321. Ezek. 38:4. I (God) will turn you (Russian Confederacy) around, put hooks into your jaws, and lead. you out, (against Israel) with all your army, horses, and horsemen, all splendidly clothed, a great company with bucklers and shields, all of them handling swords. ⁵Persia, Ethiopia, and Libya are with them, all of them with shield and helmet.

322. Isa. 51:3, Ezek. 36:35.

323. Gen. 15:18 grants the subject property over to Abraham.

324. Gen. 50:24, Deut. 30:20 & 34:4.

325. Gen. 32:28.

326. *Easton's Bible Dictionary:* Teman was a grandson of Esau, one of the "dukes of Edom" (Gen. 36:11, 15, 42). Holman's Bible Dictionary: The Temanites were renowned for their wisdom (Job 2:11; compare Jer. 49:7).

327. Psa. 137:6, Isa. 66:10, Neh. 12:43, Lam. 2:15.

328. http://ancienthistory.about.com/library/bl/bl_myth_gods_index. htm. This web site provides a brief list in alphabetical order of some of the gods of the Earth. Accessed 3/5/08.

329. http://en.wikipedia.org/wiki/Xenocide. *Xenocide:* "an act of genocide towards an alien species." Can also be searched on the internet under Genocide. Accessed 3/5/08.